CREATIVE CONCEPTS IN PSYCHOLOGY

CREATIVE CONCEPTS IN PSYCHOLOGY

An Activity and Case-based Approach

ANDREA H. GOLDSTEIN

The McGraw·Hill Companies

CREATIVE CONCEPTS IN PSYCHOLOGY: AN ACTIVITY AND CASE-BASED APPROACH

Published by McGraw-Hill, a business unit of The McGraw-Hill Companies, Inc., 1221 Avenue of the Americas, New York, NY, 10020.

Some ancillaries, including electronic and print components, may not be available to customers outside the United States.

This book is printed on acid-free paper.

1 2 3 4 5 6 7 8 9 0 WDQ/WDQ 1 0 9 8 7 6 5 4 3 2 1 0

ISBN 978-0-07-352465-8
MHID 0-07-352465-4

Vice president/Editor in chief: *Elizabeth Haefele*
Vice president/Director of marketing: *John E. Biernat*
Senior sponsoring editor: *Alice Harra*
Developmental editor: *Kristin Bradley*
Marketing manager: *Keari Green*
Lead digital product manager: *Damian Moshak*
Digital development editor: *Kevin White*
Director, Editing/Design/Production: *Jess Ann Kosic*
Project manager: *Kathryn W. Mikulic*
Manager, Media production: *Janean A. Utley*
Senior designer: *Anna Kinigakis*
Senior photo research coordinator: *Lori Kramer*
Photo researcher: *PoYee Oster*
Media project manager: *Cathy L. Tepper*
Typeface: *10/12 Bembo*
Compositor: *Laserwords Private Limited*
Printer: *Worldcolor*
Cover credit: © *Marilyn Volan/Shutterstock*

Credits: The credits section for this book begins on page 239 and is considered an extension of the copyright page.

Library of Congress Cataloging-in-Publication Data

Goldstein, Andrea H.
Creative concepts in psychology : an activity and case-based approach / Andrea H. Goldstein.
p. cm.
Includes index.
ISBN-13: 978-0-07-352465-8 (alk. paper)
ISBN-10: 0-07-352465-4 (alk. paper)
1. Psychology. 2. Psychology—Case studies. I. Title.
BF121.G618 2011
150—dc22

2010001709

The Internet addresses listed in the text were accurate at the time of publication. The inclusion of a Web site does not indicate an endorsement by the authors or McGraw-Hill, and McGraw-Hill does not guarantee the accuracy of the information presented at these sites.

www.mhhe.com

This book is dedicated to my dad, David R. Goldstein. I miss you every day.

ABOUT THE AUTHOR

Dr. Andrea H. Goldstein is a professor in the Strategies for Success General Education department at South University. She has also taught and designed courses in psychology and criminal justice for Keiser University, Everglades University, Kaplan University, and Southwest Florida College. She has won the Teacher of Distinction award at Keiser University numerous times. Dr. Goldstein has developed and taught bachelor's and master's level classes in the classroom as well as online.

Dr. Goldstein received a BA in psychology from Florida Atlantic University, a certification in education from Florida Atlantic University, an MS degree in mental health counseling from Nova Southeastern University, an MS degree in psychology from Miami Institute of Psychology, and a PsyD in clinical psychology with a specialization in forensics from Miami Institute of Psychology.

Dr. Goldstein offers workshops all over the country to faculty and staff in best practices. She is committed to helping students achieve their goals and teaching educators methodologies to enhance the learning experiences of their students.

Dr. Goldstein's spare time is devoted to cooking, baking, spending time with family and friends, and traveling. She is currently hard at work on her next big project.

Finally, Dr. Goldstein just wanted to tell her mother that it is all her fault . . . (junior Freud).

BRIEF CONTENTS

CHAPTER 1
Introduction to Psychology 1

CHAPTER 2
Biological Bases of Behavior 18

CHAPTER 3
Sensation, Perception, and Neuroscience 31

CHAPTER 4
States of Consciousness 48

CHAPTER 5
Learning 66

CHAPTER 6
Memory 83

CHAPTER 7
Motivation and Emotion 103

CHAPTER 8
Development 119

CHAPTER 9
Personality 145

CHAPTER 10
Health Psychology 166

CHAPTER 11
Psychological Disorders and Treatment 182

CHAPTER 12
Social Psychology 207

Glossary 224

Credits 239

Index 240

CONTENTS

CHAPTER 1
Introduction to Psychology 1

What Is Psychology? 2
The History of Psychology 2
Wilhelm Wundt's Structuralism 2
William James's Functionalism 3
Branches of Psychology 4
Sigmund Freud's Psychoanalytic Perspective 4
Behaviorism 5
Humanism 6
Cognitive Psychology 6
Biopsychosocial Model or Neuroscience 6
Diversity in Psychology 6
Research Methods in Psychology 7
Case Studies 7
Naturalistic Observation 7
Correlational Research 8
Survey Research 8
Experiments 8
Summary 8
Case Study #1 Psychology at Work 9
Case Study #2 Why Do People Fall in Love? 10
Case Study #3 Does TV Corrupt Your Mind? 11
Case Study #4 The Power of Persuasion 12
Case Study #5 Are You Just Lucky? 13
Activity #1 Write a Creative Story 14
Activity #2 Conduct an Experiment 15
Activity #3 Who Am I? 16
References 17

CHAPTER 2
Biological Bases of Behavior 18

Biological Bases of Psychology 19
Peripheral Nervous System 19

Central Nervous System 20
Brain Functions 21
Summary 23
Case Study #1 Too Much, Who Me? 24
Case Study #2 Sensing and Making Sense of the World 25
Case Study #3 Alzheimer's Whodunit? 26
Activity #1 Phineas Gage 27
Activity #2 What Do You See? 28
Activity #3 Are You Left Brained or Right Brained? 29
References 30

CHAPTER 3
Sensation, Perception, and Neuroscience 31

Defining Neuroscience, Sensation, and Perception 32
Thresholds 32
Sensation 32
Vision 32
Auditory Processes (Hearing) 34
Taste 35
Smell 36
Somatosensory Processing (Skin Senses) 37
Perception 37
Gestalt Principles of Perception 38
Summary 38
Case Study #1 What Can You See? 39
Case Study #2 Movie Theater Blindness 40
Case Study #3 Spring Carnival 41
Case Study #4 Illusions or Delusions? 42
Case Study #5 Tiny Trees 43
Activity #1 Taste Tests 44
Activity #2 What Can You Hear? 45
Activity #3 What Is a Blind Spot? 46
References 47

CHAPTER 4
States of Consciousness 48

Consciousness 49
Stages of Sleep 49
Why Do We Need Sleep? 50

Problems with Sleep 51
Can You Make Up for Lost Sleep? 51

Sleep Issues 51

Insomnia 51
Hypersomnia 52
Parasomnia 52

Dreams 53

Hypnosis 53

Drugs and Altered States of Consciousness 54

Stimulants 54
Depressants 55
Opioids 55
Hallucinogens 55
Marijuana 55

Summary 55

Case Study #1 Why Am I So Tired? 56

Case Study #2 Dream World 57

Case Study #3 Drugs and Consciousness 58

Case Study #4 Which Is It? 59

Activity #1 Dream Log 60

Activity #2 Dream Analysis 61

Activity #3 Meditation 62

Activity #4 Sleep Disorders 63

References 64

CHAPTER 5
Learning 66

Learning 67

Classical Conditioning 67

Acquisition and Extinction 69
Generalization and Discrimination 69

Operant Conditioning 70

Positive and Negative Reinforcers and Punishment 71
The Skinner Box 71
Schedules of Reinforcement 72
Shaping 72

Observational Learning 72

Behavior Modification 73

Summary 73

Case Study #1 Classical Conditioning: What's Wrong with Ziggy? 74

Case Study #2 Operant Conditioning: Behavior Problems 75

Case Study #3 Operant Conditioning: Who Can Train Snoopy? 76
Case Study #4 Lunch Anyone? 77
Activity #1 Maze Learning 78
Activity #2 Bells Make So Much Noise 79
Activity #3 Phobias? 80
Activity #4 Behavior Modification Contract 81
References 82

CHAPTER 6
Memory 83

Memory 84
Stages in the Formation and Retrieval of Memory from an Information-Processing Perspective 85
Types of Memory 85
Types of Memory Retrieval 86
Physiology of Memory 87
Memory Disorders 87
Memorization Versus Learning 88
Forgetting 88
Summary 89
Case Study #1 How Odd . . . 90
Case Study #2 Forget Puppy Love 91
Case Study #3 Remember That? 92
Case Study #4 Memory Loss at the Theater 93
Case Study #5 Wild Days 94
Activity #1 Implicit Versus Explicit Memory 95
Activity #2 Photos from the Past 96
Activity #3 Six Tips to Improve Memory 97
Activity #4 Numbers Game 98
Activity #5 Flashbulb Memories 99
Activity #6 Forgetful? 100
References 101

CHAPTER 7
Motivation and Emotion 103

Theories of Motivation 104
Biological Theories of Motivation 104
Cognitive Theories of Motivation 105
Humanistic Theory of Motivation 105

Conflict 106

Emotion 107

Theories of Emotion 107
Nonverbal Expression of Emotions 108

Summary 108

Case Study #1 How Quickly Can Date Night Happen? 109

Case Study #2 Retirement Life 110

Case Study #3 I Bet I Can Beat You! 111

Case Study #4 How Quickly Things Can Change 112

Case Study #5 Road Rage 113

Activity #1 Goal Setting and Achievement 114

Activity #2 Cognitive Dissonance 115

Activity #3 What Motivates Us to Eat? 116

Activity #4 Where Am I Going? 117

References 118

CHAPTER 8
Development 119

Nature via Nurture 120

Human Development from Conception to Birth 120

Genetics 121

Infancy 122

Maturation 123

Psychosocial Development 123

Stage Theories of Development 124
Social Bonds and Attachment 126

Cognitive Development 126

Piaget's Theory of Development 127
Vygotsky's Theory of Sociocultural Development 127
The Development of Language 128

Moral Development 128

Adolescence to Adulthood 129

Dementia and Alzheimer's Disease 130

Summary 130

Case Study #1 Who Knows More? 131

Case Study #2 Developmental Effects on Personality 132

Case Study #3 What, No Sleepover? 133

Case Study #4 Let's Make Applesauce 134
Case Study #5 Time Does Not Stand Still 135
Case Study #6 Wedded Bliss 136
Case Study #7 Grandma's Playing Video Games? 137
Activity #1 What's in a Name? 138
Activity #2 Lifespan Development Paper: Part I 139
Activity #3 Lifespan Development Paper: Part II 140
Activity #4 How Old Am I? 141
Activity #5 Freud Versus Erikson 142
References 143

CHAPTER 9
Personality 145

What Is Personality? 146
Biological/Evolutionary Approaches to Personality 146
Psychodynamic Approaches to Personality 147
Beyond Freud . . . Neo-Freudians 148
Trait Approaches to Personality 149
Behaviorist Perspectives of Personality 150
The Humanistic Approach to Personality 151
How Do We Assess Personality? 152
Intelligence 153
Varied Intelligences 154
Summary 154
Case Study #1 Twin Power 155
Case Study #2 Defense Mechanisms 156
Case Study #3 Who's That Guy? 157
Case Study #4 Selective Intelligence 158
Case Study #5 Intellectual Abilities 159
Activity #1 I Am . . . 160
Activity #2 How Defensive Am I? 161
Activity #3 Personality Tests 162
Activity #4 Gardner's Multiple Intelligences 163
Activity #5 How Does Personality Affect Consumer Behavior? 164
References 165

CHAPTER 10
Health Psychology 166

Health Psychology, the Biopsychosocial Model 167
The Effects of Stress 167
The Sources of Stress 168
Stress and Illness 169
Stress and Coping Skills 169
Stress Reduction and Relaxation 170
Summary 171
Case Study #1 Exhaustion Hurts 172
Case Study #2 Jog It Out 173
Case Study #3 Type A Personality, Who Me? 174
Case Study #4 Smoke Up 175
Case Study #5 Would I Lie to You? 176
Activity #1 Freudian Defense Mechanisms 177
Activity #2 Can You See the Forest Through the Trees? 178
Activity #3 Stress Workbook 179
References 180

CHAPTER 11
Psychological Disorders and Treatment 182

Defining Abnormal Behavior 183
Medical Model 183
Psychological Model 183
The Classification of Mental Disorders 184
Anxiety Disorders 185
Somatoform Disorders 186
Dissociative Disorders 187
Mood Disorders 188
Schizophrenia 189
Personality Disorders 189
Childhood Disorders 190
Therapies 191
Summary 191
Case Study #1 What Is Abnormal? 192
Case Study #2 House Fright 193
Case Study #3 How Crazy Am I? 194
Case Study #4 Is This for Real? 195

Case Study #5 Moody Much? 196
Case Study #6 Mystery Solved! 197
Case Study #7 Heightened Anxiety 198
Case Study #8 Life Is Meaningless 199
Case Study #9 What Kind of Therapist Would I Be? 200
Case Study #10 Does Therapy Make You Self-Reliant? 201
Activity #1 Diagnoses 202
Activity #2 Mental Illness Defined 203
Activity #3 Personality Disorders 204
Activity #4 Psychopathology 205
References 206

CHAPTER 12
Social Psychology 207

Why Is Social Psychology Different? 208
Attribution Theory 208
Social Relationships 209
Prosocial Behavior 210
Aggression 211
Persuasion 211
Obedience, Conformity, and Compliance 212
Group Processing 212
Summary 212
Case Study #1 Advertising That Sells 213
Case Study #2 Stereotypes 214
Case Study #3 Dog Bites and Dating 215
Case Study #4 Call You Later 216
Case Study #5 Love at First Sight? 217
Case Study #6 Dating Changes Everything 218
Case Study #7 Why Is the News So Depressing? 219
Case Study #8 Who Will Help? 220
Activity #1 A Good Deed Does Not Go Undone 221
Activity #2 Culture and Society 222
References 223

Glossary 224
Credits 239
Index 240

PREFACE

Psychology does not need to be overwhelming or scary. For many students the idea of studying psychology can be a little . . . nerve-racking. The functions of the brain, psychological theory, and core concepts of study can seem like a vast undertaking. *Creative Concepts in Psychology: An Activity and Case-based Approach* proves that this material is manageable, fascinating, and totally engaging for students.

Creative Concepts in Psychology: An Activity and Case-based Approach looks at the study of psychology in a different way than more traditional psychology texts. Rather than place the bulk of the emphasis on concepts with only a few end-of-chapter activities, *Creative Concepts in Psychology* balances theory with application in a meaningful way. Every chapter provides the core pedagogy, but also devotes substantial time and energy to case studies and student activities. By merging these concepts so seamlessly, the ability to both learn and apply is mastered in every chapter.

A successful psychology text not only teaches students, but also empowers them to use those concepts beyond the classroom. *Creative Concepts in Psychology: An Activity and Case-based Approach* strives to reach past basic understanding to full synthesis by giving students both a thorough understanding of ideas and the chance to see those ideas played out in scenarios that resemble the sorts of situations a student may encounter in his or her own life. With titles like "Why Am I So Tired?," "Wild Days," and "Exhaustion Hurts," the case studies in this text are going to have an impact because they reflect the daily struggles many students encounter.

Thorough understanding and student engagement work in harmony in this text. *Creative Concepts in Psychology: An Activity and Case-based Approach* bridges the gap between theory and practice. Students succeed because they are given the tools they need to take psychology beyond the classroom.

TEXT FEATURES

Pedagogical Groundwork: Each chapter opens with a very candid look at core concepts in psychology. The conversational tone, interesting examples, and informative visuals help students build a framework for learning.

BRAIN FUNCTIONS

How do scientists know how the brain functions? Primitive experiences studying the brain were crude and often caused more harm than good. As science progressed, however, researchers were able to determine which areas of the brain control each of the various functions. For example, they know where memory and language are stored in the brain. This information was acquired through dissection of the brain postmortem as well as through various machines that show electrical stimulation within the brain while an individual is alive.

Paul Broca (1824–1880), a French physician and researcher, worked with one case study in his research about brain functioning. His patient was a terminally ill male named Tan. He was named Tan because "tan" was one of the few sounds that he was still able to make (Davis & Palladino, 2002). Tan's vocal cords were not damaged and he could understand what was being said to him, he just could not speak. Postmortem, Tan's brain was autopsied by Dr. Broca, who located the damage to Tan's brain. The frontal lobe of his left hemisphere was severely damaged, and Dr. Broca determined that this is the area where speech is produced. Since this was a revelation in the medical field, this area was designated *Broca's area*. A second area was later found to be responsible for speech comprehension and was named *Wernicke's area* after Carl Wernicke (1848–1905), a German neurologist and psychiatrist.

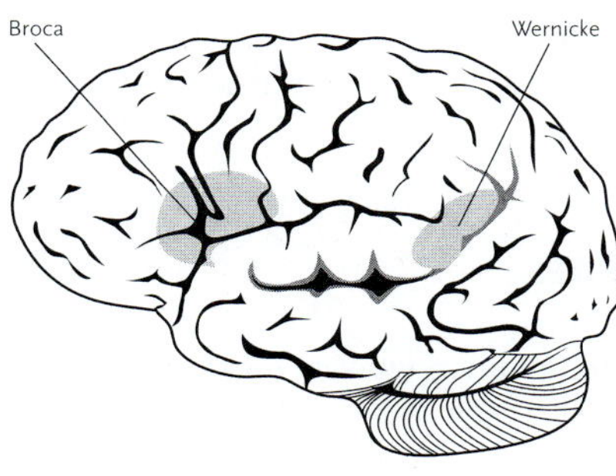

Broca and Wernicke areas.

Case Studies: The case studies in each chapter allow students to begin the process of mastery. By taking concepts and applying them to "real world" scenarios students can begin making the connection between these concepts and their own lives.

CASE STUDY #1 WHAT CAN YOU SEE?

Bernie and Leah had to drive for 45 minutes out of the city to find an isolated field suitable for stargazing. Neither of them was complaining about the drive because it was likely to be a great evening. Since Bernie and Leah did not have many interests in common, finding something that they both enjoyed doing was not always easy. Stargazing might turn out to be one of them.

Bernie was a real outdoors person and loved camping under the stars. However, his knowledge about stars, galaxies, nebulae, and so on was pretty limited. On the other hand, Leah had taken an astronomy class in high school and had a pretty good working knowledge of the names of the constellations as well as the layout of the galaxy.

For the first half hour or so, Leah pointed out constellations and taught Bernie their names. Then they made up games, such as "who can find the faintest star" and "which star is the brightest." After another hour or so, they decided that they had had enough for one night. The moon was just rising and looked gigantic as they walked back toward the car.

1. Bernie and Leah had to leave the city to stargaze. In psychological terms, what is the excess light of the city called? Why is it harder to see stars in the city?
2. Would identifying which of two stars is brighter be easier when they were both relatively dim or both relatively bright? Why? What formula is used to predict differential thresholds?
3. The moon shone off to the left as Bernie and Leah walked back to the car. At which side of their brain did the message eventually arrive? Outline the optical and neural path by which the image of the moon reached the visual cortex.
4. Leah was able to see more faint stars than Bernie. She did this by looking not directly at a star, but off to the side. Why did this trick work? What type of receptor cells are used in peripheral vision?
5. Leah tried to teach Bernie to look at a star through his peripheral vision, but he complained that the star off to the side kept disappearing. What is happening?

Activities: The activities in this text allow students to become engaged, active learners. Many of these activities will get students out of their seats and working with psychological concepts. Ultimately, students will be able to not just learn the concepts, but also experience them.

ACTIVITY #3 WHAT IS A BLIND SPOT?

We all have what is called a blind spot. This is where part of your retina is not sensitive to light. This blind spot is called the fovea and is where the optic nerve is connected to your eye. In order to find your blind spot do the following activity:

Cover your left eye and stare at the circle. Move your head closer to the page until you can no longer see the plus sign. When that happens, you have found your blind spot. Do the same thing again by covering your right eye and moving closer.

Was your blind spot in the same place for each eye? Why might there be a difference in where your blind spot occurs? Is there anything you can do to change where your blind spot occurs? What happens if you keep both eyes open and try this experiment? What if you wear corrective lenses?

ADDITIONAL RESOURCES

The Online Learning Center (OLC) provides a myriad of additional resources that will help both instructors and students succeed in the classroom. For more information visit: www.mhhe.com/goldstein

Acknowledgements

I would like to thank the following reviewers for the insightful comments that helped shape this text:

Karen Bottrill Bedell, *Baker College*

Sam Rivers Weber, *Globe University*

Loey Weber, *Globe University*

Shelly Dee Crider, *Harrison College*

John Luukkonen, PhD, *TCI College of Technology*

Mominka Fileva, *Davenport University*

Andrea H. Goldstein

CHAPTER 1

Introduction to Psychology

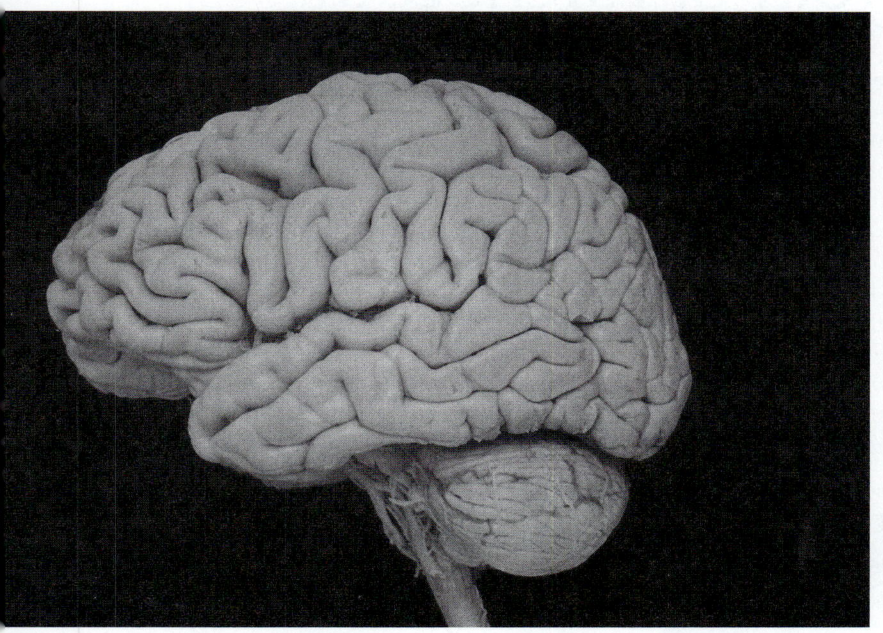

LEARNING ASSETS

Case Study #1 Psychology at Work

Case Study #2 Why Do People Fall in Love?

Case Study #3 Does TV Corrupt Your Mind?

Case Study #4 The Power of Persuasion

Case Study #5 Are You Just Lucky?

Activity #1 Write a Creative Story

Activity #2 Conduct an Experiment

Activity #3 Who Am I?

WHAT IS PSYCHOLOGY?

There are thousands of possible definitions of what psychology is and what psychology is not, but one good definition of psychology is the study of emotions, cognitions, and behavior. Thus, psychologists try to describe, predict, and explain behavior, cognitions, and emotions in order to better understand people. Psychology, known as the science of behavior and mental processes, is derived from the Greek words *psyche,* which means the soul, and *logos,* which encompasses the study of a subject. The literal translation of the term *psychology,* then, is "the study of the soul." Ancient Greeks used the word *psyche* to understand the soul, spirit, or mind as distinguished from the study and understanding of the body (Weitzen, 2002).

THE HISTORY OF PSYCHOLOGY

The reasoning behind why people do what they do has always been intriguing. However, the field of psychology is rather new. An important aspect of psychology that is often ignored is the history of psychology. The evolution of psychology has been occurring since the late 1800s. In the timeline of science, that is not very long ago. Psychology was born out of physiology and philosophy. Most of the early theorists were medical doctors who studied physiological processes in depth or philosophers who pondered the questions of the universe.

Wilhelm Wundt and William James, considered the fathers of psychology, founded the first two great schools or branches of psychology. However, neither gave their school a name. These schools later became known as *structuralism* and *functionalism,* respectively. Wundt and James were very different in their upbringings and in their perspectives, but they both had roles in creating the field of experimental psychology, which has been changing ever since. Both are credited with opening the first psychology lab in 1879. However, some historical accounts stipulate that the first American experimental laboratory at Johns Hopkins was not actually functional until 1883 (Lahey, 2003).

Wilhelm Wundt

Wilhelm Wundt's Structuralism

Wilhelm Wundt was born in Neckerau, in Baden, Germany, on August 16, 1832. A son of a Lutheran pastor, he was considered a solitary and studious boy. He was sent off to boarding school at the age of 13, and the university at age 19. He studied medicine at the Universities of Tübingen, Heidelberg, and Berlin, although he was more interested in the scientific aspect than in a medical career. In 1857 he became an instructor at Heidelberg, where he lectured on physiology; he became an assistant professor there in 1864. Three years later, he started a course he called "physiological psychology." His major work, *Principles of Physiological Psychology,* which was published in 1873 and 1874, evolved from his lecture notes. Wundt became the chair of "inductive philosophy" at the University of Zürich in 1874, and then a professor of philosophy in 1975 at the University of Leipzig, where he worked for the next 45 years. In 1875 Wundt designed the first room for experiments in sensation and perception. This is considered the founding of experimental psychology. In 1879 Wundt worked with his first graduate student to create what is considered the first real psychological research. In 1881 he started the journal *Philosophische Studien,* and he began the first course called "experimental psychology" in 1883 (Blumenthal, 2001).

Wilhelm Wundt was known as a quiet, hardworking, and methodical researcher. He was called a very good lecturer, but that is relative; Wundt would speak in a low voice for a couple of hours at a time, without notes and without pausing for questions. While Wundt was working in experimental psychology he also published four books in philosophy. Psychology was not considered a separate entity from philosophy at this time. Throughout his career, Wundt supervised 186 doctoral dissertations, mostly in psychology. Toward the end of his career, Wundt became interested in social psychology. In 1920 he wrote *Erlebtes und Erkanntes,* his autobiography. Shortly thereafter, on August 31, 1920, Wilhelm Wundt died (Boeree, 2000).

William James's Functionalism

William James was born in New York City on January 11, 1842. His father was a wealthy man who entertained the intellectuals of the time at his home. James's grandfather was an Irish immigrant who did well in real estate investments. James had a younger brother, Henry, who would also grow up to be famous; he is considered one of America's premier novelists The two brothers were sent to boarding school in Europe, and they traveled quite extensively. At 19, after a brief time as an art student, James enrolled at Harvard in chemistry, but he soon changed to medicine. Although he wanted to study the science that went with medicine, he did not want to be a physician (Boeree, 2000).

In 1865 James traveled to the Amazon River, and that trip changed his life forever because during that time he began to suffer from a whole host of health problems. After the trip, he traveled to Europe where he met Wilhelm Wundt. While in Germany he began to suffer from serious depression, accompanied by thoughts of suicide. In addition, he had serious back pain and insomnia. In 1869 he came back to the United States to finish his medical degree, but he continued to be plagued by depression. During this time, however, he seemed to improve after reading a book by a French philosopher named Charles-Bernard Renouvier. The text convinced James of the power of free will and he applied this idea to his own problems (Boeree, 2000).

William James

In 1872 James became an instructor of physiology at Harvard University. He taught his first course in psychology, called "physiological psychology," in 1875; and in 1876 he became an assistant professor of physiology.

In 1878 he married Alice Gibbons, a Boston schoolteacher. She took particularly good care of him, and his depression lessened significantly. They had five children together. Also in 1878 he signed a contract with a publisher to write a psychology textbook. It was supposed to take 2 years, but it took him 12 years to complete. In 1880 his title was changed to assistant professor of philosophy, and in 1885 he became a full professor (Boeree, 2000).

In spite of the fact that James battled openly with depression, he was very well liked by his students and was thought to have a great sense of humor. James enjoyed teaching, but he disliked research, did almost none of it, and said that labs were basically a waste of resources. In 1889 James's title was changed to professor of psychology. His book, called *The Principles of Psychology,* was finally published in 1890. Despite his dislike of research, James did raise the money for a new and expanded lab at Harvard, but rather than running it himself, he quickly hired one of Wundt's students, Hugo Münsterberg, to be its director. James did not supervise many graduate students, but several were quite successful in their own right. He retired from teaching in 1907. Two years later, James met Sigmund Freud when he came to Boston in 1909 and was very impressed by him. On August 26, 1910, William James died in his wife's arms (Boeree, 2000).

BRANCHES OF PSYCHOLOGY

Many people think that the field of psychology only has one aspect to it, the patient lying on the couch and talking to a therapist about his/her problems. However, there are many branches in psychology that have emerged as the field has gained popularity. We begin our exploration of the different psychological perspectives with Sigmund Freud.

Sigmund Freud's Psychoanalytic Perspective

When people think of psychology and its origins, they almost automatically think of Sigmund Freud. Although Wundt and James are acknowledged as the first fathers of psychology, Freud is considered the father of "modern psychology," since he created the concept of clinical therapy as we know it today. Freud was famous during his own lifetime. He was both praised and ostracized for his contributions to the field of psychology. Freud also had an egocentric air to him; if you did not agree with him and his theories, then he would have a tendency to no longer have anything to do with you. He appreciated people who believed the same theories and concepts that he did. *Psychoanalysis,* Freud's school of thought, focuses on treating maladaptive behavior by bringing unconscious causes of behavior to the conscious level. This form of therapy is still used today.

Sigmund Freud

Freud was born in 1856 to parents of modest means in Freiberg, Moravia, the firstborn child in his Viennese family of three boys and five girls. Freud's parents made sure that his intellect was fostered even though they did not have much money. Freud attended the University of Vienna and in 1881 obtained his doctorate in medicine. Then he worked as a research assistant in neurology at the Institute of Physiology from 1876 to 1882. In 1885 Freud went to Paris to study hypnosis with Jean-Martin Charcot, who was famous for his work in that area. In 1886 Freud opened a neurology office in Vienna and started to formulate his theories of the mind. He focused on what he called "hysteria," a nervous condition, publishing *Studies in Hysteria* with Josef Breuer in 1895. After his father's death, Freud published *The Interpretation of Dreams* in 1900 and the *Psychopathology of Everyday Life* in 1901. In this book Freud introduced the notion of Freudian slips, and he had a large following. Freud became an associate professor at the University of Vienna in 1902 and founded a psychoanalytic society in 1908. He published works about religion and literature, as well as his introductory lectures. The death of his daughter Sophie, in 1920, inspired the work *Beyond the Pleasure Principle*. He followed that up with *The Ego and the Id* in 1923. This work is considered his last framework of the structure of the mind. He did publish a series of papers on female sexuality in 1927 but did not discuss the formulation of the mind any further. Freud died of cancer of the mouth and jaw in 1939 (Hothersall, 1995). Although a lot of controversy surrounds Freud's work, the fact remains that he began an entire genre in the field of psychology.

One of the areas that Freud contributed most significantly to in the field of psychology was his work on dreams. He was sure that our dreams were the gateway to our unconscious and that analysis would reveal the true meanings to our dreams. He also contributed greatly in the field of childhood development, creating the first stage theory of development, which spawned many additional theories that are still considered today.

Behaviorism

The behavioral perspective focuses on observable behavior rather than mental processes. Advocates of this perspective maintain that all behavior is learned. Thus, adaptive and maladaptive behaviors are both considered learned behaviors.

Ivan Pavlov (1849–1936) is considered to be the founding father of behaviorism. A Russian physiologist who was not trying to create psychological theories of behavior, Pavlov was studying the digestive tracts in dogs when he realized that their behavior was shaped through pairing and association. Therefore, he concluded, their behavior was learned (Davis & Palladino, 2002).

John B. Watson (1878–1958) is also known as a pioneer in the field of behaviorism. Watson expanded the work of Pavlov and contributed his own theories to the field. Watson was concerned with the observable behavior of a person and not the unconscious forces underlying behavior. He felt that behavior could be controlled and predicted based on past behavior. Watson's famous study was with a child called Little Albert. In the Little Albert experiment, Watson postulated that children have three basic emotional reactions—love, fear, and rage—that can be conditioned in them through experience. To test his hypothesis, he repeatedly presented a loud noise with a white lab rat to classically condition fear of the rat into Little Albert (Hothersall, 1995). The Little Albert experiment was abruptly stopped when the child was adopted, leaving this experiment incomplete. Little Albert was never deconditioned and quite possibly lived his entire life with these conditioned fears. Although the Little Albert experiment would be considered unethical by today's standards, it was considered a breakthrough for many in the field.

B. F. Skinner (1904–1990) is another theorist who greatly contributed to the field of behaviorism. Indeed, Skinner has been identified as the greatest contemporary psychologist by many people in the field. Skinner believed that all behavior changes or continues as the result of its consequences; that is, environmental consequences, rather than free will, shape human behavior. Skinner maintained, therefore, that if there is a problem behavior and you change the environment, you change the behavior. Skinner's work has been used with mental patients as well as animals that are trained to behave specific ways.

Humanism

As the field of psychology evolved, many people questioned the psychoanalytic model as well as the behavioral model. The field of humanism was born as a reaction to the criticisms of these two previous schools of thought. The humanists rejected the notion that the environment determined behavior; rather, the humanist view emphasizes a positive view of human nature. Its roots stem from existential thought and philosophy. The works of existential philosophers such as Søren Kierkegaard, Friedrich Nietzsche, Martin Heidegger, and Jean-Paul Sartre are the foundation of this model. Carl Rogers, Abraham Maslow, and Rollo May are considered the main contributors to this psychological model. Many others have expanded these theories as they are still utilized in psychology today.

Carl Rogers (1902–1987) worked on the client's capacity for self-direction and understanding of his/her own development. Abraham Maslow (1908–1970) emphasized a hierarchy of needs and motivations. Rollo May (1909–1994) relied on existential psychology that acknowledged human choice and the tragic aspects of the human existence (Clay, 2002). A variety of psychotherapeutic techniques have arisen from this model of psychology as well.

Cognitive Psychology

Behaviorism was the leading model in psychology for most of the 20th century. Cognitive psychology was born out of a disagreement with the behavioral model. *Merriam-Webster's Medical Dictionary* defines the term *cognitive psychology* as "a branch of psychology concerned with mental processes (as perception, thinking, learning, and memory) especially with respect to the internal events occurring between sensory stimulation and the overt expression of behavior." Cognitive psychologists took exception to behavioral models that only focused on observable behaviors. They postulated that mental processes were also potential causes for behavior.

Biopsychosocial Model or Neuroscience

The biopsychosocial model, or neuroscience perspective, was introduced by George Engel (1913–1999) in 1977 and incorporated biological, psychological, and sociological perspectives for behavior. This perspective shifted the focus from disease to health. Engel (1977) believed that psychological factors could determine recovery times from biological illnesses.

This biopsychosocial, or neuroscience, model is also known as the *physiological perspective*. Physiological psychologists believe that we can best study behavior by understanding the functioning of the brain, nervous system, and hormones (Kalat, 1998).

DIVERSITY IN PSYCHOLOGY

As you have been reading about the early influences of psychology you may have noticed that all of the theorists were male. Women did not factor into the development of early theories and models of psychology. In addition, it has not been until fairly recently that psychology even looked at culture and how that can impact behavior and cognitions. There has been a lot of research in multicultural diversity recently.

There were strict barriers in the past for women and minorities in psychology. For example, Mary Whiton Calkins (1863–1930) completed the necessary requirements for a PhD in psychology from Harvard University, even studying under the great William James, but the university refused to grant her the degree. Why was Mary denied the degree? Simply because she was a woman. Mary did not let this stop her from advancing in the field of psychology. In 1905 she was the first woman elected president of the American Psychological Association (Madigan & O'Hara, 1992).

Race has also been a major factor in the development of psychology. Professional training was not allowed for African Americans during the late 1800s and early 1900s (Davis & Palladino, 2002). In 1920 Francis C. Sumner (1895–1954) was granted a PhD in psychology, and he set up the psychology program at Howard University in the late 1920s. African American women were not granted doctorates in psychology until the late 1930s. Inez Beverly Prosser (1897–1934) was the first African American woman to receive a doctoral degree in educational psychology. Sadly, she was killed in an automobile accident one year later (Warren, 1999).

RESEARCH METHODS IN PSYCHOLOGY

In psychology we use scientific research methods to add credibility to our findings. A huge criticism of Freud's work was that it did not have any scientific proof to go along with the theories. So, researchers in psychology employ these methods to ensure that the findings are relevant and relatable. Psychology is the study of cognitions, behaviors, and emotions. It is important to remember that these concepts are studied using scientific methodologies. These procedures give credibility to the field of psychology. Without this credibility, psychology would be all guesswork and not have much meaning. Researchers use the scientific method to develop explanations about phenomena. These explanations are theories that are then tested through a variety of methods. Scientists create hypotheses after the initial theory is created so that they can offer an educated guess about what they think will take place when they test their theories. The following subsections discuss some of the different methods that are used in conducting psychological research.

Case Studies

A *case study* is a clinical in-depth analysis of one person or event over time. Although there is some debate about the history of case studies, Sigmund Freud and Jean Piaget popularized the use of case studies in the psychological community. The greatest advantage to using case studies is the rich and detailed information that is received about one particular person or event, which is not as easy to do with a group. The reason that researchers follow a person or event in such detail is to gather information and then generalize it to the population at large. Case studies help researchers suggest additional research possibilities from their findings. The biggest disadvantage to case studies is that the information is not always generalizable to the population at large.

Naturalistic Observation

When we watch people working, shopping, playing, or interacting in any way, we are using observation skills. Scientifically, researchers use *naturalistic observation* to record observations of people in their natural environment. Researchers study these behaviors in order to make predictions about behavior or events. In this case the researchers do not intervene in any way with the people whom they are studying. Their job is strictly to observe and record information without being noticed. The benefits of this type of research are that researchers get a true reading of how people respond and interact naturally. However, the downside to this type of research is that it is very limited and investigators cannot get at what individuals are thinking when they behave or act in their environment.

Correlational Research

Correlational research lets us know whether two unrelated variables can be correlated; this means that we are trying to determine whether or not these variables occur together. If two items are found to occur together, then we say that there is a positive correlation between the variables. If they do not occur together, then there is a negative correlation between the variables. This allows researchers to make certain predictions about future events. For example, if we were trying to determine if going to college increases your chances of earning more money, then we would measure being a college graduate with the amount of money being earned. We would see a positive correlation between being a graduate and earning more money. Therefore, we know that these two items are positively correlated.

Survey Research

Psychologists use *survey research* to gather data that are representative of a large population. Surveys are used for a variety of reasons, and many of you have probably been part of a survey research poll. For example, if I worked for Joe Cool Wireless Company and I wanted to see how many people use my product versus how many people use other carriers, I may conduct an e-mail survey to see which provider people claim to use. I would send out my questionnaire through a mass e-mail blitz and see which carrier has the most customers. Surveys are a cheap and easy method for collecting data, but they also have a downside. People do not always tell the truth, some people would delete the e-mail, and some people just like participating in a survey because they think that they will get something free from completing it, even if they do not meet the criteria of the survey—in this case, own a cell phone. Additionally, some questionnaires are not worded well and people are unsure of how to answer. Overall, though, surveys can be quite valuable, if they are completed correctly.

Experiments

The experimental method is typically considered to be the most powerful method of data collection. With information acquired through an *experiment,* researchers can make a cause-and-effect statement about the topic being studied. The main problem with other research methods is the lack of control over situations, and the experimental method tries to overcome these issues. The experimental method is the deliberate manipulation of one specific variable while maintaining constancy of all other variables.

SUMMARY

This chapter has briefly introduced the field of psychology, its history, some of its different perspectives, and various methods used to conduct psychological research. As we progress through the chapters, you will gain insights into the various subdivisions and research in the field of psychology. Remember, each one of these chapters can be divided into its own course, or even several courses, in the field of psychology.

CASE STUDY #1 PSYCHOLOGY AT WORK

"Hey, Max, did you read the sports section online?" asked Annie of her co-worker. The two had shared an office in the information management systems department for two years and frequently discussed the results of various sporting events.

"I did read it, Annie. Did you hear about that soccer riot in England? Why does this kind of thing always happen at soccer games? You never hear about these kinds of things at tennis matches or baseball games."

"I don't know, Max. I guess the British love their soccer."

"How did you become such a huge sports fan, Annie? Girls don't usually like most sports."

1. What branches of psychology might address gender differences in behavior?
2. Consider the riot that Max read about online. What types of questions might a biopsychosocial psychologist ask about the occurrence of such behavior? What types of questions might a cognitive psychologist ask? What types of questions might a humanist psychologist ask? What types of questions might a behavioral psychologist ask?
3. When Max assumes that women do not like sports, what branch of psychology would likely address that notion?
4. How would the branch that you choose help with coping skills?
5. Have you even considered how complicated reading the newspaper online is? Which branch of psychology tries to understand the mental processes involved in reading? Which branch may address how children develop reading skills?

CASE STUDY #2 WHY DO PEOPLE FALL IN LOVE?

Turning on the TV and flipping to "Oprah," Sidney looked at her watch. It was 4:15 p.m. She had missed the beginning and would have to try to catch up.

Onstage, two "experts" argued over why people fall in love. The first speculated about what elements of another person we fall in love with and why. Do we fall in love with a face, or with a pair of eyes, or with some facet of another's personality? The second expert maintained that it is impossible to separate individual features. "It is the whole person with whom we fall in love," he said.

Comments from the audience followed these experts. One audience member commented that only after people rose above everyday concerns and worries were they capable of experiencing true love. A second audience member firmly believed people are innately driven to love certain types of people and that love is a biological not psychological response. A third person claimed that people fall in love with people who remind them of their parents. Finally, a fourth person argued that to understand why someone is in love you have to "see the world through their eyes."

1. Which school of thought does Wilhelm Wundt belong to? What methodology would Wilhelm Wundt suggest for understanding human thoughts and behaviors? Which expert would Wilhelm Wundt side with in this debate?
2. Describe the humanistic model of psychology. What would this model suggest about the first audience member's comment about love? What would the model suggest about the third member's comment?
3. Describe the psychoanalytic model of psychology. What would this model suggest about the third member's comment about love? What would the model suggest about the first member's comment?
4. Which models of psychology are most interested with the "inner mind"? What would these models think about the second audience member's comment? What would these models think about the fourth audience member's comment?
5. Why do you think we fall in love? Which theory most closely resembles your opinion on why we fall in love?

CASE STUDY #3 DOES TV CORRUPT YOUR MIND?

Brad and Stacy were having a debate about the effects that TV has on children. Brad feels that kids who watch too much TV become couch potatoes and do not become productive members of society. He also believes that watching police dramas increases the rate of crime because such shows normalize crime. He maintains that children who watch those types of TV shows start to care about others less and become less compassionate to people in trouble. Stacy thinks that kids who watch these shows do not change at all. She feels that children whose parents teach them right from wrong will not misbehave from watching TV.

1. What is a theory? What is Brad's theory on the effects of television on children? What is Stacy's theory on the effects of television on children?
2. What is a hypothesis that might come from Brad's theory? What is a hypothesis that might come from Stacy's theory? If you were asked to create an experiment designed to test each of these theories, what would it consist of?
3. A news article stated that children who watch more violent shows tend to be less compassionate. The researchers concluded that parents should not let their children watch police shows. Evaluate this conclusion.
4. Stacy suggests investigating each of their theories by studying their own children. What kind of research is this? What are the potential drawbacks to this kind of research? What are the potential advantages to this kind of research?
5. Brad is curious to know how much television children in their neighborhood watch. To find out he called 20 of his friends and asked them how much TV they let their children watch. What is this type of research called? What are the advantages and disadvantages of this type of research in general? What are the drawbacks to Brad's approach in general?

CASE STUDY #4 THE POWER OF PERSUASION

Daniel is a psychology major beginning his final semester. As part of his degree requirement, Daniel must design and conduct an experiment. Being interested in persuasion, he decides to investigate possible personality variables he believes might be associated with the ability to resist being persuaded by others.

Asking his subjects to administer increasingly large shocks to a laboratory rat, Daniel records how far he is able to persuade each person to carry the shocks. He then compares his measure to several personality scales, including a measure of aggressiveness that is obtained by recording the highest level of shock administered to the rat. Surprisingly, this measure of persuasion is correlated positively with aggressiveness; and negatively with vegetarianism and self-esteem. Daniel concludes that aggressive individuals are more likely to follow orders, whereas vegetarians are less likely to follow orders.

1. What variables from this case study do you think are important in order to draw relevant conclusions about this experiment?
2. Is the conclusion that aggressive individuals are more likely to follow orders a good one? Is the conclusion that vegetarians are less likely to follow orders a good one? Defend your answers. Which conclusion do you think is the most likely?
3. Consider the conclusion that vegetarians are less likely to follow orders. What important factor is Daniel overlooking in making this decision?
4. When discussing the implication of this study for teaching people to be resistant to persuasion, Daniel suggests, by increasing self-esteem, one can increase resistance to unwanted persuasion. Is this a reasonable implication of this study?
5. Which classic study is this mimicking with some subtle changes?

CASE STUDY #5 ARE YOU JUST LUCKY?

For the second time in four weeks, Sarah won the football pool by picking the most winning teams for the week. This wouldn't have been so frustrating for Eric except for one thing: Sarah knows nothing about football.

"I don't understand how you do it, Sarah, but I'm going to figure it out."

"I've told you before. I've always been kind of psychic about things. My mom is the same way. In fact, I think it runs in our family. Maybe it's genetic."

Eric and Sarah have had this argument a dozen times. In fact, such an argument inspired a psychology project collaboration between them. Each asked 20 people if they had ever had a psychic experience. Oddly, while only 1 of the people Eric interviewed reported having such experiences, 5 of the 20 told Sarah about a psychic experience.

"Maybe it is genetic," Eric said, returning to the conversation. "Or maybe you are just lucky."

1. Is the number of people who reported having had a psychic experience to Sarah meaningfully higher than the number of people who reported this to Eric? How do researchers determine if differences such as this are meaningful?
2. What could account for Sarah's luck in the football picks? Do you think that it is luck or is Sarah really a psychic?
3. Does the procedure that Eric and Sarah chose to use truly illuminate the issue of whether the possible source of Sarah's success is due to genetic factors?
4. Many studies have been conducted testing whether or not extrasensory perception (ESP) exists. How might a researcher draw conclusions as to whether or not it does exist?
5. If you were going to use one of the experimental methodologies to conduct your own study on ESP, which one would you use and why? Make sure you explain your answers in detail.

ACTIVITY #1 WRITE A CREATIVE STORY

Creative Thinking and Writing . . .

For this project, you will write a short story set during the time of one of the following famous people in psychology. You can write anything you want, but it needs to be time specific and include your famous person. That means you need to research the person you choose before you begin your short story.

Here are the people to choose from for this project:

William James

Wilhelm Wundt

Sigmund Freud

John B. Watson

Ivan Pavlov

B. F. Skinner

G. Stanley Hall

Carl Jung

Stanley Milgram

Fritz Perls

Carl Rogers

Anna Freud

Karen Horney

Erik Erikson

Rene Descartes

ACTIVITY #2 CONDUCT AN EXPERIMENT

In this activity, you will design a survey experiment to help you understand what psychology is about and how it differs from the popular ideas about it that most people have.

First, you are going to create a survey. Then, you will need to ask at least 20 people the questions that you have created. You should select a variety of people. These people must be volunteers!

Make sure that you record pertinent data about each subject (gender, age, what major they are in school or which position they hold on the campus) and the *exact* response to your questions. Do not add to the response or try to clarify it on your own in any way. If you are confused about what a respondent means, ask the subject to clarify!

Once you have created a survey and administered it to your selected population, you are going to spend time in your groups going over the results of your survey questionnaires. You need to analyze your findings. Were the answers to each question the same? Were they different? How were they the same or different? What does this mean? What is the point of your survey? Did your subjects figure out what you were trying to do?

Next you will write a paper based on your survey experiment. The first thing you need to do is write an introduction that explains what you studied. Remember to define the term *psychology* at the beginning of your paper. Your hypothesis should be in the introduction. You will then write the body of the paper, which will consist of the details of your experiment (what you did, what type of subjects you interviewed, the expected results, and the actual results).

Then you will do some Internet research to see if there have been any other studies that are like yours and explain what you found. Make sure that you include references for any studies that you include in your paper. You should cite at least two sources. Finally, you will write the conclusion. In your conclusion you should discuss if your hypothesis was correct or incorrect, what changes, if any, you would make if you redid the experiment, and any other conclusions you have drawn based on the research that you collected.

Here are some of the questions you will want to answer in your paper:

1. What is your hypothesis?
2. What is the definition of psychology?
3. What is the definition of a survey experiment?
4. What are some of the common elements in the statements made by your subjects?
5. What are some of the differences in the statements made by your subjects?
6. Is your hypothesis valid or not valid?
7. What happens if a hypothesis is wrong?
8. How can this information be used in the future?

ACTIVITY #3 WHO AM I?

In this activity, you will write a paper about yourself. This is not as easy as it sounds.

Some topics you may want to include in your paper are:

1. What degree are you seeking?
2. What made you choose this school?
3. What do you want to do when you graduate from school?
4. Do you want to go on for additional schooling when you are done?
5. What is your ultimate career?
6. What is your ultimate goal?
7. Do you want to marry or are you married?
8. Do you have or want to have kids?
9. What do you do for work?
10. Tell me about your family life.

The list can go on and on. . . .

This is your story. You tell it the way you want to tell it!

Remember, don't write anything that makes you feel uncomfortable.

REFERENCES

Blumenthal, A. L. (2001). A Wundt primer: The operating characteristics of consciousness. In R. W. Reiber & D. K. Robinson (Eds.), *Wilhelm Wundt in history: The making of a scientific psychology* (pp. 121–142). New York: Kluwer Academic Publishing.

Boeree, C. G. (2000). Wilhelm Wundt and William James. Retrieved from http://www.ship.edu/%7Ecgboeree/wundtjames.html.

Clay, R. A. (2002). A renaissance for humanistic psychology. The field explores new niches while building on its past. *American Psychological Association Monitor, 33*(8), 5–10.

Davis, S. F. & Palladino, J. J. (2002). *Psychology* (3rd ed.). Upper Saddle River, NJ: Pearson.

Engel, G. L. (1977). The need for a new medical model: A challenge for biomedicine. *Science, 196,* 129–136.

Hothersall, D. (1995). *History of psychology* (3rd ed.). New York: McGraw-Hill.

Kalat, J. W. (1998). *Biological psychology* (6th ed.). Pacific Grove, CA: Brooks/Cole.

Lahey, B. (2003). *Psychology* (8th ed.). McGraw-Hill.

Madigan, S., & O'Hara, R. (1992). Short-term memory at the turn of the century: Mary Whiton Calkins' memory research. *American Psychologist, 47,* 170–174.

Warren, W. (1999). *Black women scientists in the U.S.* Bloomington, IN: Indiana University Press.

Weitzen, W. (2002). *Psychology: Themes and variations: Briefer version* (5th ed.). Belmont, CA: Wadsworth.

CHAPTER 2

Biological Bases of Behavior

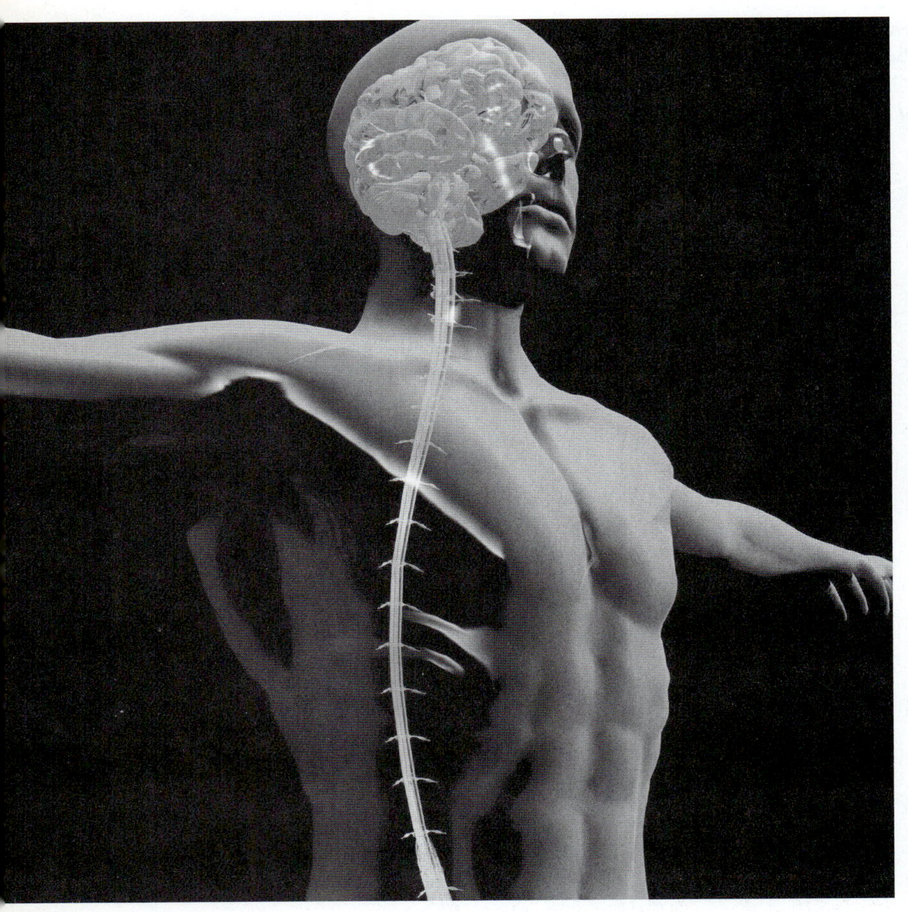

LEARNING ASSETS

Case Study #1 Too Much, Who Me?

Case Study #2 Sensing and Making Sense of the World

Case Study #3 Alzheimer's Whodunit?

Activity #1 Phineas Gage

Activity #2 What Do You See?

Activity #3 Are You Left Brained or Right Brained?

BIOLOGICAL BASES OF PSYCHOLOGY

The nervous system, which includes the brain, is the most complex of all of the organs in the human body. Scientists have been wondering about, researching, and examining the nervous system to see how it works so efficiently. When we are concerned with the hows and whys of what people do, we need to start at the most basic biological level. The nervous system allows us to sense, perceive, and react in our environment.

When we sense, perceive, and react to stimuli we offer what is known as a *response.* For example, if we go to the beach and smell the salty air, hear the waves crash in the ocean, and feel the sand beneath our toes, we are sensing and perceiving many different types of stimuli simultaneously. A response might be a sense of calmness or peace. *Receptors,* which are specialized cells, allow us to sense these stimuli. Our brain will then process this information and make sense of what we perceive. After we perceive the information, our brain tells us that we need to elicit a response. All of these processes take place within a matter of seconds and are coordinated and controlled by the central nervous system (CNS) and the peripheral nervous system (PNS). The CNS is composed of the brain and the spinal cord, and the PNS comprises the nerves that connect the brain and spinal cord to the rest of the body.

Peripheral Nervous System

The PNS has two main components. These two components are sensory and motor. Sensory, or afferent, pathways provide input from the body to the CNS. The motor, or efferent, pathways carry signals to the muscles and glands. We call these muscles and glands *effectors.* The PNS has two major divisions: the somatic nervous system (SNS) and the autonomic nervous system (ANS). The somatic division of the PNS is responsible for deciphering all of the contact with the environment that we encounter. This includes the nerves that connect receptors to the spinal column and brain and the nerves that run from the brain and spinal cord to the muscles. The SNS regulates how we sense and respond to stimuli. Many of our responses are known to be planned and coordinated, so the SNS is said to be a voluntary system, which just means that it is in our control.

The ANS interacts with the organs and glands that regulate our bodily functions. We are not able to plan or coordinate these functions, so they are not voluntary or in the realm of our control. So we say that this is an autonomic, or involuntary, system. The ANS can be further divided into two main components: the sympathetic division and the parasympathetic division. The sympathetic division is in control of getting us out of trouble, which is what we often call the *fight-or-flight response.* The fight-or-flight response, first identified by Walter Cannon (1914), is described by Cannon as the body's response to impending danger—we either prepare to fight or flee the dangerous situation. As identified by Cannon, the physical changes that occur during this response are outlined as follows:

- Our senses sharpen. Pupils dilate (open out) so we can see more clearly, even in darkness. Our hairs stand on end, making us more sensitive to our environment (and also making us appear larger, hopefully intimidating our opponent).
- The cardiovascular system leaps into action, with the heart pump rate going from one up to five gallons per minute, and our arteries constrict to maximize pressure around the system while the veins open to ease return of blood to the heart.
- The respiratory system joins in as the lungs, throat, and nostrils open up, and breathing speeds up to get more air in the system so the increased blood flow can be reoxygenated.

The blood carries oxygen to the muscles, allowing them to work harder. Deeper breathing also helps us to scream more loudly!

- Fat from fatty cells and glucose from the liver are metabolized to create instant energy.
- Blood vessels to the kidney and digestive system are constricted, effectively shutting down systems that are not essential. A part of this effect is reduction of saliva in the mouth. The bowels and bladder may also open to reduce the need for other internal actions. (This might also dissuade our attackers!)
- Blood vessels to the skin constrict, reducing any potential blood loss. Sweat glands also open, providing an external cooling liquid to our overworked system. (This makes the skin look pale and clammy.)
- Endorphins, which are the body's natural pain killers, are released. (When you are fighting, you do not want be bothered with pain—that can be put off until later.)
- The natural judgment system is also turned down, and more primitive responses take over—this is a time for action rather than deep thought.

When the fight-or-flight response is no longer in question, the parasympathetic division then returns the body to its normal, balanced state, by slowing the functions that were aroused by the sympathetic division. This allows the body to return to its previous state before the danger was presented.

Central Nervous System

The central nervous system (CNS) consists of the brain and the spinal cord. Fluid and tissue insulate the brain so that it is not as prone to injury. The spinal cord is encased in a protective shield called the *vertical column,* which consists of 24 bones known as *vertebrae.* Sensory nerves enter the dorsal, or back, of the spinal cord; the motor nerves exit the ventral, or front, of the spinal cord between the vertebrae. Reflexes, which are automatic responses, are produced when the sensory nerves provide information that does not travel all the way to the brain.

The brain consists of three parts: the *cerebrum* (known as the seat of consciousness), the *cerebellum* (part of the unconscious brain), and the *medulla oblongata* (also part of the unconscious brain). When information needs to travel through your body to the brain, it travels upward through a group of nerves known as a *tract.* The information passes through the hindbrain, which is the medulla, the pons, and the cerebellum. The medulla is responsible for very important functions such as breathing, swallowing, and blood circulation. The pons connects the two halves of the brain at the hindbrain, and the primary function of the pons is sleep and arousal. The cerebellum is responsible for skilled movements and balance. If you drink too much alcohol, the most deeply affected area of the brain is the cerebellum.

The message we have been referring to continues to travel through the midbrain region, which is known as the brain stem when combined with the hindbrain. The tectum, where sensory information is processed, is found on the roof of the midbrain. The nerve pathways that are a complex network of fibers are known as reticular formation and this controls arousal and alertness.

As information continues to travel, it leaves the brain stem and moves upward to the forebrain. The forebrain is divided into two separate and distinct halves with exact replicas in each half. The corpus callosum connects these two hemispheres and is in charge of communication for each side. The first region within the forebrain to receive information is the subcortical structures. The subcortical structures are underneath the other main division of the forebrain, which is known as the cerebral cortex, or cerebrum. The cerebrum is the outer covering of the brain. The cerebral cortex is very wrinkled and distinctive in humans and serves as the separation of the various lobes within the brain. The brain has four lobes: the frontal lobe, the temporal lobe, the parietal lobe, and the occipital lobe. It is important to note that there are two hemispheres of the brain, and there are four lobes.

A group of interrelated subcortical structures that are involved in the regulation of hunger, emotions, thirst, aggression, and sexual behaviors is known as the *limbic system*. The limbic system consists of the amygdala, the hippocampus, and the septum. The exact functioning of the limbic system is still a highly debated area of interest. However, most scientists agree that the limbic system is involved in emotional reactions, memory storage, and experiencing pleasure. The thalamus is deeply situated in the forebrain. There is one on either side of the midline of the brain. The thalamus relays to the cerebral cortex information received from various areas of the brain.

BRAIN FUNCTIONS

How do scientists know how the brain functions? Primitive experiences studying the brain were crude and often caused more harm than good. As science progressed, however, researchers were able to determine which areas of the brain control each of the various functions. For example, they know where memory and language are stored in the brain. This information was acquired through dissection of the brain postmortem as well as through various machines that show electrical stimulation within the brain while an individual is alive.

Paul Broca (1824–1880), a French physician and researcher, worked with one case study in his research about brain functioning. His patient was a terminally ill male named Tan. He was named Tan because "tan" was one of the few sounds that he was still able to make (Davis & Palladino, 2002). Tan's vocal cords were not damaged and he could understand what was being said to him, he just could not speak. Postmortem, Tan's brain was autopsied by Dr. Broca, who located the damage to Tan's brain. The frontal lobe of his left hemisphere was severely damaged, and Dr. Broca determined that this is the area where speech is produced. Since this was a revelation in the medical field, this area was designated *Broca's area*. A second area was later found to be responsible for speech comprehension and was named *Wernicke's area* after Carl Wernicke (1848–1905), a German neurologist and psychiatrist.

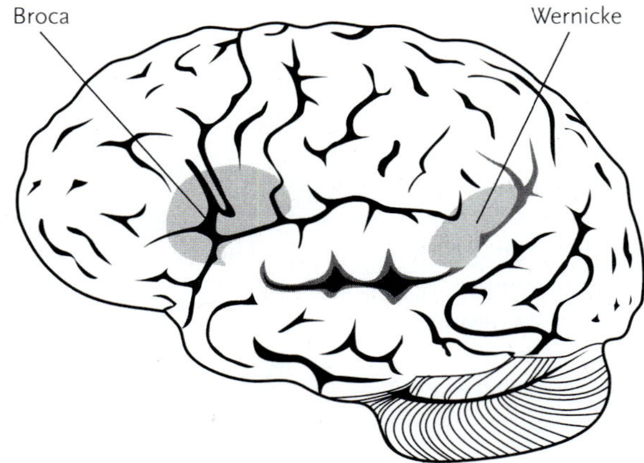

Broca and Wernicke areas.

The most extensive knowledge that researchers have gained is through working with people who have had some type of brain damage. People who have suffered strokes have offered a plethora of knowledge that has aided in many of the breakthroughs people now take for granted. A stroke is the rapidly developing loss of brain function(s) due to a disturbance in the blood supply to the brain. As a result, the brain loses its ability to function properly.

In the past, stroke was referred to as cerebrovascular accident, or CVA, but the word *stroke* is now preferred (Donnan, Fisher, Macleod, & Davis, 2008). Scientists are also able to learn a lot about the brain through other incidents that cause damage.

A variety of tests are used to evaluate brain functioning and also to determine the severity and longevity of the damage. An electroencephalograph (EEG), which monitors and records electrical activity in the brain, can examine brain functions without a patient having to have surgery. The use of computer imaging to assess brain function also has increased. There are PET scans, CT scans, and MRI scans. PET, or positron emission tomography, provides information about the brain's metabolic activity by utilizing nuclear medicine imaging. A PET scan measures things like blood flow, oxygen use, and glucose metabolism. A CAT scan, or CT imaging, stands for computerized axial tomography; it uses x-ray equipment to produce images of the inside of the body. MRI stands for magnetic resonance imaging; it is also used to see the inside of the body, but it is better able to determine the soft tissues (Novelline, 1997).

Neurons, which have nuclei, are cells that compose the nervous system. The nuclei are encased in membranes and contain many smaller structures. Neurons can communicate with one another and come in a variety of shapes and sizes, a quality that sets them apart from other cells. Interneurons are small, and many of them are able to occupy one area, whereas motor neurons are quite large and travel longer distances. The composition of all neurons includes a cell membrane, dendrites, a soma, an axon, and synaptic buttons. Cell membranes usually surround the entire neuron and give it shape. It is filled with cytoplasm and is semipermeable. *Semipermeable* means that the neuron allows some substances to pass through it. The dendrites are short, branchlike structures that receive information from the receptors. The soma, which is the cell body, relays the neural signal from the dendrites to the axon. The axon transmits signals to other neurons, glands, and muscles. The synaptic buttons store neurotransmitters before they are released as well as transmit signals from one neuron to the next.

The myelin sheath of a neuron can make all of these neurons different. It consists of fat-containing cells that insulate the axon from electrical activity, which increases the rate of the transmission of signals. There is a gap between each myelin sheath cell along the axon. The myelin sheath makes the white matter of the brain appear white. Included in the myelin cells are glial cells, which are called *oligodendrocytes* in the central nervous system and *Schwann cells* in the peripheral nervous system. The gaps formed between the myelin sheath are called the *nodes of Ranvier.*

A well-developed and healthy myelin sheath is critically important. For example, multiple sclerosis is a neurological disorder that is characterized by what we call *demyelination* of axons in places throughout the central nervous system. This loss of the myelin sheath typically results in different types of symptoms. The symptoms depend on the areas that are affected by the neurons. Common symptoms include lack of muscle control, difficulty with speech, and various visual disturbances.

Now we will focus on how neurons are organized and how information is transmitted from neuron to neuron. Neurons need to be properly aligned and organized in a particular manner when sending messages. A synapse is the most common arrangement for the messages to occur naturally. It consists of the synaptic buttons being near each other, but not touching. The presynaptic membrane is the membrane on the side that sends the message. A commonly occurring type of synapse consists of three parts: the synaptic button that sends the signal, a dendrite to receive the signal, and the synaptic cleft, which is the space between the synaptic button and the dendrite.

Charles Scott Sherrington (1857–1952) was the first scientist to discover neurotransmitter activity. He was studying the reflexive foot raising in dogs when he observed that reflexes occurred more slowly than the speed of the neural impulse in the axon would predict. So he correctly predicted that another process must be involved (Davis & Palladino, 2002). After this prediction, Sherrington found that the synapse involved consisted of special chemicals that we now call *neurotransmitters.* Synaptic vesicles, located in the synaptic buttons, are where neurotransmitters are stored in tiny packets. An influx of calcium ions rush into the synaptic buttons when neuron signals reach them. The neurotransmitter is then released into the synaptic cleft. As the neurotransmitter enters the synaptic cleft, it makes contact with the postsynaptic membrane of another neuron. These neurotransmitters contact specially shaped receptor sites, and this allows the signal to be transferred from one neuron to another.

In order to understand the importance of neurotransmitters, we must look at the myriad roles they play in our everyday lives. Moving, walking, and sitting are all affected by neurotransmitters. Parkinson's disease involves an issue with the neurotransmitters and results in reduced levels of the neurotransmitter dopamine. L-dopa is a drug that is often prescribed to Parkinson patients to try to reduce the effects of the disease. People suffering from Parkinson's disease often report stiffness, tremors, and slow movements due to a lack of the neurotransmitter dopamine.

As mentioned earlier, the brain consists of two hemispheres that are connected by what is called the *corpus callosum*. People often use the phrase "split brain" to refer to the two hemispheres of the brain. For many years, scientists wondered what would happen if the corpus callosum were severed, so in the 1960s two neurosurgeons did just that. Phillip Vogel and Joseph Bogen were the two surgeons who found that when they severed the corpus callosum, epilepsy seemed to be reduced for some patients. These findings allowed for Nobel Prize winner Roger Sperry and his colleague Michael Gazzaniga to do additional research. They found that severing the corpus callosum revealed that each hemisphere was responsible for different processes. They also found that severing the corpus callosum did not reduce intelligence or motivation. Even more specifically, they learned that the left hemisphere is responsible for speech and language production and operates in a logical, sequential, and analytical manner. The right hemisphere was shown to be the center for our emotions. It is also responsible for spatial abilities and creativity.

SUMMARY

The chapter has focused on the biological bases of behavior. These functions are central in our processing and perceiving the world. The next chapter focuses specifically on how these biological functions contribute to how we sense and perceive the world.

CASE STUDY #1 TOO MUCH, WHO ME?

On Friday evenings Dennis liked to join his friends at the Beach Sider, a bar near campus that has a wide selection of beers on tap as well as bottled beer from 30 countries on six continents. This Friday was no exception. After enjoying two beers at home to start the evening, Dennis made the short walk to the Beach Sider. As it turned out, his friends Jackie and Matthew were there celebrating; they had taken a midterm exam in their English literature class that afternoon and both had studying all week to get ready. As the night, and the drinking, progressed, Dennis's behavior began to change in predictable ways: His speech became slurred, his balance began to go, and his thinking became narrowly focused. Additionally, many social inhibitions were shed, and Dennis approached people and made statements that he never would have made when sober.

1. From a physiological viewpoint, why will Dennis's behavior go back to normal when he sobers up?
2. Why did alcohol consumption affect Dennis's ability to walk with a normal, smooth balance? What region of his brain was affected and in what ways?
3. What physiological effects does alcohol consumption have on the body's neurotransmitters? Can these effects be traced to any quality that is characteristic of drunkenness? Which qualities?
4. Alcohol is often called a depressant. However, most people who drink say that it does not depress them. In what ways is alcohol a depressant? Can you postulate any physiological basis for alcohol-induced effects on mood?
5. From a psychological viewpoint, why is Dennis more confident when he drinks alcohol in large quantities?

CASE STUDY #2 SENSING AND MAKING SENSE OF THE WORLD

Returning from vacation, Drew was disappointed to discover that she had gained 7 pounds. Reasoning that it had taken a month to gain the weight, she resolved to begin a one-month regimen of diet and exercise. In a symbolic gesture, Drew dug out a pair of running shoes that she had not worn for six months. Changing into gray sweats, she was ready to go. After briefly stretching her leg muscles, she headed toward her favorite coffee shop. The coffee shop was three quarters of a mile away and she reasoned that the mile and a half run would be a good length for her first day. Drew was running for a short period of time when she noticed a slight pain in her stomach. Drew immediately remembered why she had given up jogging six months ago—abdominal cramps. Slight at first, the cramps increased noticeably as she made her way to the coffee shop. Approaching the coffee shop she felt certain that she was not going to be able to complete her trip. Unexpectedly, just as she thought about stopping to dig out her cell phone to call for a ride, her pain began to subside. The pain was replaced with a pleasant, almost euphoric feeling. Drew was going to make it after all.

1. Drew's cramps began to increase as she approached her favorite coffee shop. On a biological level, what mechanisms allow the body to differentiate degrees of pain? What does this suggest about the treatment of severe pain?
2. The cramps, being replaced by a "runner's high," began to subside as Drew approached the coffee shop. What neurological changes might have occurred to cause this "second wind"?
3. Is it possible that it was no coincidence that Drew's second wind occurred as she approached her favorite coffee shop and recognized it as being the halfway mark? How might the recognition of being half finished reduce feelings of pain?
4. What types of drugs do you think interfere with the nervous system?
5. It is a well-known fact that there is an optimal level of physical exercise for burning calories and that by exercising too rigorously you will actually burn fewer calories. Use your knowledge of the nervous system to explain this counterproductive relationship.

CASE STUDY #3 ALZHEIMER'S WHODUNIT?

It was just past 10:00 p.m. when Detective Livingstone received a call to proceed to the home of Charlie Hallifax, now the late Charlie Hallifax. When he arrived, he was greeted by Officers Hogan and McCaffey.

In the reading room, sprawled out in an awkward position in the center of the room, Mr. Hallifax's body was an unsettling sight.

"It looks like Mr. Hallifax had a seizure. Of course we can't be sure, but that's what it looks like," offered Officer Hogan.

Livingstone's attention was elsewhere. Next to Mr. Hallifax's body was a broken brandy snifter.

"What do we know about Mr. Hallifax's mental health as of late?" asked Detective Livingstone.

"Apparently Mr. Hallifax has suffered from depression for a number of years," said McCaffey. "Lately he's been frustrated with forgetfulness. His neighbor tells us that he's been losing his memory, and that it bothered him greatly. Why do you ask, sir? Do you have any ideas?"

"Just one," said Livingstone as his face began to glow triumphantly. "Did Mr. Hallifax have a maid?"

"Yes, he did!" exclaimed Hogan.

1. What neurological transmitters are associated with depression? What does this imply about the effectiveness of drug treatments for depression?
2. Mr. Hallifax's slow memory loss may be due to Alzheimer's disease. What might account for the degeneration of these memory processes?
3. Detective Livingstone suspects that the maid poisoned her employer. What effects will poison have on the internal system of a human being?
4. Which part of the nervous system is responsible for controlling muscles, such as the heart, which were affected by the maid's poison?
5. The sight of Mr. Hallifax's contorted body alarmed Detective Livingstone. What physical reactions did he probably experience? Which part of the nervous system is responsible for these changes?

ACTIVITY #1 PHINEAS GAGE

For this activity you will research the case history of Phineas Gage on the Internet and present the findings. Make sure you use reliable sources that detail Phineas Gage's life before his accident and after his accident. There have been some fairly recent findings about what may have actually occurred with Phineas Gage. Find this information and include it in your presentation.

Your professor will outline the specific details of your presentation. However, you should always use reliable sources, cite your sources, and have as many facts and details as possible for this presentation.

ACTIVITY #2 WHAT DO YOU SEE?

http://www.michaelbach.de/ot/

http://kids.niehs.nih.gov/illusion/illusions.htm

http://www.optillusions.com/

Go to one of the above sites and choose any five optical illusions. Take your time and really pay attention to the details and what the instructions for each optical illusion ask you to find. Then, answer the following questions:

1. Were you able to find what the site told you to find in the pictures?
2. Are some illusions more difficult to see than others?
3. What is the process that is taking place in your brain to decipher these illusions?
4. Is everyone able to see these illusions and decipher them?
5. What may stop someone from being able to decipher these illusions?

ACTIVITY #3 ARE YOU LEFT BRAINED OR RIGHT BRAINED?

http://www.wherecreativitygoestoschool.com/vancouver/left_right/rb_test.htm

Go to the site listed above and take the short quiz to see if you are left brained or right brained. When you are finished, answer the following questions:

1. Which side does the test say is more dominant?
2. Do you agree or disagree with the test?
3. How would you describe yourself in regard to which hemisphere you favor?
4. Why does determining which hemisphere you are dominant in matter?

REFERENCES

Cannon, W. B. (1914). The emergency function of the adrenal medulla in pain and the major emotions. *American Journal of Physiology, 33,* 356–372.

Davis, S. F., & Palladino, J. J. (2002). *Psychology* (3rd ed.). Upper Saddle River, NJ: Pearson.

Donnan, G. A., Fisher, M., Macleod, M., & Davis, S. M. (May 2008). Stroke. *Lancet, 371*(9624): 1612–1623.

Novelline, R. (1997). *Squire's fundamentals of radiology* (5th ed.). Cambridge, MA: Harvard University Press.

CHAPTER 3

Sensation, Perception, and Neuroscience

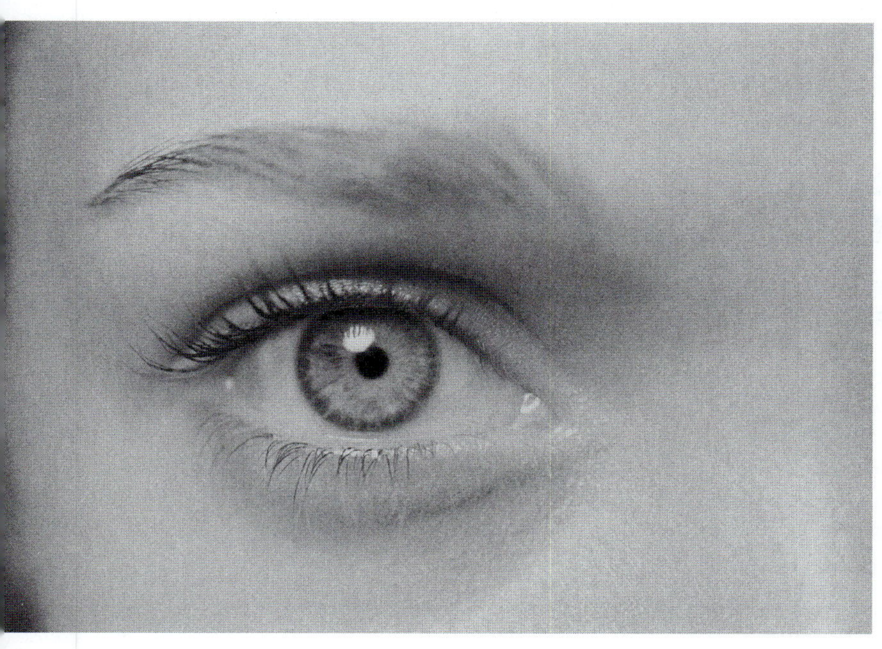

LEARNING ASSETS

Case Study #1 What Can You See?

Case Study #2 Movie Theater Blindness

Case Study #3 Spring Carnival

Case Study #4 Illusions or Delusions?

Case Study #5 Tiny Trees

Activity # 1 Taste Tests

Activity # 2 What Can You Hear?

Activity # 3 What Is a Blind Spot?

DEFINING NEUROSCIENCE, SENSATION, AND PERCEPTION

The concepts of sensation, perception, and neuroscience are quite fascinating and explain how we process information and make sense out of it. *Neuroscience* can be defined as the study of the brain and central nervous system. *Sensation* can be defined as the activation of the sense organs by a source of physical energy, and *perception* can be defined as the sorting out, interpretation, analysis, and integration of stimuli by the sense organs and brain (Feldman, 2009). Once stimulated, receptor cells transmit information to the brain. Physical energies like sound and light must first be changed into an electrochemical form for the nervous system to translate them. This change, which is necessary for processing information, is called *transduction*. If a stimulus is continually presented, then the body will use a process known as *adaptation* to accommodate the information being presented. For example, when you go into a dark movie theater from the sunlight, it is difficult to see, but your eyes adapt and soon you can see better in the dark. The same thing holds true if you listen to loud music with earphones for a period of time. Eventually, it does not seem that loud. This, however, is not good for your ears!

THRESHOLDS

For receptors to react to a stimulus there must be some amount of intensity. This is called the *absolute threshold,* which is the smallest amount of energy that must be present for perception to occur 50 percent of the time. The *difference threshold* is defined as a noticeable difference that occurs 50 percent of the time in an existing stimulus that has been changed by either adding or subtracting energy. The difference threshold can also be called *just noticeable difference* since it refers to the minimum change in stimulation necessary to detect a difference between two stimuli (Nittrouer & Lowenstein, 2007). It is important to realize that thresholds are not the same for all people. Everyone has a unique threshold that allows for these differences to be noticed.

SENSATION

This section examines the role of the senses in our lives. The neuroscience and the biological, physiological, and cognitive aspects behind each sense are discussed.

Vision

Vision is typically considered to be the most valuable of the five senses. Much research has been devoted to vision and its processes. We are able to see due to electromagnetic waves that have been transmitted from visual receptor cells. Wavelengths are considered energy that travels in waves and varies in length. They are measured in nanometers, which are billionths of a meter. The perception of colors also depends on different wavelengths, which are referred to as *hues.*

The visual system is quite a complex system that takes place fairly instantaneously. First, light waves must pass through the cornea of the eye, which serves as a protective coating that helps us to focus on light waves. These light waves then enter the anterior chamber and pass through the aqueous humor. The aqueous humor, a clear fluid with a jellylike consistency, supplies nourishment to the eye. The light waves are then transported through the pupil. The pupil is surrounded by a colored membrane known as the iris. The pupil is regulated by the iris's ability to change shape and control the amount of light that is let in.

The light then passes through the lens, which changes shape to focus on the visual image. Accommodation is the process by which the lens changes its shape to support the focusing process. The posterior chamber is where the light goes after it has passed through the lens; this structure is also filled with a clear and jellylike substance, which is called the *vitreous humor*. The vitreous humor offers nourishment to the eye as well as helps shape it. After all of this, the light waves finally reach the retina, which is the part of the eye that converts the electromagnetic energy of light to electrical impulses for transmission to the brain (Feldman, 2009).

The optic nerve—located on the underside of the brain, in front of the pituitary gland—is a bundle of ganglion axons that carry visual information to the brain. The rods and cones in the eye shape what we see. Rods are thin, cylindrical receptor cells in the retina that are very sensitive to light; cones are cone-shaped, light-sensitive receptor cells in the retina that are responsible for sharp focus and color perception. There are many more rods than cones. Rods and cones both contain photopigments, which are light-sensitive chemicals. Because rods have a lower threshold than cones, less light is necessary to activate them. Thus, cones are primarily used for color vision.

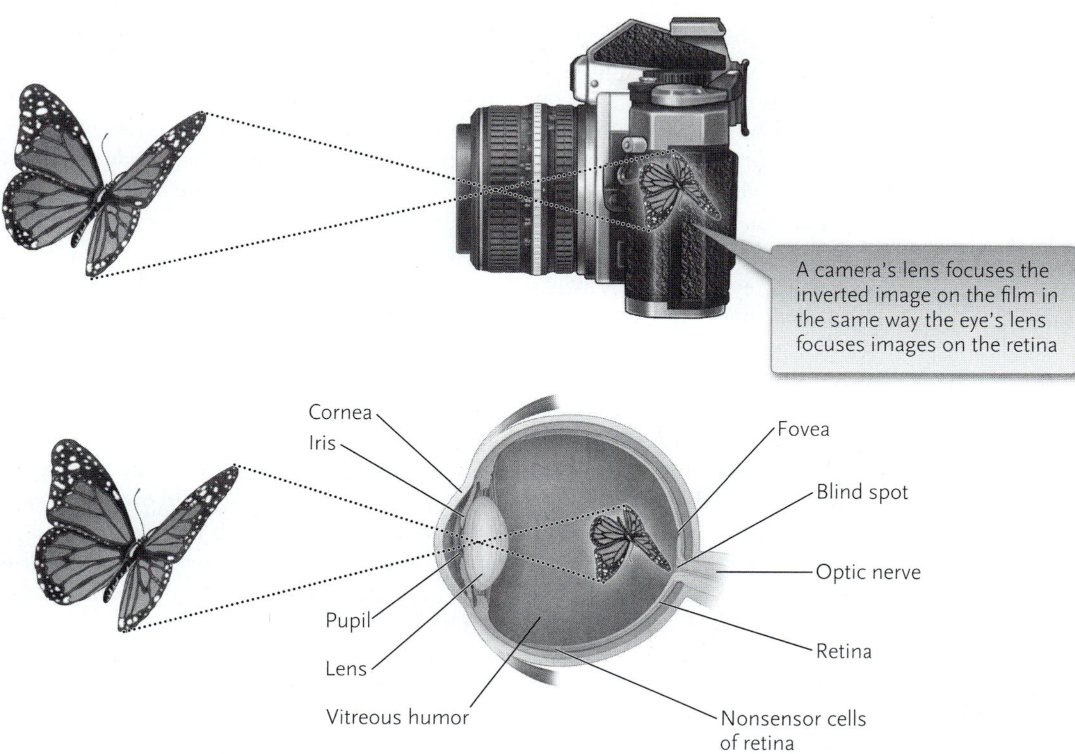

Although human vision is far more complicated than the most sophisticated camera, in some ways basic visual processes are analogous to those used in traditional, nondigital photography.

Color Vision

When discussing color vision, psychologists and other scientists often refer to the trichromatic theory of color vision, developed by Thomas Young in 1802 and modified by Hermann von Helmholtz in 1852 (Brown & Wald, 1964). This theory refers to the fact that the retina has three kinds of cones, each of which responds primarily to a specific range of wavelengths. The theory postulates that different shades are created when we receive sensory information in different amounts or proportions from the three types of cones. Eventually, another theory of color vision was proposed in 1870 by Ewald Hering; it is referred to as the opponent process theory. This theory states that the cones are arranged in pairs. It further states that red is paired with green while blue is paired with yellow. This means that one member of the pair directly influences the other member of the pair.

Seeing in color is taken for granted by most people. However, not everyone has that privilege. There are people who are considered color deficient. Some people are unable to see any color at all, known as being a *monochromat,* but this is a rarity. These people are only equipped with one type of cone, which forces the brain to process the light waves the same, so they only see in shades of gray. There are also *dichromats,* who are people who have difficulty seeing one of the primary colors (red, blue, or green). In addition, there are *trichromats,* who see three distinct colors, but one of the colors is not processed the same way it would be with a regularly sighted person. Therefore, trichromats perceive colors differently from how others with normal color vision see them.

Auditory Processes (Hearing)

How do we hear what is going on around us? Why is it important that hearing is processed so quickly? What is a sound wave? A sound wave is moving air due to an object's vibrations. The vibrations cause the molecules to move, which makes the air move, and this makes up the sound waves. Sound waves have three distinct characteristics: wavelength (frequency), amplitude (intensity), and purity (timbre). Shorter wavelengths are produced due to faster vibrations, which are sensed as high pitches. Longer wavelengths are produced due to slower vibrations and are sensed as low pitches. Frequency is measured in cycles per second and represented as hertz (Hz).

Sound waves are primarily gathered outside of the ear in what is called the *pinna,* which starts them on their journey to auditory receptors. The sound waves then travel down the *auditory canal* where they reach the *eardrum,* which causes the eardrum to move. The movement causes three bones (the *hammer,* the *anvil,* and the *stirrup*) in the middle ear to vibrate. These three bones are jointly known as the *ossicles.* The hammer (malleus) is attached to the eardrum and strikes the anvil (incus), and the anvil strikes the stirrup (stapes). The stirrup is connected to what is called the *oval window,* which connects the middle ear to the *cochlea* found in the inner ear. If the stirrup causes a vibration in the oval window, then the fluid in the cochlea is set in motion and produces a vibration in the basilar membrane. This vibration creates another set of reactions. The *organ of Corti* begins to rise and fall with this vibration, and when it moves upward, the hair cells that project from it brush against the tectorial membrane located just above it. The hair cells here are the auditory receptors. When there is contact with the tectorial membrane, the hair cells bend and then they depolarize (Fettiplace, 1990). *Depolarization* is a change in the potential where the charge becomes less negative. The auditory nerve transmits auditory information to the higher-order brain regions. The auditory nerve leads to the cochlea and then it travels to the medulla. Then, the auditory nerve is able to cross over to the opposite hemisphere and travel to the

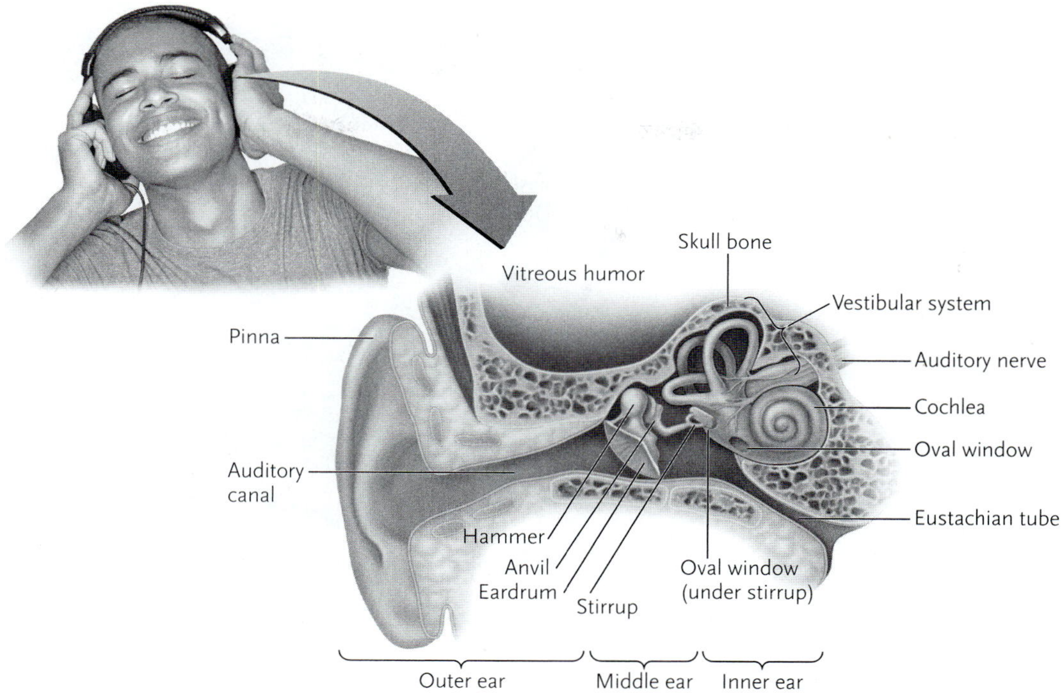

The major parts of the ear.

SOURCE: Brooker et al., 2007, p. 956.

thalamus, which then sends the information to the temporal lobe of the cortex for final processing. This is a very complex process that occurs quickly.

Taste

Our sense of taste is often taken for granted. Think about what happens when you are sick and you cannot taste your food. You usually do not want to eat when you cannot taste what you are eating. Taste, or gestation, is a complex process that allows us to sense what we are ingesting and to respond to dissolved molecules and ions called *tastants*. We detect taste with what is called *taste receptor cells*. These taste receptor cells are clustered in taste buds. Each taste bud has a pore that opens out to the surface of the tongue, which enables molecules and ions taken into the mouth to reach the receptor cells inside. We can discern four primary taste sensations: salty, sour, sweet, and bitter. In addition, a new sense of taste, called *umami,* has recently been found. Umami is a meaty or savory taste that occurs when foods with glutamate (like the preservative MSG) are eaten. Different parts of the tongue can detect all types of tastes. Moreover, the simple tongue "taste map" that is found in many textbooks has been criticized for many reasons.

A single taste bud contains 50–100 taste cells representing all five taste sensations (which is why the classic textbook pictures showing separate taste areas on the tongue are wrong). Transmembrane proteins admit the ions that give rise to the sensations of salty and sour as well as bind to the molecules that give rise to the sensations of sweet, bitter, and umami. A single taste cell seems to be restricted to expressing only a single type of receptor

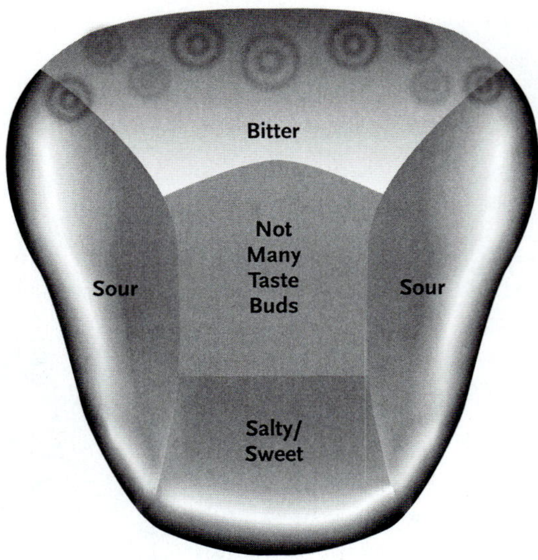

A classic textbook picture showing separate taste areas on the tongue.

(except for bitter receptors). Taste receptor cells are connected through an adenosine triphosphate (ATP)–releasing synapse to a sensory neuron leading back to the brain. However, a single sensory neuron can be connected to several taste cells in each of several different taste buds. The sensation of taste, like all sensations, resides in the brain.

Smell

Did you know that your sense of smell, also called *olfaction,* is least acute in the morning and that your ability to sense odors increases as the day wears on? It is true. Smell depends on sensory receptors that respond to airborne chemicals. These chemoreceptors are located in the olfactory epithelium, which is a patch of tissue about the size of a postage stamp located high in the nasal cavity. The olfactory epithelium is made up of three kinds of cells: sensory neurons, the supporting cells between them, and basal cells. Basal cells divide regularly, producing a fresh batch of sensory neurons to replace those that die. This is unusual since neurons are seldom replaced.

Anosmia is a loss in the ability to smell, which can result from genetic defects, aging, allergies, a side effect from certain drugs, or illnesses such as a virus or cold. Head trauma, however, is the leading cause of anosmia. We have about 10 million receptors in the olfactory system, each of which has 6 to 12 hairlike projections known as *cilia.* It is interesting that the olfactory system takes a different route to the brain than the other systems discussed so far. The nerve enters the olfactory bulb, which is located near the optic chiasm on the underside of the brain. Then some of the nerve fibers go to the amygdala, which is part of the limbic system, and then travel to the thalamus and hypothalamus. These nerve fibers travel even farther still to the cerebral cortex for higher-level processing. That is why smells can be very powerful reminders of past events. Also, how do we determine flavors? The senses of smell and taste have to commingle to reveal tastes to us that have meaning.

Somatosensory Processing (Skin Senses)

The skin senses (somatosensory processing) are involved in sensing information from our receptors in the skin. Somatosensory processing helps us with basic survival because it allows us to realize dangers that may be occurring around us. These skin senses include touch, pressure, pain, and temperature. Pressure receptors are known as *mechanoreceptors,* and temperature receptors are called *thermoreceptors.* When scientists look at the deeper levels of the skin, they can find all sorts of additional receptors that help humans make their way in the world, including the following:

- *Free nerve endings,* which are receptors that are sensitive to temperature and pain.
- *Meissmer corpuscles,* which are receptors for light touch.
- *Merkel receptors,* which are activated by steady pressure from small objects.
- *Pacinian corpuscles,* which are receptors that are very sensitive to the touch.
- *Ruffini endings,* which are receptors that are activated by pressure from larger objects and stretching of the skin.

Finally, people need to be able to distinguish pain. If we experience an event that causes pain, we must get out of that situation as quickly as possible. The gate control theory is a popular theory of pain and has explained how the sensation of pain occurs. According to this theory, the particular nerve receptors in the spinal cord lead to specific areas of the brain related to pain. When these receptors are activated due to an injury or an issue with a specific part of the body, a "gate" to the brain is opened. This gate allows us to experience the sensation of pain (Melzack & Katz, 2004).

PERCEPTION

Sensations have no meaning until they are perceived. Thus this section follows up our discussion on sensation with an examination of perception. Have you ever heard the philosophical debate about a tree falling in the woods? It goes like this: If a tree falls in the woods and there is no one there to hear it, does it make a sound? If we answer this philosophically, we may have many answers, but if we look at this dilemma from a biological perspective, it is easily answered with one answer. The tree falling produces sound waves, but if there is no one there (humans or animals) to perceive it, then it does not make a sound, only sound waves that vibrate without perception.

Think about how many stimuli occur in the environment. It would be impossible to focus on every single sight, sound, smell, or even taste that we encounter. So we have to focus our attention on certain details and even learn how to drown out some of the others. Attention is one of the most widely studied areas in cognitive neuroscience, since it is amazing how we are able to tune in and tune out stimuli in our environment. In *The Principles of Psychology* (1890, pp. 403–404), William James wrote, "Everyone knows what attention is. It is the taking possession by the mind, in clear and vivid form, of one out of what seem several simultaneously possible objects or trains of thought. Focalization, concentration, of consciousness are of its essence. It implies withdrawal from some things in order to deal effectively with others, and is a condition which has a real opposite in the confused, dazed, scatterbrained state which in French is called *distraction,* and *Zerstreutheit* in German."

When we delve further into perception, we look at pattern perceptions. Pattern perception is the basic ability to discriminate among different shapes, objects, and figures. The ability to detect certain types of stimuli, like movements, shapes, and angles, requires specialized cortical cells in the brain that we call *feature detectors*. If we did not have these feature detectors, it would be virtually impossible to detect an object that is being thrown at you at a quick pace. There are many theories to explain how these feature detectors work. One theory, offered by Hubel and Wiesel (2005) stated that specific cells in the occipital lobe are responsible for how we determine patterns. The theory states that simple cells respond to bars or edges and then send a message to the complex cells, which then respond to the more intricate patterns. The brain is then able to assemble them so that individuals can identify the object being presented as one they recognize or one they do not recognize (Goldstein, 2001). Another popular theory is known as the feature-analysis theory, which states that individuals perceive the basic elements of an object and then mentally assemble them to create a complete object (Lindsay & Norman, 1977).

When we see something we have to determine if we recognize it, but it is a rather instantaneous event. *Perceptual constancy* refers to the phenomenon of seeing familiar objects as having a standard size, shape, color, or location regardless of changes in the angle of perspective, distance, or lighting. We can store these memories so that every item that we see is not new every time we see it. If we had to identify the same objects as new every time we encountered them, we would be unable to function very well.

Perceptual constancy also helps us with *depth perception,* which is the ability to see the world in three dimensions. Depth perception occurs with the help of depth cues. There are two main types of depth cues: binocular cues and monocular cues. Binocular cues include both eyes, and monocular cues occur with the processing of only one eye. Our eyes view items differently based on range and perception. Each eye may see things just a bit differently. Each eye also sees from a different angle, which is known as *binocular disparity*. The images form from each eye and when they are processed together, depth perception occurs.

Gestalt Principles of Perception

The term *gestalt* is German for "unified whole." Gestalt psychology was founded by Max Wertheimer, Wolfgang Kohler, and Kurt Koffka and focused on how people perceive and interpret the world. Max Wertheimer in particular found that rapid sequences of perceptual events create the illusion of motion even when there is none. This is known as the *phi phenomenon*. Movies are based on the phi phenomenon and are in practice every day.

The most common aspect of the gestalt laws of organization is the concept of closure, which is how we usually group elements to form enclosed or complete figures rather than open or incomplete ones. The principle of proximity in Gestalt psychology refers to how we perceive elements that are closer together as grouped together. We also have a tendency to group items that we perceive to be similar in appearance into one group. Finally, there is the principle of simplicity, which refers to the fact that when we see a pattern we tend to perceive it in the most basic way that we can. Gestalt psychology is no longer a popular theoretical perspective in current trends, but the physiological implications remain valid and important.

SUMMARY

Sensations, perceptions, and neuroscience are a complex set of systems and processes that incorporate our everyday interactions and assign them meaning. The biological, physiological, and cognitive aspects must be integrated to form important interactions. Behavior is determined by all of these processes that are taken for granted since they are so automatic. These systems take us one step closer into explaining why people do what they do.

CASE STUDY #1 WHAT CAN YOU SEE?

Bernie and Leah had to drive for 45 minutes out of the city to find an isolated field suitable for stargazing. Neither of them was complaining about the drive because it was likely to be a great evening. Since Bernie and Leah did not have many interests in common, finding something that they both enjoyed doing was not always easy. Stargazing might turn out to be one of them.

Bernie was a real outdoors person and loved camping under the stars. However, his knowledge about stars, galaxies, nebulae, and so on was pretty limited. On the other hand, Leah had taken an astronomy class in high school and had a pretty good working knowledge of the names of the constellations as well as the layout of the galaxy.

For the first half hour or so, Leah pointed out constellations and taught Bernie their names. Then they made up games, such as "who can find the faintest star" and "which star is the brightest." After another hour or so, they decided that they had had enough for one night. The moon was just rising and looked gigantic as they walked back toward the car.

1. Bernie and Leah had to leave the city to stargaze. In psychological terms, what is the excess light of the city called? Why is it harder to see stars in the city?
2. Would identifying which of two stars is brighter be easier when they were both relatively dim or both relatively bright? Why? What formula is used to predict differential thresholds?
3. The moon shone off to the left as Bernie and Leah walked back to the car. At which side of their brain did the message eventually arrive? Outline the optical and neural path by which the image of the moon reached the visual cortex.
4. Leah was able to see more faint stars than Bernie. She did this by looking not directly at a star, but off to the side. Why did this trick work? What type of receptor cells are used in peripheral vision?
5. Leah tried to teach Bernie to look at a star through his peripheral vision, but he complained that the star off to the side kept disappearing. What is happening?

CASE STUDY #2 MOVIE THEATER BLINDNESS

This movie is really terrible, Derrick thought to himself. Bad acting, bad directing, bad effects; this movie had it all. During what was intended to be a dramatic rescue scene, Derrick decided he needed to take a break, rose quickly out of his seat, and walked briskly toward the lobby.

Standing too quickly, Derrick was a little dizzy at first, but it passed quickly. Not knowing exactly where he was going, he headed to the men's room to use the bathroom and wash his hands. Still not wanting to go back yet, he decided to stop at the concession stand and buy some popcorn and a drink. The popcorn, which filled the room with a buttery aroma, was actually a little stale.

Not knowing what else he could do, Derrick decided to go back to his seat. Entering the theater, his eyes adjusted to the darkness quickly and he found his seat.

1. Why did Derrick experience a brief dizziness when he rose to leave the theater? What parts of the body are involved?
2. What are the five sensations of taste? Which one(s) would respond to eating popcorn? In what area(s) of the tongue are these taste buds located? What does Derrick actually mean when he says the popcorn "tastes" stale?
3. While getting Derrick's popcorn, the concession worker burned her hand on the heating element. She grabbed the burned area on her skin and held it very tightly. Why might this help reduce the pain?
4. How many sensations are mentioned in this story, either explicitly or implicitly? Can you identify more than five? Can you identify more than seven?
5. How sensitive is the sense of smell? How many different types of receptor cells are involved in the olfactory system? At age 22, is Derrick's sense of smell improving or declining? Why?

CASE STUDY #3 SPRING CARNIVAL

Emily was excited to be going to the annual spring carnival that came to her town in mid-May. Besides providing good live music, the carnival boasted a dozen or so smaller side shows as well as games and even a few rides. The event always reminded her of the state fair that she attended as a child with her father. Picking up a newspaper, Emily searched for information about this year's carnival.

Among last year's shows that had been Emily's favorites was one with a young comedian who had performed some very funny ventriloquism. For days afterward she would remember his act and laugh aloud. Another show she had thoroughly enjoyed was a hologram exhibit. She was still amazed how holograms portrayed images in three dimensions. Emily hoped these shows would be here again this year.

Finding the listing of events, Emily was disappointed to discover that the "Sights and Sound" booth with the hologram exhibit had been replaced with the pointillist paintings of the French Neo-Impressionist Georges-Pierre Seurat.

1. Using your knowledge of speech reception, can you explain how ventriloquists create the illusion of making a stuffed or wooden doll speak? Would a person who has slightly impaired hearing be more or less susceptible to a ventriloquist's tricks?
2. How do 3-D movies create the appearance of having a third dimension? Is this the same process that underlies hologram technology? In what ways must the two techniques differ? In what ways must they be the same?
3. The time that elapsed as Emily read the newspaper article about the carnival was very short. What does this suggest about the feature-analysis approach to understanding reading?
4. Which of the four gestalt laws of organization can be implicated in the phenomenon that causes pointillist paintings to appear like orderly scenes at a distance?
5. Based on the principles of psychology, what emotions does the carnival create in Emily? Is this why she enjoys the shows and events? If Emily had bad experiences in the past at carnivals, would it change her perception of the events?

CASE STUDY #4 ILLUSIONS OR DELUSIONS?

Samantha walked around the neighborhood with her two boys, George, 11, and Simon, 6. They had three more houses to visit on their annual Halloween trick-or-treating outing. Simon was busy counting up how many chocolate bars he had collected when George suddenly cried, "Simon, look how big the moon is! That means that the werewolves are coming out early this year!"

Simon looked up, wide-eyed. The moon did look huge and orange, too. "Then I want to go home now," he yelled." I don't want the werewolves to get me!"

"George, don't scare your brother," said Samantha. "That's just called a harvest moon, Simon. It isn't scary."

George turned serious and said, "How come the moon gets so big sometimes, Mom? Is it closer to the earth today?"

Samantha explained, "Well, it is really just an illusion. Depth cues, like those trees you see over there, make you think the moon is farther away than it really is. Your brain tries to compensate for this far distance, but since the moon really isn't that far away, your brain ends up making it appear bigger. When the moon is higher in the sky, the depth cues aren't there, so you see the moon at the size you're used to."

1. As the night goes on, and the moon rises more, the harvest moon disappears and appears to be its normal size again. Explain how you could teach George to use his thumb (or some other item) to measure the retinal image of the moon and prove that it remains the same size as it rises.
2. Many optical illusions do not work for all people, such as people from non-Western cultures. Why do some illusions not work in these cultures? Do you think all cultures see the harvest moon illusion?
3. Imagine that you lived on a planet with a moon that was usually low on the horizon. Would the harvest moon effect happen there? On this planet, how would the moon appear to us on a day when it rises high in the sky? Would it appear smaller or larger?
4. Even though Samantha knew why the moon appeared bigger, her eyes were still "fooled" by the harvest moon. What does this say about the level of processing that perceptual processes follow? Can they be interrupted by concentrating very hard?
5. What neural processes are occurring when Samantha and her boys are looking at the moon? Would these processes be the same if the moon were a different size that night?

CASE STUDY #5 TINY TREES

The cry of a nearby infant awakened Melissa from her nap. *The gentle rocking motion of the train must have lulled me to sleep,* she thought. She rubbed her eyes and peered out the window at the sun rising over a foreign landscape. Melissa was on a long train ride from Seattle to the most northern region of British Columbia, a place with beautiful and unfamiliar scenery.

Still a little tired, she stared absently down at the rocks and flowers that lay close to the train tracks, but the train was going so fast that the blur made her dizzy. Looking up, she noticed a patch of trees on a nearly bare horizon, several miles away. Sooner than she expected, the train approached and passed the little grove. "Wow, those trees weren't so far away," she said. "They're just really tiny! I wonder what they are called." The new countryside was indeed very strange and beautiful.

1. Why did the objects close to the tracks appear to be moving faster than objects farther in the distance? What is this phenomenon called? Is it a monocular or binocular depth perception cue?
2. What perceptual cues caused Melissa to think the trees were very far away when they were actually close? What role did her previous knowledge play in her perception of the trees? Would she have made the same mistake if the trees were close to a house, car, or some other familiar object?
3. When the baby's cry woke her up, Melissa was able to tell that the baby and its mother were to her left rather than to her right. Describe the perceptual processes that might have led to this inference.
4. Although she could have looked out the windows on the opposite side of the train, Melissa focused on the scenery out of her own window. What is this phenomenon called? Do you think Melissa might be able to recall any of the scenery from the other side of the train? Defend your answer.
5. Compare the different theories of perception to explain Melissa's perception of the small trees.

ACTIVITY #1 TASTE TESTS

For this activity you will need three different flavors of juice, soda, or tea. You will also need a blindfold, something on which to record your results, a packet of sugar, some salt water, and your taste buds.

Directions: Have someone blindfold you and then one by one have you taste each type of beverage. Find out how well you were able to identify the different flavors. Once you have completed this aspect of the experiment, wipe your tongue so that it is dry and then put some sugar on the dry part of your tongue. You will not be able to taste it. Your tongue must be wet for your taste buds to work. Now put some salt water on the back of your tongue and you will find you can hardly taste it. But if you put some salt water on the front of your tongue, it will taste very salty.

Since your sense of smell helps you to taste things, put the blindfold back on and hold your nose and taste the beverages again. You will not be able to tell what they are anymore! If you let go of your nose you should be able to identify the beverages again.

ACTIVITY #2 WHAT CAN YOU HEAR?

Directions: Write down all of the sounds that you currently hear. Make sure you pay attention to each sound and include it in your list. Then, go to a quiet room and pay attention to the sounds that you hear when it is supposed to be quiet. Finally, create as much noise as you can and see how long it takes before it bothers you, or someone else!

When you have finished this exercise, write down the processes involved in what you did for each step of your research experiment.

ACTIVITY #3 WHAT IS A BLIND SPOT?

We all have what is called a blind spot. This is where part of your retina is not sensitive to light. This blind spot is called the fovea and is where the optic nerve is connected to your eye. In order to find your blind spot do the following activity:

Cover your left eye and stare at the circle. Move your head closer to the page until you can no longer see the plus sign. When that happens, you have found your blind spot. Do the same thing again by covering your right eye and moving closer.

Was your blind spot in the same place for each eye? Why might there be a difference in where your blind spot occurs? Is there anything you can do to change where your blind spot occurs? What happens if you keep both eyes open and try this experiment? What if you wear corrective lenses?

REFERENCES

Brooker, R. J., Widmaier, E. P., Graham, L. E., & Stiling, P. D. (2007). *Biology*. New York: McGraw-Hill.

Brown, P. K., & Wald, G. (1964). Visual pigments in single rods and cones of the human retina. *Science, 144,* 45–52.

Feldman, R. (2009). *Psychology and your life*. New York: McGraw-Hill.

Fettiplace, R. (1990). Transduction and tuning in auditory hair cells. *Seminars in the Neurosciences, 2,* 33–40.

Goldstein, B. (2001). *Sensation and perception* (6th ed.). London: Wadsworth.

Hubel, D. H., & Wiesel, T. N. (2005). *Brain and visual perception: The story of a 25-year collaboration* (p. 106). New York: Oxford University Press.

James, W. (1890). *The principles of psychology* (Vol. 1). New York: Henry Holt.

Lindsay, P., & Norman, D. A. (1977). *Human information processing: An introduction to psychology* (2nd ed.). San Diego: Harcourt Brace Jovanovich.

Melzack, R., & Katz, J. Z. (2004). *The gate control theory: Reaching for the brain*. Mahwah, NJ: Erlbaum.

Nittrouer, S., & Lowenstein, J. H. (2007). Children's weighting strategies for word-final stop voicing are not explained by auditory sensitivities. *Journal of Speech, Language, and Hearing Research, 50,* 58–73.

CHAPTER 4

States of Consciousness

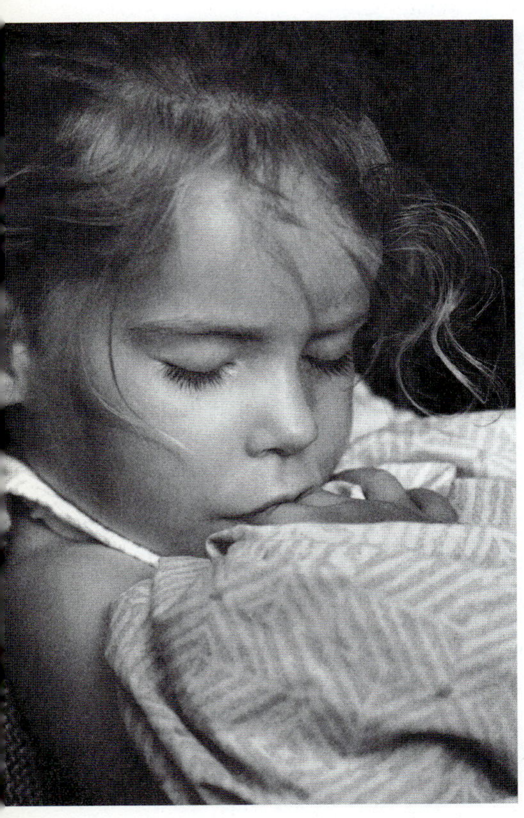

LEARNING ASSETS

Case Study #1 Why Am I So Tired?

Case Study #2 Dream World

Case Study #3 Drugs and Consciousness

Case Study #4 Which Is It?

Activity #1 Dream Log

Activity #2 Dream Analysis

Activity #3 Meditation

Activity #4 Sleep Disorders

CONSCIOUSNESS

The last chapter focused on the basic biological processes involved in sensation and perception; this chapter explores the various states of consciousness that we use to perceive these events. *Consciousness* refers to your awareness of sensations, perceptions, and cognitions. We are always conscious, but various states change the level and function of our consciousness. These states, as well as how they alter our consciousness, are examined next.

STAGES OF SLEEP

Most people are concerned with the stages of sleep and what occurs during every phase. Do dreams occur in all of the stages? What is the difference between nightmares and night terrors? Does everyone need the same amount of sleep? Can you make up sleep that you previously lost? These questions and many others are asked when the stages of sleep are discussed. We will now answer them all!

Individuals go through five stages of sleep every time they completely cycle through the stages of sleep. We go from light sleep to deep sleep to what is known as *rapid eye movement (REM) sleep*. If scientists attach someone to electrodes, they can watch and determine which stage of sleep he or she is in at any given time. Stages 1 through 4 are known as non-REM (NREM) sleep. We always start in Stage 1 and progress through each stage until we are deeper and deeper into the sleep cycle. Stage 1 is referred to as the *drowsiness stage* and only lasts for a few minutes. In this stage, you often feel like you do when you are watching television and your eyes keep closing and your head starts to bob up and down; your eyes move slowly and your muscle activity all but diminishes. This is often the stage where you feel like you are falling, and sometimes you feel a part of your body jolt. These are just muscle contractions that occur because your body is not yet used to the restful state. It is very easy to become fully awake during Stage 1, but if you continue into the cycle past Stage 1, you enter into Stage 2, which is known as *light sleep.* It is still easy to wake someone who is in light sleep, but in this stage eye movement stops and brain waves actually become much slower. Sudden bursts of rapid brain waves can be seen in this stage, but they are starting to diminish as the person heads into deep sleep. You continue into Stages 3 and 4, which are collectively known as *deep sleep.* It is extremely difficult to wake someone who is in deep sleep. If you are awakened during these stages, you are likely to be groggy and not know who you are or where you are! In Stage 3, scientists can see delta waves, which are extremely slow brain waves interspersed with smaller, faster waves. In Stage 4, the brain produces delta waves almost exclusively. No eye movement or muscle activity occurs in Stages 3 or 4. In these stages, individuals may experience bed-wetting, night terrors, and sleepwalking.

Night terrors are not the same as nightmares. What makes them different? Night terrors can result in an apparently rapid awakening with fear, confusion, rapid heart rate, and sweating. They are not dreams. Although night terrors are more common in children aged 3 to 5 years old, adults may experience them as well. Typically children outgrow night terrors as they get older. Since individuals who have night terrors get up in a frightened state, it may appear as though they are awake, but they typically have trouble communicating and seem confused. Breathing may be fast and the pupils may be dilated, but the person is actually still asleep. These night terrors typically last for approximately 15 minutes, and then the person appears to lie down and fall back asleep. However, he or she was never actually awake in the first place!

A person who experiences night terrors usually does not remember the event the next morning. The incidence of night terrors may increase in an adult who is experiencing emotional stress or using illegal substances. As mentioned, these night terrors occur exclusively during Stages 3 and 4 of the sleep cycle. Nightmares occur during REM sleep. People typically remember their nightmares, but they usually have no recollection of night terrors.

The fifth stage of sleep, rapid eye movement (REM) sleep, is where the bulk of a person's dreams occur. When you enter REM sleep, your breathing becomes more rapid and shallow, your eyes have a tendency to jerk around rapidly, and your limbs are temporarily paralyzed. Your brain waves look the same in REM sleep as they do when you are fully awake. Heart rate increases, blood pressure rises, males develop erections, and the body loses some of its natural ability to regulate its temperature.

According to many of the current sleep studies, infants spend about half of their sleep in REM sleep, whereas adults only spend about 20 percent of their time in REM. Adults typically spend 50 percent of their time sleeping in Stage 2, and the remaining 30 percent is divided up among the other three stages. The REM cycle was not discovered until 1953 when new tests, called *electroencephalogram (EEG) tests,* were developed to track brain waves. Before 1953, people thought that brain activity actually stopped during sleep. (See Table 4.1 for a summary of the percentages of sleep at the various sleep stages.)

The average length for a complete sleep cycle is 90 to 110 minutes. After a person falls asleep, the REM stage typically occurs about 70 to 90 minutes later. So an average person who sleeps for eight hours will go through the stages four to five times a night. According to recent sleep studies, the amount of sleep a person needs depends on the person. Eight hours is the old standby, but it is not always correct. Each person knows how much sleep he or she requires to function well.

Why Do We Need Sleep?

Sleeping seems like a waste of time to many people. Why do we need to sleep? Sleep actually helps the body to restore and repair itself in many different ways. In addition, sleep helps our memory, learning, and social processes. When we sleep, we encode new information and store it properly in our long-term storage. REM actually helps to control learning. The locations in the brain that control social interactions, decision making, and emotions slow during sleep, which allows us to be fresh when we are awake. Some theories assert that the nervous system regenerates during sleep and that without sleep it may cause nervous system damage. Our immune system also regenerates during sleep. While we are sleeping our cells increase production while proteins break down at a slower rate. Without sleep we become more susceptible to infection and disease. Growth and development in children occurs during sleep as well. That is why babies and children who are still growing require much more sleep than a fully grown adult. Sleep is a necessary part of life, and scientists are still learning all of its value.

TABLE 4.1 STAGES OF SLEEP

Stage Number	Stage Name	Percentage of Overall Sleep Cycle
1	Drowsiness	30%—divided among Stages 1, 3, and 4
2	Light sleep	50%
3 and 4	Deep sleep	30%—divided among Stages 1, 3, and 4
5	Rapid eye movement (REM)	20%

Problems with Sleep

Many things can go wrong with sleep. Sleep deprivation can cause many different problems that we are no longer sharp enough to realize. Have you ever been sleep deprived and feel cranky, tired, and frustrated? The body is telling you that you need to sleep to repair your internal processes. Some of the signs of sleep deprivation include difficulty getting up in the morning, falling asleep during work or class, lack of focus and concentration, and being moody, irritable, depressed, or anxious. If you feel the need for a nap in the middle of the day, need an alarm clock to wake up, or fall asleep as soon as you lie down, you may be sleep deprived. Sleep deprivation can cause numerous cognitive and physical problems. Some of these include: poor decision making; increased risk taking; poor performance in work or school; impaired driving abilities; increased incidence of diabetes, high blood pressure, heart disease, and obesity; impaired memory; physical impairment; anxiety, depression, or emotional problems; increased symptoms of ADHD; and magnification of the effects of drugs or alcohol (de Benedictis, Larson, Kemp, Barston, & Segal, 2007).

Can You Make Up for Lost Sleep?

One of the most frequent questions involved in discussions of sleep is, Can you make up for lost sleep? How would you answer that question based on what has been discussed so far? The answer is actually yes and no. You can never get back the sleep that you lost because you cannot go back in time and regain the lost sleep, but you can catch up on your lost sleep by sleeping more in the future. All of the reparations that occur during sleep would not occur if we were not allowed to catch up on lost sleep. If you lost sleep one night and could never catch up, then you would continue to fall in a downward spiral forevermore. Therefore, we can regain the benefits of sleep when we are able to sleep a little extra. Many people are sleep deprived during the work or school week but make up the sleep on the weekends. If you sleep later on the weekends than you do during the week, consider yourself catching up!

SLEEP ISSUES

Many people suffer from sleep issues. These can range anywhere from having trouble falling asleep to not sleeping. Sleep issues are categorized into three major categories: insomnia, hypersomnia, and parasomnia.

Insomnia

The American Insomnia Association states that *insomnia* is defined as trouble falling asleep (called *sleep-onset insomnia*) or staying asleep (*sleep-maintenance insomnia*). It is likely that about one third of the American population suffers from some type of insomnia. However, only about 10 percent of those people are actually being treated. Insomnia has a tendency to occur more frequently as people get older and seems to affect women more frequently than men. Insomnia deals with the quality of a person's sleep, not the amount of time sleeping. Causes of insomnia vary by person, but some common causes include anxiety, stress, worry, drugs or alcohol, environmental factors, menopause, and medical problems.

Many treatments are available for people who experience insomnia. Treatment is necessary in one form or another because if you do not sleep, you will die. Sleep is required to

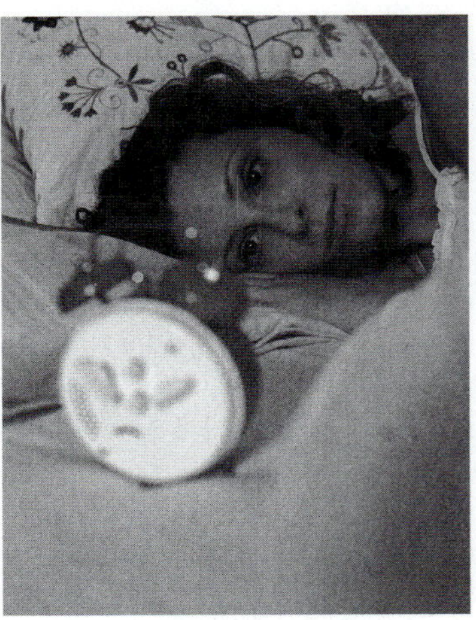

maintain our lives. Extreme sleep deprivation will cause the organs in the body to systematically shut down. One of the treatments offered is known as *sleep restriction,* a behavior modification process that helps a person focus on sleeping. When people use sleep restriction, they are only allowed in their bed when they are sleeping; they must try for 25 minutes to fall asleep or they need to leave their bed. Another treatment, stimulus control therapy, reserves the bedroom for sleep and sex only. Still other treatments include relaxation techniques, biofeedback, avoidance of caffeine and alcohol, cognitive-behavioral therapy, and medication. Medications should be used very cautiously since they are typically highly addictive and may lead to other problems down the road.

Hypersomnia

Hypersomnias are disorders characterized by prolonged nighttime sleep or excessive sleepiness. Individuals with hypersomnia feel as though they need to nap throughout the day; however, this usually occurs during work or school, during a meal, or in the middle of a conversation. Hypersomnia may be caused by another sleep disorder that falls within this category, such as sleep apnea or narcolepsy. Sleep apnea is when breathing stops during sleep and is the most studied sleep disorder because of its potentially lethal effects. It is said to affect nearly 20 million Americans, mostly males. Sleep apnea is often associated with loud snoring, although snoring does not always occur. Flow of air to the lungs stops for at least 10 to 15 seconds and can be fatal. Most people are unaware that this is occurring other than noticing that they are tired after a full night's rest. Sleep apnea is associated with heart attack, high blood pressure, congestive heart failure, coronary heart disease, stroke, pulmonary hypertension, and psychiatric impairment. Narcolepsy consists of being sleepy and falling asleep during the day spontaneously even if a normal amount of sleep was experienced during the night. These episodes are often called "sleep attacks" and can last from several seconds to more than 30 minutes. This is typically a hereditary disorder. Treatments vary depending on the cause and nature of these sleep disorders.

Parasomnia

Parasomnia refers to a disorder that occurs during sleep. Parasomnias are seen most frequently in children, but adults do experience them as well. Some examples of parasomnias are sleepwalking (somnambulism), night terrors, muscle twitching (myoclonus), sleep talking (somniloquy), and bed-wetting (enuresis). Let's look at these more in-depth. Sleepwalking is still a mystery to us, but scientists believe it is brought on by stress, fatigue, sleep deprivation, and some medications. It typically occurs early in the night during Stages 3 and 4. Sleepwalking occurs more frequently in children, but it is seen in adults. Those who sleepwalk typically have no memory of the sleepwalking event the next day. As discussed earlier, night terrors also occur in Stages 3 and 4 and include physiological changes that often cause the sleeper to appear to awaken. Muscle twitching is an involuntary jerking of a muscle or group of muscles and cannot be controlled. Often associated with a feeling of falling, muscle twitching typically happens as people fall asleep, but it can occur throughout the night. It often wakes the person up and can occur throughout the sleep cycle. The exception is that it does not occur during the REM stage of sleep. Sleep talking actually has no medical or psychological consequences. It can occur during any of the stages of sleep but typically will not occur in REM sleep. In Stages 1 and 2, the speech may be intelligible; however, in Stages 3 and 4, the "talking" may be moans or gibberish. People who talk in their sleep typically do not have any memory or recollection of doing it. Finally, bed-wetting frequently occurs in children under the age of 5 during the sleep cycle. This parasomnia disorder may be due to weak bladder muscles or nervous system development delays. When bed-wetting occurs after a child is 5 years old, it is considered to be a potentially psychological issue due to stress or anxiety.

DREAMS

Dreams typically occur during the REM stage of sleep. There is, however, some mental activity that occurs during the NREM stages as well. REM dreams are considered to be very vivid, visual, active, and emotional. Dreams fascinate laypeople and researchers alike, and most people wonder what their dreams mean. Countless theories have been created to interpret dreams. Dream interpretation first gained recognition with Sigmund Freud in 1900 when he wrote *The Interpretation of Dreams.*

Sigmund Freud (1856–1939) discussed the *manifest content* of dreams, defining it as the obvious information that individuals remember from their dreams. But he felt that the manifest content is just the base level of a person's dream and that individuals need to dig deeper to find the true meanings of their dreams. Freud referred to this true meaning of dreams as the *latent content.* He maintained that if individuals undergo the process of dream work, then they can take the manifest content, analyze it, and come up with the latent content of their dreams. Freud further said that dreams are based on wish fulfillment and occupy humans' wishes, hopes, and fears.

Dream theories also propose that we dream to work through our problems in a less threatening environment (Cartwright & Lamberg, 1997). Seeking solutions to everyday problems through our dreams may be a daunting task for many people. Another theory, proposed by the research of Hobson and McCarley (1977), entitled the activation-synthesis theory, states that dreams arise during REM sleep from random bursts of brain activity and the brain attempts to make sense of these haphazard signals. This means that dreams would not have any value whatsoever. Obviously, this varies differently from both Freud's and Cartwright and Lamberg's interpretations.

HYPNOSIS

What is hypnosis? Why are there claims that you can stop smoking, stop eating, or focus better if you undergo hypnosis? Hypnosis comes from the work of Franz Mesmer. Have you ever heard someone say that they are mesmerized? That is because Mesmer discovered what he called *animal magnetism.* Using animal magnetism, he claimed that he could cure everything from blindness to paralysis. Mesmer's theory was that the environment was charged with an invisible magnetic force that could accumulate in his own body and then transfer to other people's bodies. Mesmer would often sit facing the person and stare into their eyes for up to hours at a time (Darnton, 1968). The name *hypnosis* emerged in 1843 when a Scottish surgeon named James Braid changed it from *mesmerism.*

According to the American Psychological Association (2005), hypnosis

> typically involves an introduction to the procedure during which the subject is told that suggestions for imaginative experiences will be presented. The hypnotic induction is an extended initial suggestion for using one's imagination, and may contain further elaborations of the introduction. A hypnotic procedure is used to encourage and evaluate responses to suggestions. When using hypnosis, one person (the subject) is guided by another (the hypnotist) to respond to suggestions for changes in subjective experience, alterations in perception, sensation, emotion, thought or behavior. Persons can also learn self-hypnosis, which is the act of administering hypnotic procedures on one's own. If the subject responds to hypnotic suggestions, it is generally inferred that hypnosis has been induced. Many believe that hypnotic responses and experiences are characteristic of a hypnotic state. While some think that it is not necessary to use the word "hypnosis" as part of the hypnotic induction, others view it as essential.

Details of hypnotic procedures and suggestions will differ depending on the goals of the practitioner and the purposes of the clinical or research endeavor. Procedures traditionally involve suggestions to relax, though relaxation is not necessary for hypnosis and a wide variety of suggestions can be used including those to become more alert. Suggestions that permit the extent of hypnosis to be assessed by comparing responses to standardized scales can be used in both clinical and research settings. While the majority of individuals are responsive to at least some suggestions, scores on standardized scales range from high to negligible. Traditionally, scores are grouped into low, medium, and high categories. As is the case with other positively-scaled measures of psychological constructs such as attention and awareness, the salience of evidence for having achieved hypnosis increases with the individual's score. (APA, 2005; note that this definition and description of hypnosis was prepared by the Executive Committee of the American Psychological Association, Division of Psychological Hypnosis; permission to reproduce the preceding is freely granted).

DRUGS AND ALTERED STATES OF CONSCIOUSNESS

When we talk about drugs, we typically think about illegal drugs, but drug consumption also includes prescription drugs. Oftentimes prescription drugs are misused and taken in incorrect dosages. Sometimes it is accidental, other times it is on purpose. One thing is definite: Psychoactive drugs alter consciousness, cognitions, and behaviors in many different forms. Drugs may have physiological addictive qualities, and then there is a potential psychological dependency on the drug.

Stimulants

Stimulants are drugs that have an effect on the central nervous system. They are often referred to as *uppers* because of the effect that they have on the body. Stimulants increase or speed up the mental and physical processes in the body. A person taking a stimulant may talk really fast, move really quickly, or seem jittery. Think that it can't be you? Do you drink coffee or soda or smoke cigarettes? These are all legal stimulants. Some prescription stimulants that are often misused are Ritalin, Dexedrine, and Meridia. Some illegal stimulants include methamphetamine, amphetamines, cocaine, and crack. All of these substances increase brain activity and heart rate, and trigger the nervous system.

Depressants

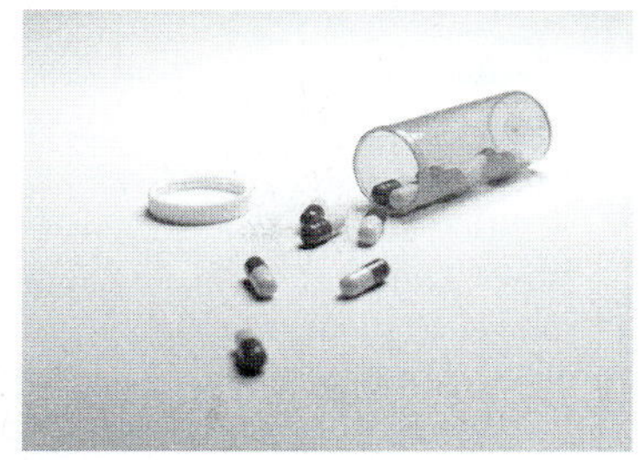

Depressants are substances that slow down, or depress, the central nervous system. Depressants are often referred to as *downers,* which is the opposite of stimulants. Depressants have a sedative, hypnotic, and tranquilizing effect on people. Think this can't be you? Have you ever had an alcoholic beverage, taken a sleep medication, or taken an antianxiety medication? These are all legal depressants. Some prescription depressants become illegal when they are not used for their intended purpose. For example, this includes very controversial drugs called R*ohypnol* and *GHB,* date rape drugs. Due to its sedative properties, a date rape drug is sometimes used to sedate another person so that person doesn't resist a sexual assault. Other prescription depressants include barbiturates, Xanax, Valium, and Librium.

Opioids

Opioids are analgesics that are both naturally occurring and synthetic substances that create a loss of sensitivity to pain and make a person sleepy. They are typically prescribed for the relief of pain but are often misused due to their euphoric, sedating, and numbing effects. Some typical opioids are OxyContin, Vicodin, and Percocet. These drugs create a dependence that is both physiological as well as psychological, and withdrawal symptoms are severe.

Hallucinogens

Hallucinogens alter a person's state of mind and mood. They are often referred to as *psychedelic drugs* or *dissociative drugs.* They can cause a person to hallucinate, which means to hear, see, or feel things that are not really there. People who take these drugs often detach or dissociate from their surroundings. LSD, mescaline (peyote), psilocybin, and psilocin (mushrooms) are some of the popular hallucinogens. Ketamine and PCP alter mood and mind but do not create hallucinations.

Marijuana

Marijuana does not fall into one of these neat categories, because its effects mainly depend on what is included in the plant that is consumed for psychoactive purposes. It is most often referred to as a *stimulant,* but it also has depressive qualities as well. Marijuana is considered a stimulant because it increases heart rate, but it can be classified as a depressant because it lowers blood pressure. It does impair psychomotor coordination, concentration, and short-term memory. The long-term effects of marijuana use are unclear and highly debatable.

SUMMARY

This chapter has focused on the sleep cycle and dreams, and the biological and psychological effects of these processes. We have looked at how the body produces natural effects, as well as at how they can be altered with psychoactive substances. Overall, it is necessary to see how we impact the processes that our bodies undergo at all times.

CASE STUDY #1 WHY AM I SO TIRED?

Vincent met his friend Rick in line waiting for coffee one weekday morning before work.

"Boy, am I exhausted," Vincent moaned. "I felt like I would never get to sleep last night. When I finally did, I had the most horrible dream. I was walking home from the library when somebody started to chase me, but I couldn't run because my books were way too heavy. I felt like I was running underwater. It was really frightening. Now this morning I feel so tired!"

"Maybe you can take a nap in class this afternoon to make up for it," Rick joked as he passed the condiment bar, stopping to get some cream and sugar, then handed the coffee to Vincent. "At least have a cup of coffee to make it through the morning."

1. Did Vincent experience a nightmare or a night terror? What is the difference between the two? How often do most people have frightening dreams?
2. At what stage of sleep did Vincent's frightening dream occur? During what part of the night is this stage of sleep most likely to occur?
3. How might Freud interpret Vincent's dream? What is the dream's manifest content? What might be the latent content of the dream? To what processes would activation-synthesis theory attribute Vincent's dream?
4. How common is the kind of insomnia that Vincent experienced? Given what you know about insomnia, how long do you suppose it really took Vincent to get to sleep that night?
5. Think about Rick's suggestions to Vincent for dealing with his sleepiness. Will they help Vincent in the short run? Will they help Vincent overcome a chronic insomnia problem? What alternative suggestions would you make to Vincent?

CASE STUDY #2 DREAM WORLD

Raindrops began to fall as Jennifer pulled out of the parking lot and began her long commute home.

"What a way to start the weekend," she muttered, turning on her lights and windshield wipers. Soon she was happily distracted by thoughts about the upcoming weekend. She had been planning a surprise party for her husband, Scott, for weeks, and as she drove she imagined how excited and pleased he would be when he walked through the door and saw all of his friends. In her mind Scott's face would light up with surprise and he would turn to her and say, "How did you plan all of this without me knowing?"

Jennifer turned on the radio and found a one-hour news show. She followed the first few stories, but before she knew it she was almost home. She had safely driven almost 10 miles, but couldn't remember any of it!

1. How was Jennifer's daydream about the party different from dreams she may have had at night? In particular, which dreams are more controllable? How does the content differ?
2. How would you describe what happened to Jennifer as she listened to the news? Was she in an altered state of consciousness? Why or why not?
3. How often do most people daydream, on the average? Do you see any important functions of this particular dream of Jennifer's? Should Jennifer be concerned about daydreaming?
4. Do you think Jennifer was in a state of hypnosis? What features does her state have in common with a hypnotic state? What features may be different? If you had to guess, what stage of wakefulness or sleep would you say Jennifer's brain waves resembled during those 10 miles?
5. What features does Jennifer's experience have in common with meditative states? What features may be different? How does people's memory for meditative states differ from their memory for hypnosis sessions?

CASE STUDY #3 DRUGS AND CONSCIOUSNESS

As Jake walked through the solarium at work he heard an argument among two co-workers that caught his attention. One co-worker was seated behind a table displaying literature and information promoting the legalization of marijuana. Before long several other co-workers began to participate in the discussion.

"Marijuana is as safe as alcohol. Everyone uses it anyway, so why shouldn't it be legalized?" a nearby student was asking.

"But if you legalize it, you might as well legalize every other drug, too. They are all the same," another co-worker offered.

"Marijuana is not addictive at all and it has no harmful side effects either," said another bystander.

"Well, I heard that pot makes you just want stronger and stronger drugs. So, if we legalize it, we're just inviting worse trouble."

"Oh, that's silly. It has the same effect as beer. They're practically the same thing," someone from the back shouted.

"I think you all had better get your facts straight," said the person behind the table. "Check out these flyers and then we can discuss this issue fairly."

1. What classification of drug is marijuana? How are its effects different from alcohol? How are they different from narcotics? From stimulants? Which of the classifications of drugs is the most addictive?
2. What makes a drug addictive? What are some of the major symptoms of drug addiction? How addictive is marijuana?
3. How common is marijuana use compared with alcohol use? Why do you suppose alcohol is socially accepted whereas marijuana is largely not?
4. What is your own opinion about whether marijuana should be legalized? Be sure to defend your opinion with sound, research-based evidence and *not* the faulty arguments that were given by the co-workers in the story.
5. What are the potential psychological impacts of marijuana and other illegal substances? What are the potential psychological impacts of alcohol?

CASE STUDY #4 WHICH IS IT?

Marilyn wasn't sure if she should be worried about her friend Jodi or not. A lot of times Marilyn found Jodi fun to be with, full of energy and confidence. Jodi could stay up all night talking or studying. Other times Jodi slept all day and acted really depressed, grumpy, and worried. There were times when Jodi wasn't home for days and she skipped out on work. Marilyn wasn't sure how Jodi was doing at her job, but she didn't think Jodi was doing all that well. She also suspected that Jodi had money problems. Jodi used to ask to borrow money from Marilyn occasionally, but now Marilyn suspected that she just "borrowed" directly from people at work without asking. Maybe Jodi was just going through a rough time. Then again, maybe it was something more serious.

1. Which of Jodi's behaviors seems consistent with a drug problem? What common symptoms of drug abuse are missing in this description? Many of Jodi's behaviors could be explained by non-drug-related reasons. Should Marilyn be suspicious of a drug problem? What features might help you decide?
2. Given Jodi's behavior, what classification of drug would you suspect her to be using? Which of her symptoms are common to most drug use?
3. How would drugs or alcohol alter Jodi's behavior? Is this considered an altered state of consciousness? Could Jodi's behavior change if she stopped taking drugs or drinking alcohol?
4. What psychological disorder(s) might account for Jodi's behavior? What kind of treatment would Jodi require if her behavior is not drug or alcohol induced?
5. Would hypnosis or meditation change Jodi's behavior? Explain.

ACTIVITY #1 DREAM LOG

Directions: Record the answers to each question about your dreams. In order to maintain accuracy, you should record your dreams as soon as you wake up so that they are clear in your mind.

1. What was the manifest content of your dream(s)? Explain what happened and who was in your dream(s).
2. What were you doing before you went to bed? Do you think this had any impact on your dream(s)?
3. Will your dream(s) affect your day? Explain.
4. Examine your dream(s) and discuss your analysis of the dream(s).
5. What is the latent content of your dream?

ACTIVITY #2 DREAM ANALYSIS

Directions: Write your answers to the following questions in essay format. Make sure you research your answers and include references to support your points.

1. Who created dream analysis?
2. What does dream analysis entail?
3. Name at least three prominent figures in dream analysis and outline their theories and concepts.

ACTIVITY #3 MEDITATION

Daily meditation is a proven technique to encourage and promote relaxation. Relaxation can create restful sleep patterns. Try this meditation exercise and then write a journal entry to explain how you felt immediately after you completed the exercise.

- Find a quiet room.
- Sit in a comfortable position on the floor (use a cushion if needed).
- Sit with your hands resting lightly in your lap.
- Close your eyes and relax.
- Take deep breaths in and out through your nose.
- Try to focus on your breathing.

  Count each breath as you exhale.

  Count to 10.

  Repeat several times until relaxation sets in.
- Clear your mind of everything and think only of counting each breath as you exhale.
- Acknowledge any other thoughts that enter your mind, and then gently let them go and concentrate once again on your breathing.
- At the end of your daily meditation, gently stretch and become aware of your body before standing up.

ACTIVITY #4 SLEEP DISORDERS

Directions: Look at the following list of sleep disorders and choose any four disorders. Research each disorder that you choose and create some discussion questions to go along with your research. When you have completed the research, be prepared to have an interactive discussion with your classmates. Make sure you use credible sources and cite them properly.

Insomnia

Narcolepsy

Sleep apnea and snoring

Nocturnal myoclonus

Parasomnias

Restless leg syndrome

Circadian rhythm sleep disorders

Sleepwalking

Sleep eating

Bruxism

Sleep talking

Rhythmic movement disorder

Sleep paralysis

Sleep onset association disorder

Hypersomnia

Kleine-Levin syndrome

REFERENCES

American Psychological Association. (2005). The Division 30 definition and description of hypnosis. Retrieved from http://www.apa.org/divisions/div30/define_hypnosis.html.

Cartwright, R. D., & Lamberg, L. (1997). *Crisis dreaming: Using dreams to solve your problems.* New York: HarperCollins.

Darnton, R. (1968). *Mesmerism and the end of the enlightenment in France.* Cambridge, MA: Harvard University Press.

de Benedictis, T., Larson, H., Kemp, G., Barston, S., & Segal, R. (2007). *Understanding sleep: Sleep needs, cycles, and stages.* Retrieved from http://www.helpguide.org.

Freud, S. (1900). *The interpretation of dreams.* New York: Macmillan.

Hobson, J. A., & McCarley, R. (1977). The brain as a dream state generator: An activation-synthesis hypothesis of the dream process. *American Journal of Psychiatry, 134,* 1335–1348.

LaBerge, S. (1985). *Lucid dreaming.* New York: Ballantine.

Mellinger, G. D., Balter, M. B., & Uhlenhurth, E. H. (1985). Insomnia and its treatment. Prevalence and correlates. *Archives of General Psychiatry, 42,* 225–232.

CHAPTER 5

Learning

LEARNING ASSETS

Case Study #1 Classical Conditioning: What's Wrong with Ziggy?

Case Study #2 Operant Conditioning: Behavior Problems

Case Study #3 Operant Conditioning: Who Can Train Snoopy?

Case Study #4 Observational Conditioning: Lunch Anyone?

Activity #1 Maze Learning

Activity #2 Bells Make So Much Noise

Activity #3 Phobias?

Activity #4 Behavior Modification Contract

LEARNING

Learning is a lifelong process that begins at birth and progresses in complexity as we age. In psychological terms, learning typically means a relatively permanent change in behavior. Learning has been broken down into smaller parts known as classical conditioning, operant conditioning, and observational learning.

CLASSICAL CONDITIONING

If I start discussing a wonderful meal that I had in great detail, I bet I can get your mouth to water. Or, if I ask you to describe your favorite dish, you may be able to get both of our mouths to water. Seeing commercials on TV that show freshly baked pizza, right-out-of-the-oven chocolate lava cake, or a big plate of nachos and cheese will certainly cause a reaction in most people. When we salivate at the thought or sight of these foods, we are exhibiting a learned response. We have associated these foods with their tastes and how they make us feel when we eat them. This is the classic example of what is known as *classical conditioning.* Classical conditioning occurs as a result of pairing two stimuli, one neutral and one unconditioned, together to form an association.

Classical conditioning was first explained by Ivan Pavlov (1849–1936), a Russian scientist who was working in the field of physiology, not psychology. Pavlov was studying the digestive tracts in dogs and came to conclusions that shaped how we looked at learning forevermore. The experiments on digestion earned Pavlov the 1904 Nobel Prize in Physiology and Medicine, and he became well known for defining the concept of "conditioned reflex."

Ivan Petrovich Pavlov was born at Ryazan, where his father, Peter Dmitrievich Pavlov, was a village priest. Although Pavlov went to the church school and then studied at the theological seminary there, he eventually abandoned his religious career and decided to devote his life to science. In 1870 he enrolled in the physics and mathematics department at the University of Saint Petersburg to take the course in natural science. Thus, Pavlov's primary interest became physiology, and he stuck with that throughout another study on the physiology of pancreatic nerves.

Pavlov's research with dogs focused on investigating saliva's role in dogs' digestion. While doing this research, however, Pavlov accidentally found a much greater phenomenon. In his initial experiments, dogs were presented with food, which was placed on their tongues, to get them to salivate. After several days, however, Pavlov realized that the dogs began salivating before the food was presented. First he noticed that they would begin to salivate as he entered the room, and then he recognized that they also began to salivate when they heard his footsteps in the hallway before he entered the room. This made Pavlov think that further research was necessary to see why this was happening.

Pavlov started one of his experiments by ringing a bell, which had no meaning to the dogs at this point. He referred to this as a *neutral stimulus (NS).* Pavlov then started feeding the dogs immediately after ringing the bell, and the food became what he called an *unconditioned stimulus (UCS).* An unconditioned stimulus is an event that automatically produces a response without any previous training. After several pairings of ringing the bell with producing the food, the dogs would start to salivate at the sound of the bell; they knew that the bell meant that food would be produced immediately after the sound. Pavlov said that the dogs had been classically conditioned to salivate at the sound of the bell, which had become a *conditioned stimulus (CS).* It was a conditioned stimulus because it elicited salivation, which then became a *conditioned response (CR).* Pavlov called this a *reflexive behavior to*

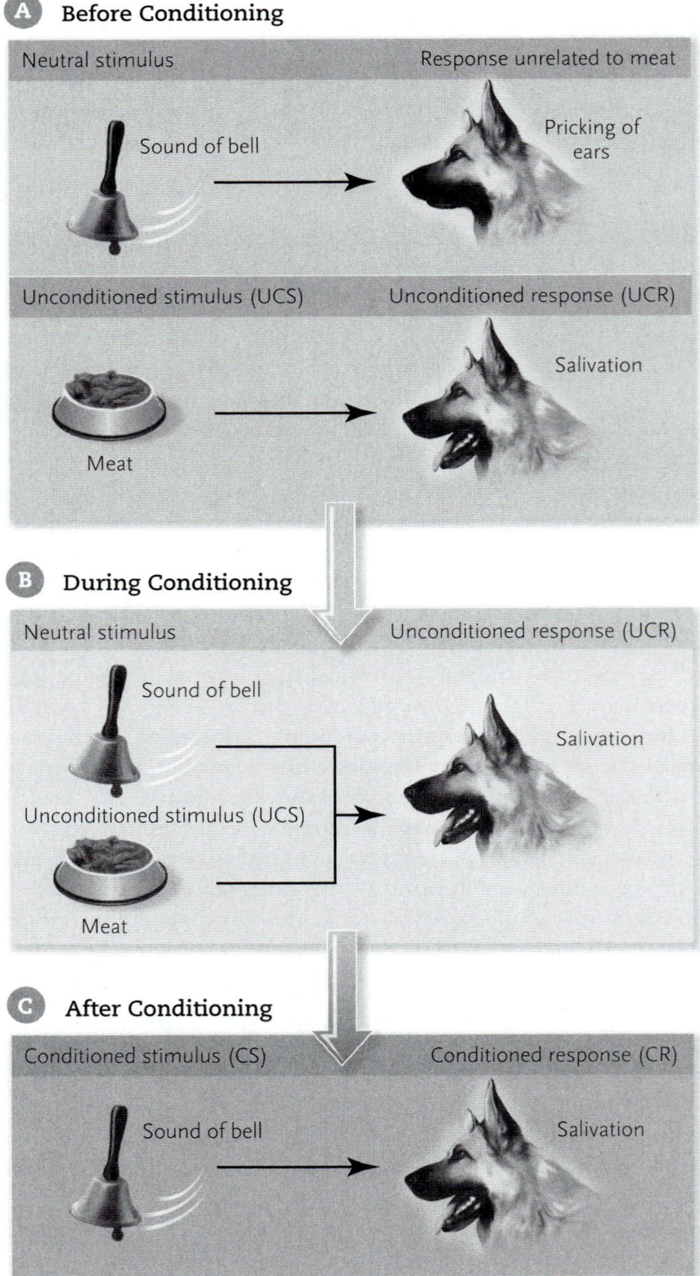

The basic process of classical conditioning. (A) Before conditioning, the ringing of a bell does not bring about salivation—making the bell a neutral stimulus. In contrast, meat naturally brings about salivation, making the meat an unconditioned stimulus and salivation an unconditioned response. (B) During conditioning, the bell is rung just before the presentation of meat. (C) Eventually, the ringing of the bell alone brings about salivation. We now can say that conditioning has been accomplished: The previously neutral stimulus of the bell is a conditioned stimulus that brings about the conditioned response of salivation.

a new association. The bell previously had no connection to the food but was shown to have a connection when they were paired together. Therefore, classical conditioning is learning through associations and pairings. New behaviors are not learned in classical conditioning.

A great example of classical conditioning is if you eat tempura shrimp and it results in food poisoning and you become violently sick, and then you feel ill every time you see tempura shrimp on the menu. You will generally not eat any kind of shrimp at all after your bad experience. This type of learning is so strong that it can last a lifetime. In classical conditioning, the shrimp was a neutral stimulus before you became ill; after conditioning, it became a conditioned stimulus. The response, feeling ill, is an unconditioned response. After conditioning, if the conditioned stimulus is presented by itself, it produces a response, the conditioned response, which is very similar to the unconditioned response.

Have you ever been afraid of something for no real reason at all? Classical conditioning can account for many of these responses. Fears that are irrational in nature are called *phobias,* and they are typically learned behaviors in response to specific stimuli. For example, many people are deathly afraid of spiders. However, most spiders are harmless and will not cause impending doom. It is important to make a distinction here. If you are afraid of something that has imminent and real danger, it is not a phobia. For example, if you are in the woods and you run into a bear, it is natural, and smart, to be afraid of the bear and try to make a hasty retreat. If you have a fear of pictures of bears in books or on television, then it is likely a phobia.

Acquisition and Extinction

Classical conditioning was further enhanced by Pavlov's earlier research. He included acquisition, which is how people develop a conditioned response, and extinction, which is how they eliminate these responses (Rescorla, 2004). *Acquisition* of behaviors is where a response is initially learned. Many factors are associated with whether or not a behavior will be acquired and how strong the learning is that takes place. The opposite of acquisition is known as *extinction.* Extinction is unlearning already learned behaviors, and it has many different aspects. Pavlov created extinction when he wanted to extinguish salivation at the sound of a bell. To do this, he rang the bell without giving food numerous times. Eventually, the dogs learned that the bell would not produce food and, therefore, salivation was eliminated.

Pavlov also identified another phenomenon after he discovered that extinction was possible. He called it *spontaneous recovery.* Spontaneous recovery is the reappearance of a conditioned response (CR) that has previously been extinguished. The recovery may occur after a period of nonexposure to the conditioned stimulus (CS). In his dog experiments, after Pavlov extinguished the pairing of the bell with food, and thus salivation, he could wait for two weeks and pair the bell with food, and spontaneous recovery produced salivation in the dogs every time the bell was rung once again.

Generalization and Discrimination

John B. Watson (1878–1958) was an American psychologist who created behaviorism as a field of study in psychology. In 1920 Watson, along with his assistant Rosalie Rayner, conducted an experiment known as the Little Albert experiment, which was briefly discussed in an earlier chapter. When they chose Albert from a hospital for the study, he was nine months old. First Albert was given a series of emotional baseline tests before the experiment began. Then he was exposed for the first time to a white rat, a white rabbit, a dog, a monkey, masks with and without hair, cotton wool, and burning newspapers. During these baseline tests, Albert showed no fear to any of the objects being presented. The experiment began about two months later when Albert was about eleven months old. The researchers would place Albert on a mattress on a table in the middle of a room. Next, a white laboratory rat was placed near Albert, and he was allowed to play with it. Albert did not show any fear of the rat at this time. He began to reach out to the rat and tried to hold it.

After this initial trial, a second interaction had the same setup, except Watson and Rayner made a loud sound behind Albert's back by striking a steel bar with a hammer when Albert touched the rat. Albert would cry and show fear when he heard the noise. These two stimuli were paired on numerous occasions, and then Albert was presented with just the rat and not the noise. Now, Albert became very distressed when he saw the rat alone. He would cry, turn away from the rat, and try to get away from it. Albert was associating the white rat (an original neutral stimulus, now a conditioned stimulus) with the loud noise (unconditioned stimulus); that produced the emotional response of crying (originally the unconditioned response to the noise, now the conditioned response to the rat). Continuation of this experiment showed that Little Albert learned to *generalize* his response so that when other white furry objects were placed in front of Albert, he would cry and exhibit fear. Watson did notice that the objects had to have white fur or white hair to invoke the generalized fear reaction (Watson & Rayner, 1920).

Albert was taken from the hospital before he was desensitized to the white furry objects. Therefore, it was not known if Albert maintained his fear of white furry objects throughout his entire life! Many current research studies show that the likelihood of Little Albert generalizing this fear over long periods of time without reinforcement of the noise is unlikely. However, it is a hotly debated point that has shaped ethics in psychology as well. Therefore, this experiment reveals that stimulus generalization is the likelihood of a subject to respond to stimuli that are similar, but not necessarily exactly the same as the original conditioned stimulus. Stimulus discrimination occurs when the subject realizes that the object is not the same as the feared object and that a fear response is not necessary.

OPERANT CONDITIONING

Operant conditioning is another form of learning that is sometimes referred to as *instrumental conditioning.* A great way to think of operant conditioning is how individuals operate on their environment. In essence, it is what people learn from their experiences. One of the most influential theorists of operant conditioning is B. F. Skinner (1904–1990). Skinner created the school of radical behaviorism, so named because his theories were more extreme than his predecessors' behaviorism theories. In his experiments, Skinner focused on learning through schedules of reinforcement. Different reinforcers would elicit specific behaviors. According to Skinner, a *reinforcer* is an event or a stimulus that makes the behavior it follows more likely to occur (Skinner, 1938). The behaviors that come before the reinforcer are known as *target responses.*

Reinforcers are either primary or secondary. A *primary reinforcer* is something that is naturally considered satisfying, whereas a *secondary reinforcer* is something that is learned to satisfy the subject. An example of primary reinforcement would be receiving money as a reward for good behavior. An example of secondary reinforcement is buying something with the money you received as a reward. These reinforcers can both be either positive or negative (Skinner, 1938). Behaviors typically increase regardless of whether a primary or secondary reinforcer is motivating the behavior.

Positive and Negative Reinforcers and Punishment

Positive reinforcement is an increase in the likelihood that a behavior will occur in the future due to the addition of a stimulus immediately following a response. An example would be rewarding a dog with a treat immediately after you tell it to sit and it does. *Negative reinforcement* is an increase in the likelihood that a behavior will occur when the consequence is the removal of an aversive, or negative, stimulus. An example of a negative reinforcer is if your mother asks you every Monday to remember to take out the garbage and nags you until you do, then you take out the garbage each week to avoid her nagging, rather than because you are just being helpful.

Skinner noted that punishment is not the opposite of reinforcement. He felt that punishment decreases undesired behavior as well as has other effects. Skinner said that punishment occurs in two different forms. In the first form, a given behavior is followed by the presentation of an aversive stimulus; in the second form, a given behavior is followed by the removal of a pleasant stimulus. An example of the first form of punishment is when a student misbehaves in class and is removed from the classroom and sent to the principal's office. An example of the second form is not allowing a child who misbehaved to watch television with the family.

The Skinner Box

B. F. Skinner was largely influenced by the work of John B. Watson, but Skinner took Watson's work to a whole new level. Watson believed that psychology focused on how to predict and control behavior. Skinner looked for stimuli that controlled behavior. In order to work on the theories of reinforcement, Skinner created what is known as a *Skinner box* to experiment with these phenomena. The box contains one or more levers that an animal can press, one or more stimulus lights, and one or more places in which reinforcers like food can be delivered.

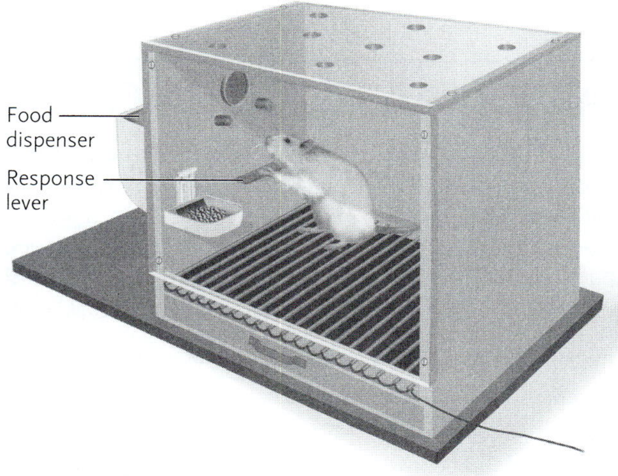

B. F. Skinner used a Skinner box to study operant conditioning. Laboratory rats learn to press the lever in order to obtain food, which is delivered in the tray.

Schedules of Reinforcement

When Skinner created the Skinner box, he also created what he called schedules of reinforcement to test behavioral responses. These schedules of reinforcement are the guidelines used to present or remove reinforcers or punishment following specified operant behavior. These guidelines outline the time and/or the number of desired responses that go along with the learning component. The first is an interval schedule, and it requires a minimum amount of time that must pass between successive reinforced responses. Responses made before the time has elapsed are not rewarded. Fixed-interval schedules produce a more frequent rate of responses as the time of the reinforcement approaches. Variable-interval schedules produce a steady rate of responses. Ratio schedules require a certain number of responses to produce a reinforcer. Fixed-ratio schedules produce a high rate of responses until the reinforcer is received, and then it is likely that a pause in responses will occur afterward. Variable-ratio schedules produce a high and steady rate of responses. Finally, there is extinction, where the reinforcement of a response is discontinued. This leads to a decline in the occurrence of a the previously reinforced response.

Shaping

Skinner referred to *shaping* as "the method of successive approximations." This means that you reinforce a behavior that is similar to the behavior that you are trying to produce. Then you look for alterations that are similar to the behavior that you are trying to create until you find the exact behavior that you want (Boeree, 2006). The method of shaping is the same as that used in *systematic desensitization,* which was created by Joseph Wolpe (1915–1997). Systematic desensitization is often used to treat phobias. For example, it could be used with someone who is very afraid of flying. First the person would be asked to come up with 10 scenarios that involve flying and the feelings that are evoked from these scenarios. They should be in successive order from least scary to most scary. The individual then learns how to do relaxation techniques to calm down. The person works on that for a few sessions and then goes through each of his or her scenarios utilizing the relaxation techniques that have been learned. An individual does this until he or she can fly without the extreme fear.

OBSERVATIONAL LEARNING

The original beliefs in psychology were that a response must be performed for learning to occur. The work of Albert Bandura (1925-) changed this pattern of thinking. Bandura's theory is known as *observational learning,* or *social learning theory,* which is learning that occurs as a function of observing, retaining, and replicating new behaviors that are observed. We learn to copy, or model, behavior that we see others performing (Westen, Burton, & Kowalski, 2006). Bandura felt that there were four key processes of observational learning:

1. The person must pay attention to another person's behavior and consequences.
2. A mental representation of what the person has witnessed must be stored in his or her memory.
3. The person must be able to convert stored mental images into overt behavior.
4. The person must have a certain level of motivation to reproduce the behavior.

Bandura's famous experiment is known as the *Bobo doll experiment,* which he conducted to study the aggressive behavior patterns in children. This experiment has had great impact on the study of violence and children. In this experiment, Bandura used a blow-up doll that was a little larger than the children whom he was studying. He included 48 boys and 48 girls between the ages of 3 and 6 years old. Children were exposed to the experiment individually so that they were not influenced or distracted by the other children.

The first part of the experiment involved bringing a child and an adult model into a room with highly appealing activities and a Bobo doll. The experimenter told the child that the toys were only for the model to play with. After about a minute, the model attacked the Bobo doll by hitting it with fists and a mallet and offering negative verbal messages. After about 10 minutes, the experimenter came back into the room and dismissed the adult model.

Next, the child was taken into another playroom with a nonaggressive model who simply played nicely for 10 minutes. The Bobo doll was completely ignored by this nonaggressive model. After the 10 minutes were over, each child was taken into another playroom and was allowed to play with the attractive toys for a few minutes before being told that they were reserved for other children. The child was also told that there were toys in the next room that he or she could play with.

The final phase of the experiment took place in the last room in which the child was left for 20 minutes with a series of aggressive and nonaggressive toys to play with. Judges watched the children through a two-way mirror. The judges based their decisions on eight different measures of aggression. The results showed that children who witnessed the aggressive model were more likely to imitate the model's aggressive behavior. Also, males were more likely than females to act aggressively.

BEHAVIOR MODIFICATION

Behavior modification is a treatment modality that is often used to change unwanted behaviors. Edward Thorndike (1874–1949) first introduced the concept in 1911 (Thorndike, 1911). Behavior modification referred to psychotherapeutic techniques derived from empirical research, and it has come to mean increasing adaptive behavior through reinforcement and decreasing maladaptive behavior through punishment. It is extremely effective when applied properly.

SUMMARY

This chapter has focused on the various aspects of learning new behaviors. We have looked at classical conditioning, operant conditioning, and observational learning. Although the responses that occur with classical conditioning, operant conditioning, and observational learning mostly occur automatically, we are able to break them down to reduce the likelihood and occurrence of maladaptive behaviors.

CASE STUDY #1 CLASSICAL CONDITIONING: WHAT'S WRONG WITH ZIGGY?

The phone on the other end of the line rang four times before someone answered. "Hello, Renatta Pet Hospital." Katie recognized the voice as belonging to Dr. Mark Renatta, the veterinarian for her dog, Ziggy.

"Hi, Dr. Renatta, this is Katie Golden. I brought my dog, Ziggy, in yesterday afternoon for some shots." Katie paused to give Dr. Renatta a chance to think.

"OK, sure, I remember now. Ziggy hadn't been feeling very well," he said.

"Right, well, you told me that Ziggy might feel a little sick to his stomach for a few hours, but that if he didn't get over it in twenty-four hours to give you a call. Well, it's been twenty-six hours now and he won't eat.

"The funny thing is that he acts like he's hungry. I've been cooking, and every time I start the blender he comes running, but when I show him that his bowl has food in it, he just sniffs but won't eat it."

Dr. Renatta thought for a moment, then he seemed to get an idea. "Tell me, Katie, did you feed Ziggy just before you brought him in to us?"

1. What is Dr. Renatta's idea about the cause of Ziggy's refusal to eat his food, despite showing signs of being hungry? What are the implications of this for classical conditioning theory?
2. Why does Ziggy run into the kitchen when he hears a can being opened? What is the conditioned stimulus in this instance? What is the unconditioned stimulus?
3. Is Ziggy's running to the kitchen a conditioned response, an unconditioned response, or both? Explain your answer.
4. As a puppy, Ziggy would sometimes run into the kitchen when the blender was turned on. However, he only did this a few times. Explain this behavior in classical conditioning terms.
5. Katie started Ziggy on a dry food diet two years ago, and for the past year Ziggy has not bothered to chase after the sound of the blender. According to classical conditioning theory, what happened to cause Ziggy to stop responding to this sound, and why did he start again?

CASE STUDY #2 OPERANT CONDITIONING: BEHAVIOR PROBLEMS

Isabella and Joshua sat quietly in their bedroom. Joshua was reading the letter that Isabella had read half a dozen times since it arrived from the school this morning. The school had written to them to inform them that their son, Ethan, had been skipping classes again. Apparently the talk the three of them had before the school year began hadn't been very effective. The timing couldn't have been any worse for Ethan. Last weekend, after he borrowed Isabella's car, Ethan drove home drunk.

Taking it one problem at a time, Isabella and Joshua brainstormed about how to deal with these situations. Because Ethan had driven while drunk, they could take away his driving privileges for a month or make him spend the next two Saturdays working around the house. For skipping class, they could ground him for a week, or they could offer to increase his allowance if his attendance is perfect for a while. Or they could combine the two punishments: revoke his driving privileges and tell him that the only way to get them back is for perfect attendance.

1. What are the differences between negative reinforcement and positive reinforcement? Give an example of each from the story.
2. What is the difference between a negative punishment and a positive punishment? If Ethan was forced to do housework for two weekends, which type of punishment would that be?
3. When is punishment the best choice in dealing with unwanted behaviors? Should either of Ethan's behavior problems be handled by the use of punishment? Explain your answer.
4. When is reinforcement more effective than punishment in shaping behavior? Why? Should either of Ethan's behavior problems be handled by the use of reinforcement?
5. What role do cognitions play in operant conditioning? Consider the effect of forcing Ethan to mow the lawn as a punishment if he happens to enjoy mowing the lawn.
6. What are the potential consequences of all of Ethan's problem behaviors?

CASE STUDY #3 OPERANT CONDITIONING: WHO CAN TRAIN SNOOPY?

As Lucy released the Frisbee, her puppy, Snoopy, ran after it. Leaping slightly, Snoopy caught the falling Frisbee and returned it to Lucy.

"Wow, he's some catcher," mused Lucy's friend Linus. "How did you teach him to catch like that?"

"Well, I started off by feeding him out of the Frisbee so he'd go to it," Lucy said. "Later I would give him a treat when he chewed on it, then if he caught it when I dropped it, and finally he would get the treat only if he chased it down when I threw it.

"Then I had to train him to bring it back, so I started giving him treats every time he returned the Frisbee so he got used to dropping it in order to get the reward. I rewarded him only every other time, then less often. Now he gets a treat only once or twice per Frisbee game. He's a fully trained Frisbee-catching machine," said Lucy.

1. If an animal was taught a totally unnatural trick, what type of conditioning would you use to attempt this feat?
2. What type of conditioning did Lucy use to teach Snoopy to catch a Frisbee? What type of reward schedule did she use?
3. What type of conditioning and reward schedule did Lucy use to teach Snoopy to return the Frisbee? Why does Snoopy continue to catch and return the Frisbee despite receiving almost no rewards for doing so?
4. Lucy jokingly calls Snoopy a Frisbee-catching machine. In what way is this analogy appropriate to the principles of operant conditioning?
5. Will Snoopy continue to catch the Frisbee if there are no rewards given at all? Explain your answer.

CASE STUDY #4 LUNCH ANYONE?

The front door of the apartment opened, and Eve heard her father's voice call out. "Is anybody home?" he mockingly asked, knowing that Eve was eagerly awaiting his return.

"Daddy's home! Daddy's home," she shrieked.

In one loving motion, Noah swept his daughter up into his arms. While Eve hugged him tightly, he whispered into her ear, "Where's your mom?"

Eve responded softly, "She's in your bedroom." Then somewhat louder Eve said, "Daddy, you missed my birthday!"

"Then I guess it's too late to give you this," he said, pulling out a play kitchen set from a bag. Eve shrieked again. Noah opened the box and started to set up the play furniture and appliances. Eve knew just what to do with each new piece.

"I'll cook you a hamburger, Daddy," she said, flipping a plastic hamburger with her new toy spatula in her new kitchen.

"You're a pretty good cook, Eve. Who taught you how to cook?" Noah asked.

Eve laughed at his joke. He knew that she was not allowed near the stove when it was turned on.

1. Eve proceeded to cook a nine-course meal for her father, and from that day on the kitchen set was her favorite toy. How would operant conditioning theory explain her love for this toy?
2. How would classical conditioning theory explain Eve's attachment to her new toy? Identify the conditioned and unconditioned stimuli and responses.
3. How would cognitive learning theory explain Eve's being able to pretend to cook her father a hamburger, despite having never been allowed near a stove while it was on?
4. How would observational learning theory explain Eve's ability to "cook" for her father? Identify the four stages of observational learning theory in this story.

ACTIVITY #1 MAZE LEARNING

Directions: Follow the maze below from the center to the exit. Do not lift your pen from the paper once you start, and do not start over once you make a mistake. Just work at the maze continuously until you have found your way out. Work as fast as you can.

Completing the maze employs the concept of operant conditioning. Furthermore, the Premack Principle is applied here. The Premack Principle states that some behavior that happens without the interference of a researcher is actually a reinforcer for this behavior.

ACTIVITY #2 BELLS MAKE SO MUCH NOISE

Directions: For this experiment you need a bell or something that makes noise. You will choose one person to go outside of the room for approximately five minutes. While this person is outside of the room you should hide something in the room and make sure the other students know what it is and where it is hidden. Bring the person back inside the room. This person will be told to locate a hidden object. He or she will have to listen to the bell for directions. The ringer will ring the bell slowly when the person is far away from the hidden object and more rigorously as the person nears the object. When the person finds the hidden object, the ringing will stop.

ACTIVITY #3 PHOBIAS?

Directions: Look at the phobias listed at the following link: www.phobia-fear-release.com/phobia-list-2.html. Choose any three phobias that interest you and research their origin and symptoms. Then, explain how these phobias were generated in the first place. Finally, explain how you would go about eliminating these phobias.

ACTIVITY #4 BEHAVIOR MODIFICATION CONTRACT

This contract is a tool that can help you lead a healthier lifestyle. You need to assess your behaviors and determine your goals. This contract will help you change your undesired behaviors.

Complete the following sentence. Be as specific as you can.

In _____ week(s), my goal is to ______________________
____.

Objectives

Make a list of the lifestyle changes that are necessary to accomplish your goal. For instance, if your goal is to quit smoking, you might want to make these changes in lifestyle: cut smoking in half and then eventually quit completely.

1.
2.
3.
4.
5.

Evaluation

To realize your goals, it is important to measure your progress. Make a list of the ways in which you will track your progress.

1.
2.
3.
4.
5.

Reward

Rewards are a great way to change behavior. Complete the following. Again, be specific.

When I meet my goal, I will reward myself by
____.

I am entering into this agreement with myself to change my behavior. I will stick to the goals that I have outlined throughout this behavior modification contract.

Name: ______________________________________

Date: ______________________________________

REFERENCES

Bandura, A., Ross, D., & Ross, S. A. (1961). Transmission of aggressions through imitation of aggressive models. *Journal of Abnormal and Social Psychology, 63*(3), 575–582.

Boeree, C. G. (2006). B. F. Skinner 1904–1990. Retrieved from http://webspace.ship.edu/cgboer/skinner.html.

Nobel Lectures, Physiology or Medicine 1901–1921. (1967). Amsterdam: Elsevier Publishing Company.

Rescorla, R. (2004). Spontaneous recovery. *Learning and Memory, 11,* 501–509.

Skinner, B. F. (1938). *The behavior of organisms: An experimental analysis.* Upper Saddle River, NJ: Prentice Hall.

Thorndike, E. L. (1911). Provisional laws of acquired behavior or learning. In E. L. Thorndike, *Animal intelligence.* New York: Macmillan.

Watson, J. B., & Rayner, R. (1920). Conditioned emotional reactions. *Journal of Experimental Psychology, 3*(1), 1–14.

Westen, D., Burton, L., & Kowalski, R. (2006). *Psychology: Australian and New Zealand edition.* Milton, Queensland: John Wiley and Sons.

CHAPTER 6

Memory

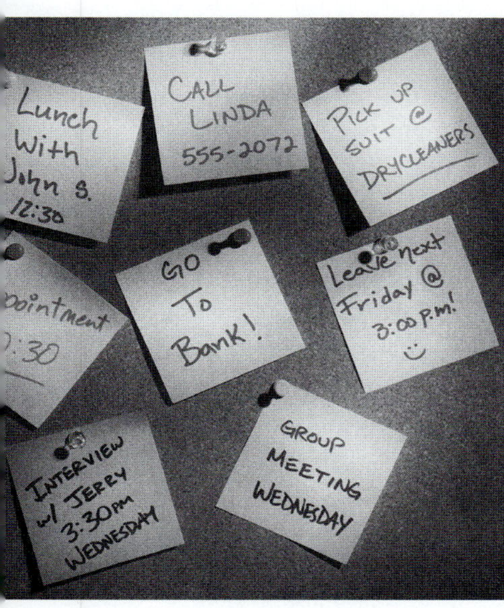

LEARNING ASSETS

Case Study #1 How Odd . . .

Case Study #2 Forget Puppy Love

Case Study #3 Remember That?

Case Study #4 Memory Loss at the Theater

Case Study #5 Wild Days

Activity #1 Implicit Versus Explicit Memory?

Activity #2 Photos from the Past

Activity #3 Six Tips to Improve Memory

Activity #4 Numbers Game

Activity #5 Flashbulb Memories

Activity #6 Forgetful?

MEMORY

The last chapter's focus was on the learning process and how it takes place. In this chapter, the focus is on the various types and stages of memory. For learning to have a lasting effect on us, it must be acquired first and then stored in one of our memory receptors. Hence, the discussion here explores how we encode, store, and retrieve memory to use it in our daily activities. Memory is one of the activities of the human mind, and it is studied quite often by cognitive psychologists. Cognitions involve the thinking process, perception, learning, and reasoning.

Traditional studies of memory actually began with the philosophers, as much of psychology did in its early days. Herman Ebbinghaus (1850–1909) was the first person in the history of psychology to experiment on and study memory. Ebbinghaus believed that memory involved forming new associations that would be strengthened through repetition. To study and test his ideas about memory processes, he conducted an experiment from 1879 to 1880 and again in 1883 through 1884, using himself as the subject. Ebbinghaus's work set the scientific standard for careful work that is still used today (Shakow, 1930).

Ebbinghaus's experiment consisted of creating a set of items to be committed to memory. To ensure the items would not have any previous associations tied to them, he used nonsense syllables. They were in the form of consonant, vowel, consonant and did not spell anything. He created about 20 lists of these types of items and then memorized them systematically. To do that, he would read them first, go on to the next item, and then repeat it to himself over and over again throughout each list of nonsense syllables. Each time through this process was considered one repetition. After several repetitions, he would attempt to recall the items on the list. As the number of repetitions went up, so did his recall of the nonsense syllables. At first recall was rapid and then became more slow as the list was mastered. This learning process is considered a *learning curve,* and its description was the first time that it was considered as a learning concept.

Herman Ebbinghaus

Ebbinghaus wanted to test his retention of these nonsense syllables, so he practiced the list until he was able to repeat the items correctly two times in a row. He waited different periods of time before testing himself again and found that forgetting occurred most rapidly after the end of practice, but the rate of forgetting slowed as time went on and fewer nonsense syllables could be recalled. He called this the *forgetting curve;* once again, Ebbinghaus's description of this process was the first time the forgetting-curve concept was identified.

Another phenomenon that Ebbinghaus found was what he called the *overlearning effect*. You can continue to practice memorizing the list beyond what is necessary once you have sufficiently learned the information. The benefit of the overlearning effect is that it takes longer to forget the material when you have stopped working on it than if you did not overlearn the material. Ebbinghaus also discovered what he called the *serial position curve*. This concept refers to the serial position of an item and the ability to recall it; that is, the place on the list where an item is located affects the learning of that item. Thus, items that are closer to the top of the list are often easier to remember than items lower down on the list, such as the middle of the list (the primacy effect). The items near the end of the list are also easier to recall than those in the middle of the list (the recency effect) (Ebbinghaus, 1885).

Stages in the Formation and Retrieval of Memory from an Information-Processing Perspective

The greatest creation that was born in the image of the human brain is the computer. Computers were built using the complicated processes that occur within our brains. The analogy is often used to explain how the brain works, when in actuality, it should be used to explain how a computer works! Regardless, we can look at memory processing in relation to computer processing because our brains, after all, are the most complicated computer ever built.

There are three main stages in the formation and retrieval of memory that help explain this process. First is encoding, the processing of received information through one of our five senses. We must touch, taste, hear, smell, or see something first in order to process it—perception of one of these senses is paramount to the process.

Next, encoding relies on rehearsal, which is repeating the input and then organizing it into a meaningful manner. Once we have perceived one of these sensations, it networks into our storage area where we build a permanent record of received information as a result of merging this information together in a meaningful manner. Think about this; if every time we smelled a new flower we had to start the process of identifying first that it is a flower, that it might smell nice, that it is pretty, it would take forever to get through the day. But we already have a stored notion that flowers, in general, usually smell nice regardless of the type, so we are able to process new items with relative ease.

Finally, none of this collected information would matter if we were not able to easily retrieve it from our storage center. Retrieval can be a tricky component in this process since we encounter a lot of sensory information on a regular basis. We often have to rely on memory cues to help us jog our memories to find the information we are looking for. For example, have you ever smelled a cologne or perfume that reminded you of an ex-boyfriend or ex-girlfriend? Have you ever seen an old movie and it reminded you where you were when you first saw it? These are all memory cues that help us to remember details that are stored in our storage vault.

Types of Memory

Humans use three types of memory to remember information: *sensory memory, short-term memory,* and *long-term memory*. There is a subcategory in short-term memory, called *working memory,* that helps us to sort out information as well. The first stage corresponds to the initial moment that an item is perceived. Once again, sensory information is anything acquired through one of our five senses: sight, touch, smell, taste, or hearing. This information does not require any further processing, and we encounter an overload of sensory information all of the time. Sensory memory is retained for only milliseconds to a few seconds. If this were not the case, we would be bogged down by everything we encounter. The sensory information may either be sent forward through the process or it decays quickly and is abandoned for new sensory information. Attention plays a large role in this process, since what we put forward and what we pay attention to varies greatly from person to person.

Once we determine what will move forward and what will be discarded, the next stage of memory is short-term memory. Short-term memory can last from a few seconds to a minute. George A. Miller (1920–present) worked at Bell Laboratories and conducted experiments to see how much information we can store in our short-term memory. His results indicated that most individuals can store seven, plus or minus two, items (Miller, 1956). If you think about that for a moment, that is how we wound up with seven-digit phone numbers. We also see the phenomenon of chunking in phone numbers. Chunking is grouping numbers into smaller blocks to make them easier to remember.

Working memory is an interesting process that is not synonymous with short-term memory. It is based on the duration of memory retention and how it is applied to daily life. For example, if we go shopping and see that there is sale where we can take 25 percent off the already reduced sale price, then we have to perform a variety of complex equations in our head to come up with the final cost of the item (checking the price in a price retrieval machine is cheating). This process is the essence of working memory.

Long-term memory allows people to store memory for a period of days to years and can be permanent. Our capacity for storage of long-term memories is potentially limitless. Our long-term memories affect how we process new information, how we process old information, and how we see the world. Information in long-term memory is stored in networks known as *schemas.* A schema is a cognitive model of the world. We use these schemas to categorize information. Some schemas are separate but related, and they affect how we perceive blocks of information as well; that is, we can focus on the important information and disregard information that is meaningless. As you can clearly see, we also process through what is known as *top-down processing*. This means that our prior knowledge influences how we perceive new stimuli. We also develop bias through this manner. Since retention of information is important in long-term memory, we work on rehearsal through the transfer of learning. Transfer of learning occurs because we access prior knowledge to help us decipher new information.

Long-term memory can be classified further into two different types (Anderson, 1976): declarative memory (explicit) and procedural memory (implicit). Explicit memory requires what is known as *conscious recall.* Just as long-term memory can be broken down into further types, so can declarative (explicit) memory. It includes episodic memory, which is information about our own lives, and semantic memory, which concerns our knowledge about the world. Flashbulb memories occur within episodic memory. These memories offer very emotional reactions to events that we can "see" in our minds. Procedural (implicit) memory, the other type of long-term memory, relies on unconscious experience with a task. So, for example, when you are driving home from a friend's house and you are listening to the radio and just magically arrive in your driveway, your implicit memory got you home without you even paying much attention to where you were going. Remember classical conditioning? That is considered a form of implicit memory.

Types of Memory Retrieval

Sensory and short-term memory are both considered bioelectrical types of memory because they store information in the form of electrical signals in the brain. Long-term memory, however, is considered a biochemical type of memory because it accesses a deeper region of the brain for recollection. This brings us to the memory retrieval process that must take

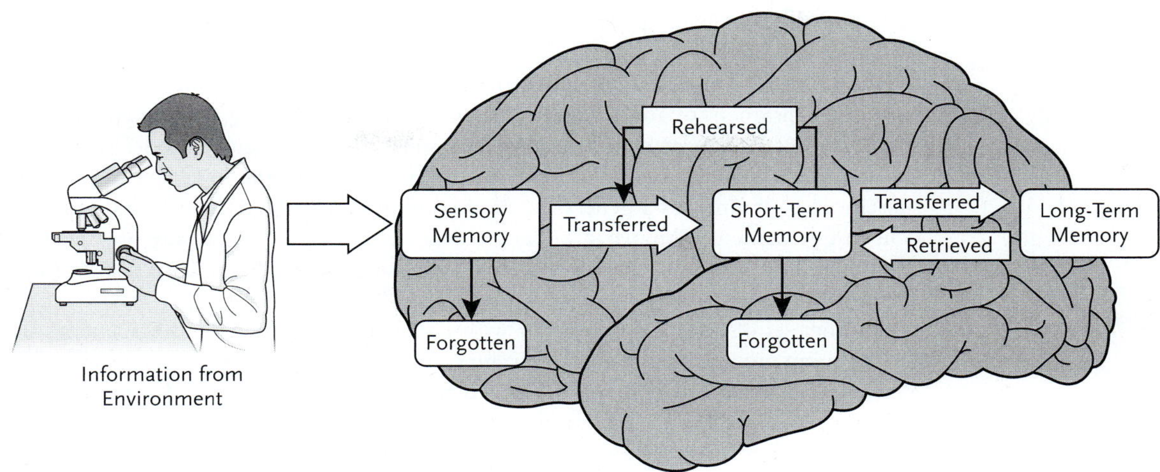

Memory is a complex system that follows a specific path as highlighted here.

place for these systems to have any importance. Research shows that there are four types of memory retrieval. In *recollection,* which is a type of remembering used in reconstructive memory, pieces of memories are pieced together and information is determined based on the organization of that material (Benjamin, Hopkins, & Nation, 1994, pp. 250–290). *Recall* is the ability to regenerate memory without being offered any part of the memory first (Loftus, 1990). *Recognition* is the ability to identify something as a memory once the experience is repeated (Loftus, 1990). Finally, there is *relearning*, which occurs when someone has an easier time remembering material when it is learned for the second time. This happens even if the material was completely forgotten (Loftus, 1990).

PHYSIOLOGY OF MEMORY

The mechanisms of memory are still not that well understood. Scientists have made a lot of advancements over time, but they are still unsure of some of the exact processing that occurs in order for memory to have meaning. Psychologists believe that the hippocampus, the amygdala, and the mammillary bodies are involved in certain kinds of memory, but more research has to be conducted. They also believe that the hippocampus is involved in spatial learning and declarative learning because when there is damage to that area of the brain, these memory systems are affected. Learning and memory are directly connected to neural synapses, so researchers are unsure whether these parts are the cause or just nearby the regions that memory travels to have meaning.

MEMORY DISORDERS

The study of memory disorders has offered most of the information that psychologists know about memory itself. Amnesia, of which there are many different types, is a memory disorder that results in memory loss. One of the more interesting types of amnesia, which often results in psychiatric intervention, is known as a *fugue state.* According to the American Psychiatric Association's *Diagnostic and Statistical Manual of Mental Disorders* (2000), a fugue state is a rare psychiatric disorder characterized by reversible amnesia for personal identity, including the memories, personality, and other identifying characteristics of individuality. The state is usually short-lived (hours to days), but it can last months or longer. Dissociative fugue usually involves unplanned travel or wandering and is sometimes accompanied by the establishment of a new identity. After recovery from fugue, previous memories usually return intact; however, there is complete amnesia for the fugue episode. Importantly, an episode is not characterized as a fugue if it can be related to the ingestion of psychotropic substances, to trauma, to a general medical condition, or to psychiatric conditions such as delirium or dementia, bipolar disorder, or depression. Fugues are usually precipitated by a stressful episode, and upon recovery there may be amnesia for the original stressor (dissociative amnesia).

Another set of disorders that occur with memory are dementia and Alzheimer's disease. *Dementia* can be defined as a group of symptoms caused by brain disorders. Dementia is not a disease, it is an interruption in normal activities. These activities include simple events like eating or complex events such as problem solving and critical thinking. Memory loss is a symptom of dementia; however, forgetfulness is not always dementia related. Many diseases cause dementia, such as Alzheimer's disease and stroke. *Alzheimer's disease* is the most common form of dementia. It tends to begin slowly and is seen in the part of the brain that controls memories and language. This may lead to forgetting recent events but having clear pictures of events that took place long ago. It typically occurs after the age of 60 and the risks increase with age. There is no cure for dementia or Alzheimer's disease, but there are drugs that help reduce the symptoms.

MEMORIZATION VERSUS LEARNING

What is the difference between memorizing information and learning information? There is a huge difference, actually. When you *memorize* information, you store it in your short-term memory or working memory. We know that means it does not last that long. However, when you *learn* information, you store it in your long-term memory and that means that you can own that for a lifetime. Memorization is known as rote learning and still requires repetition to be stored at all.

FORGETTING

Why do we forget information? That is an age-old question. However, psychologists today can offer some simple answers, since they now have a handle on how information is processed and stored. For example, forgetting can be due to weak encoding. If we were not paying attention to something in the first place, then we have a greater chance of forgetting it. Forgetting also could be due to a lack of a retrieval cue. Sometimes we need a retrieval cue to help us remember specific items or events. If that cue is missing or not strong enough, then we are not likely to be able to produce the memory. Forgetting may be due to time. Over time our memories may fade or become unclear. This is not due to dementia, but rather to a lack of time spent on that item or event. Forgetting may be caused by repetitive experiences. This means that you will not likely remember what you ate for lunch two weeks ago on Monday unless it was a special event. You can probably remember what you did on your last birthday, holiday, or vacation, but that is because they are special occasions and not repetitive events like eating lunch daily. Finally, we forget because it keeps us sane! If we remembered every event that occurred, we would have sensory overload. We tend to throw out information that is not important to us (hopefully).

SUMMARY

This chapter has focused on the process that must take place for all of the different types of memory to function properly. The various aspects that cause memory to disintegrate, deteriorate, or disappear were examined. Memory is a complex process that requires more than just studying.

CASE STUDY #1 HOW ODD . . .

Jamie was just returning from her first golf lesson.

"How did it go?" asked her husband, who seemed preoccupied watching his favorite television news show.

"Fine," she said, laying down her heavy golf bag. "But I noticed something odd about the way the golf pro answered my questions. I thought he would be able to just tell me what to do. Instead, it seemed that in order to remember anything, he would have to act it out himself. Only then could he describe what I was supposed to do."

"That's nice, dear," said her husband, as he stared at an over-the-top news story on the screen.

Later, when Jamie's husband tried to recall how her lesson had gone, all he could remember was that the golf pro had seemed "odd."

1. What form of long-term memory was Jamie showing when she told her husband how the golf pro had acted?
2. The golf pro seemed to have trouble describing how something was done unless he performed the action himself. What form of memory code was he probably relying on?
3. Jamie seemed surprised by the golf pro's memory process. If the golf pro had been unable to answer her questions immediately, without acting them out first, what kind of memory would he probably have been showing?
4. Jamie's husband seemed to have trouble remembering what she had said about her lesson because he had not considered it very carefully. Which type of memory does this explanation most closely resemble?
5. Which of the three memory processes seems to have caused Jamie's husband's memory problem? Why?

CASE STUDY #2 FORGET PUPPY LOVE

Mary liked to draw, even during class. From her desk, if she leaned backward and peeked a bit to the left, she could make out the magnificent profile of her classmate Johnny, the most popular boy in the school. Then she would try to draw Johnny in the margin of her notebook. She noticed that after each glance, she could almost see his face for a short while, even though she had looked away.

"Mary, you weren't even listening!" said the teacher, awakening Mary from her reverie.

"Yes, I was," said Mary. "You just asked if anyone could name the nine planets." Actually, Mary had not been listening, but the sound of the teacher's last question had seemed to ring in her ears even so.

"Well, can you name the nine planets?" challenged the teacher.

"No," said Mary, "because they already have names." The class erupted in laughter.

"I know!" Johnny called out. "Mercury, Venus, Earth, Mars, Jupiter, Saturn, Uranus, Neptune, and Pluto. I know because the first letters match the sentence 'Mary's violet eyes make Johnny stay up nights period.'"

Mary blushed.

1. Mary seemed to be able to see Johnny's profile "in her mind's eye" for a short time after she looked away. What form of sensory memory might she have been using?
2. Later, Mary was also able to remember the sound of the teacher's question, even though she had not been listening. What form of sensory memory might she have been using this time?
3. Explain the memory process that Johnny used to remember the names of the nine planets.
4. Johnny was able to combine the names of the planets into a meaningful group of information. What type of memory is Johnny now using to recall this information?
5. Although Mary did not know the names of the planets, she knew for certain that there were nine of them. What type of long-term memory did she use to store this information?

CASE STUDY #3 REMEMBER THAT?

Pam had been nervous ever since she had accepted the invitation to stop in for tea from her aunt Sadie and her aunt Mimi. Now, late and frantically looking for their house, Pam fretted. How was she going to recognize their house when she hadn't been there for 15 years? All she could remember about the house were some red flowers on the porch. Unfortunately, it was now the middle of winter. Once again, Pam promised herself to be more careful writing down directions. Suddenly, she saw a house she knew belonged to them.

Once everyone was settled, tea went well. Aunt Sadie, it seemed, remembered the day John F. Kennedy died "as if it were yesterday." She spoke at length, recalling an amazing amount of detail. She and Mimi had been together when they had first heard the news.

"It is a wonder," said Pam, who was genuinely amazed, "that you remember so vividly."

"It is a wonder that you remember so wrongly," sputtered Mimi, breaking her long silence. "My dear Sadie, I too remember that day as if it were yesterday. Unfortunately, many of your so-called details are incorrect!"

1. Why might Pam have been able to recall the flowers when she forgot everything else about the appearance of the house?
2. Why might Pam have been able to recognize the house when she saw it, even though she had not been able to remember what it had looked like?
3. Both Sadie and Mimi had vivid memories of what they were doing when they first heard of John F. Kennedy's death. What is the name for this kind of memory?
4. Apparently Sadie and Mimi disagreed on several details of what they were doing when they first heard of John F. Kennedy's death. Why might they disagree?
5. On what kinds of details might Sadie and Mimi be especially likely to disagree?

CASE STUDY #4 MEMORY LOSS AT THE THEATER

Nathan liked to act in his local theater. In a new play, his character, Ralph Rigley, has been in an automobile accident and suffered complete memory loss for two hours afterward. During those two hours, someone had committed a murder. Despite his memory loss, Ralph was a suspect.

In the opening scene, Ralph is lying in a hospital bed. The doctor allows Police Inspector Fenley only three questions, because of Ralph's delicate condition. Nathan's lines in this scene are: "I think, Fenley, she served a strudel," "I can't remember," and "No."

The night before the first performance, Nathan fell asleep repeating his lines. He even dreamed about them.

Arriving at the theater opening night, Nathan found that the order of his lines had been changed. Then the order was changed again. Confused and worried, Nathan mentally associated the order of his lines to a walk through the rooms of his house. Each room he mentally passed through would remind him of the next line.

The scene arrived. Everything went well, until Nathan's last line.

"Can you remember," asked Police Inspector Fenley, "what the victim served for dessert that night?"

Nathan mentally walked upstairs to his bedroom. "I think, stairway," said Nathan, "she served a frudel."

1. Why do people forget what they have learned?
2. Nathan originally learned his lines to a degree far beyond what he needed to say them correctly. Do you think it is possible to overlearn material?
3. Once having learned the order of his lines, Nathan found it difficult to learn a new order. What type of memory was Nathan having trouble with?
4. On opening night Nathan was expected to relearn his lines. What type of memory makes this possible?
5. Even though he had worked very hard, Nathan incorrectly recited his lines. Was there anything about the way Nathan memorized his lines that might have made the mistake more likely?

CASE STUDY #5 WILD DAYS

Lilian and Faye are sisters. Now, both in their seventies, they found themselves living together once again. Most days they sat and argued. Today, the issue was whether Lilian, the "prettier" one, had ever been interested in a married man.

"What was his name?" Faye mused, looking out the window. "I am certain I know it." Just then an art gallery truck drove by. "Oh, I remember!" she cried. "His name was Fine, Marty Fine! I saw that look in your eye, and his marriage wasn't very happy."

Lilian feigned horror, as she exclaimed, "Why, I never! You know that I was happily married to Irving for 50 years, and I never missed a Sunday sermon, unlike some people."

"True," said Faye, ignoring the barb. "This was before you even met Irving. I think you may have forgotten your wilder days. And you must have known that he wasn't happy in the marriage. You yourself told me once that he said that since getting married, life had gone downhill."

"Faye, Faye, Faye," Lilian said, with a chuckle. "He said marriage was like riding a bicycle downhill, meaning that things got easier, not worse."

1. At first Faye had trouble remembering the "suitor's" name, even though she was sure she knew it. What might help her remember his name?
2. When Faye saw the art gallery truck, she suddenly recalled that the man's name was "Fine." How did the truck jog her memory?
3. Assume that Lilian had really forgotten her "wilder days." Why might she have been more likely to forget them than her sister?
4. What is the exact memory process that is necessary to recall someone's name after seeing them in person?
5. What process might explain why Faye's memory for something Lilian said might be inferior to Lilian's memory for the same thing?

ACTIVITY #1 IMPLICIT VERSUS EXPLICIT MEMORY?

Directions: Define implicit memory and explicit memory on the following lines. Then, in the boxes below write tasks that you perform that would fall into either the implicit memory category or the explicit memory category. There are examples offered to get you started.

Definition of Implicit Memory:

____

____

____

____

Definition of Explicit Memory:

____

____

____

____

Tasks Requiring Implicit Memory	Tasks Requiring Explicit Memory
Example: Singing a familiar song	Example: Writing a term paper

ACTIVITY #2 PHOTOS FROM THE PAST

Directions: Gather photos from your life that occurred at different stages of your life. Look at the photos that you collected. Do you remember the events that led up to that photo being taken? Write down as much information as you can about each photo. Is it easier to remember the more recent photos? What phenomena are occurring with each memory that you conjure?

ACTIVITY #3 SIX TIPS TO IMPROVE MEMORY

Directions: In the following spaces, write six tips that will help others improve their memories. Explain why this is important when you have finished each one.

1. Tip #1 and Explanation:

2. Tip #2 and Explanation:

3. Tip #3 and Explanation:

4. Tip #4 and Explanation:

5. Tip #5 and Explanation:

6. Tip #6 and Explanation:

ACTIVITY #4 NUMBERS GAME

Directions: Work with a group on this activity. Once you have chosen your group, choose one person to read this sheet while the other group members do not have access. The person reading this sheet needs to ask the group members to take out a pen and paper and get ready to work on this activity. The group should be told that they will listen to a set of numbers and after you are done reading, they need to write down the numbers in the exact order based on what they remember. Make sure you do not chunk the numbers for them. Try to read the numbers as though they are all separate numbers and not a group set. Read each set of numbers separately.

Here are the number sets:

1. 5 1 9 2 3
2. 9 1 9 2 5 8
3. 9 8 2 2 9 3 1
4. 3 8 5 4 9 6 5 7
5. 3 8 0 4 7 1 3 6 9
6. 5 3 3 1 9 6 1 2 1 6
7. 6 7 4 6 2 9 0 4 3 2 8

When you are done with this activity, check to see how many people in the group got each number set correct. Ask the group how difficult they felt this exercise was.

ACTIVITY #5 FLASHBULB MEMORIES

Directions: First define a flashbulb memory. Next, report a flashbulb memory that is especially vivid for you. Explain the details of the event as you remember it unfolding. What role did emotion play in the formation of the memory? Have you rehearsed and retold the memory unusually often?

Definition of Flashbulb Memory:

Flashbulb Memory Explanation:

ACTIVITY #6 FORGETFUL?

Directions: Go to the Alzheimer's disease website (http://www.alz.org/alzheimers_disease_what_is_alzheimers.asp) and answer the questions that follow:

1. Define Alzheimer's disease and explain the most recent findings.
2. What are 10 signs that someone has Alzheimer's disease?
3. What are the risk factors of Alzheimer's disease?
4. What are the myths surrounding Alzheimer's disease?
5. What is the difference between a dementia and Alzheimer's disease?

REFERENCES

American Psychiatric Association. (2000). *Diagnostic and statistical manual of mental disorders* (4th ed., text rev.). Washington, DC: Author.

Anderson, J. R. (1976). *Language, memory, and thought.* Mahwah, NJ: Erlbaum.

Benjamin, L. T., Jr., Hopkins, J. R., & Nation, J. R. (1994). *Psychology* (3rd ed.). New York: Macmillan College Publishing.

Ebbinghaus, H. (1885). *Über das Gedächtnis. Untersuchungen zur experimentellen Psychologie.* Leipzig: Duncker & Humblot; the English edition is Ebbinghaus, H. (1913). *Memory. A contribution to experimental psychology.* New York: Teachers College, Columbia University.

Loftus, E. F. (1990). Memory. In *World Book Encyclopedia* (Vol. 13). Chicago: World Book, Inc..

Miller, G. A. (1956). The magical number seven, plus or minus two: Some limits on our capacity for processing information. *Psychological Review, 63,* 81–97.

Shakow, D. (1930). Hermann Ebbinghaus. *American Journal of Psychology, 42,* 505–518.

CHAPTER 7

Motivation and Emotion

LEARNING ASSETS

Case Study #1 How Quickly Can Date Night Happen?

Case Study #2 Retirement Life

Case Study #3 I Bet I Can Beat You!

Case Study #4 How Quickly Things Can Change

Case Study #5 Road Rage

Activity #1 Goal Setting and Achievement

Activity #2 Cognitive Dissonance

Activity #3 What Motivates Us to Eat?

Activity #4 Where Am I Going?

THEORIES OF MOTIVATION

Where does motivation come from? What motivates you? Are motives positive or negative? Motivation is a very important aspect of psychology and has received a lot of attention in recent years as people try to find the secret to success. Several distinct theories of motivation exist that try to explain these interesting behaviors. We will focus on these theories and explanations throughout this chapter.

Although many different definitions of motivation exist, there is a lot of consistency when it comes to most of the research on motivation. One good definition of motivation is that it is an internal state or condition (sometimes described as a need, desire, or want) that serves to activate or energize behavior and give it direction (Kleinginna & Kleinginna, 1981). Motivation theorists generally accept that motivation is involved in all learned responses. The major issue is whether or not motivation is a primary or secondary influence on behavior.

Biological Theories of Motivation

The biological theories of motivation look at the physiological processes that guide behavior. Instinct theory is often used to help describe motivation and its relation to behavior. This theory relies on the notion that all thoughts and actions can be traced back to instincts; that is, inferences can be made about all behaviors in regard to how they serve a survival purpose for humans. An example of instinct theory in action would be a bully on the playground. The leader (i.e., the bully) tries to hold all of the power and will belittle others to gain this power and control. This can be seen in the animal world when two males fight for dominance to be the leader of the pack. The attempts to explain human behavior strictly through instinct has failed, however, and it is not considered the sole guiding principle to behavior.

In the early 19th century, Sigmund Freud (1856–1939) offered a very broad view of instincts and how they contribute to our survival. His psychoanalytic theory views bordered on drive theory (see the description of the drive-reduction theory later in this section), but he believed further that human behavior was motivated by two biologically energized instincts. These are Eros, the life instinct, and Thanatos, the death instinct. The life instinct was the basis for sexual motivation; that is, humans try to continue the survival of the species by engaging in sexual relations to produce progeny. The death instinct was at the opposite end of the spectrum and involved aggressive motivation. Freud felt that these instincts remained in our unconscious and, therefore, were carried out unbeknownst to us.

William James (1842–1910) also offered instinct theory explanations in his work. James, if you recall, held a functionalist perspective. He emphasized the survival value of instinctive motivation, arguing that humans were born with a score of instincts that are at the core of all complex behavior. Some of the instincts that he offered in his theory were fear, sociability, cleanliness, and love.

Instinct theory fell out of favor in the 1930s. The critics claimed that instinct theories failed to explain behavior. Also, since instincts are not observable and could not be subjected to empirical testing or behavior evaluation, there was no scientific proof of their existence. In the 1930s the behaviorists were studying environmental stimuli in regard to motivation. Behavior is complex and contains a lot of variety; therefore, instinct theory was considered much too simplistic. The sociobiological model, which is more modernized, looks at behavior as being motivated by individuals' instinctual need for survival.

Drive-reduction theories also attempt to explain motivation and behavior. In these theories, drives are defined as internal states created by a physiological need. These drives may be met in different ways. For example, someone who is hungry works 10 hours at his or her job to make money to buy groceries, whereas someone else steals the food from

the grocery store. So, in drive-reduction theory, the basic biological needs that people have are hunger, thirst, sleep, and sexuality. We work to reduce the drives that we are encountering. If we are hungry, we try to find food. If we are thirsty, we try to find water, and so on. Drive theories become less viable in trying to explain behaviors such as gambling, competitive sports, or engagement in risky behaviors. These theories are troublesome when it comes to explaining why we engage in certain behaviors even when we do not have to. For example, some people eat when they are not hungry or drink when they are not thirsty.

Arousal theory is a term used to explain a general state of physiological activation. This can be thought of in terms of how a person's body and mind are geared up and ready for some type of action or occurrence. This theory contends that people behave so as to bring about an optimal level of arousal for themselves. If they are too aroused, they act to reduce arousal. For example, if we are hungry, we eat. If individuals are not aroused enough, they act to increase arousal. For example, if we are bored, we watch television.

Cognitive Theories of Motivation

The cognitive approach to motivation and behavior maintains that people think about, plan, and control their behavior. For example, if you are bored, then you think of plans that will be exciting; that is, you decide what you like to do and then go about doing it. You do not just jump out of the window to solve your boredom! The cognitive consistency theories attempt to explain behavior from this point of view. If we have imbalanced, inconsistent, or contradictory opinions or beliefs, a tension or energy is created that serves as a force that motivates behavior (Festinger, 1957).

Leon Festinger (1919–1989) created the theory of cognitive dissonance, which states that when individuals have two inconsistent or incompatible thoughts, they try to resolve this incompatibility because dissonance is unpleasant or aversive to them. An example of cognitive dissonance would be if you eat too much and explain that you eat because it stops you from feeling nervous. However, you feel bad because overeating has caused considerable weight gain. Cognitive dissonance is a state of tension that we try to resolve.

A whole host of theories exist that do not rely on drives, instincts, or resolving cognitive dissonance. One of these theories is called incentive theory. Incentive theory states that behavior is motivated by the pull of external goals and rewards. An example of incentive theory is seen right here as you read this textbook. You are likely going to school to gain new skills for a good-paying job. Therefore, you are motivated to read this book, do well in this class, and all of the others, in order to graduate and obtain a high-paying job. Incentive theory is based on operant learning theory. This means that it can be tested with experiments. The main criticism of incentive theory is that it has a problem explaining behavior that has no external goals, such as playing; behaving altruistically; satisfying curiosity; or acquiring mastery of a new task.

Humanistic Theory of Motivation

Another popular theory of motivation is humanistic theory. This theory suggests that people are motivated to satisfy needs in progressive levels to realize their highest potential. Abraham Maslow (1908–1970), who is considered the founder of humanistic psychology, created a hierarchy of needs that includes basic physiological needs, safety needs, a need for belonging, a need for self-esteem, and, finally, a need to become self-actualized. This approach is rather comprehensive and is a long journey that is never complete for most people.

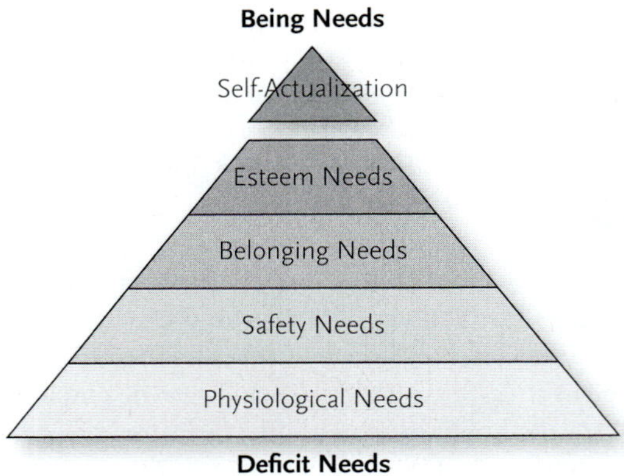

Maslow's Hierarchy of Needs, as he called it, starts out with humans' basic physiological needs, which include oxygen, water, protein, salt, sugar, calcium, and other minerals and vitamins. This level also includes the need to maintain a pH balance and proper temperature. These basic needs include the motivation to be active, to rest, to sleep, to get rid of wastes, to avoid pain, and to have sex. If individuals satisfy all of these basic needs, they move up the hierarchy to the next level: safety and security needs. Here people become increasingly interested in finding safe circumstances, stability, and protection. They may even develop a need for structure, order, and limits. Moving up the pyramid, individuals go into love and belonging needs. This is when people feel the need to make friends, have a love interest, have children, and have affectionate relationships in general, and even a broader sense of community. They next climb the ladder to the level that involves esteem needs. Maslow suggested that there are different types of esteem needs. There is a lower one, which is the need for the respect of others, and the need for status, fame, glory, recognition, attention, reputation, appreciation, dignity, and even dominance. A higher form involves confidence, competence, achievement, mastery, independence, and freedom. Finally, if people can achieve all of these levels, they embark on what Maslow termed *self-actualization.* Needs at this level do not involve balance or homeostasis, like the preceding motivations. Rather, it is a matter of becoming the most complete, the fullest individual possible (Maslow, 1970). Criticisms of Maslow's concept of self-actualization is that it is hard to define and even more difficult to test. Other criticisms include that it gives too little weight to incentives that motivate people to behave in specific directions.

CONFLICT

We humans have come to realize that conflict is inevitable when we interact with others in our everyday lives. Thus, conflict can be a motivating factor in people's behavior outcomes. The nature of conflict is difficult to define, but in essence, it involves opposing forces with different objectives. Moreover, we encounter different types of conflict. For example, there is psychological conflict, which is internal, and there is social conflict, which occurs between an individual and one or more people. These conflicts often propel people into action. That is, we try to balance out the conflict because we do not like the feelings of worry and tension that typically accompany conflict. These uncomfortable feelings motivate us to return to what is called *homeostasis.* Homeostasis is a sense of equilibrium or status quo.

If we have conflict, and we want to return to homeostasis, then we turn to various approaches to help us overcome these conflicting feelings. In an *approach-approach conflict,* which states that two desirable things are wanted, only one option can be chosen. For example, you are asked to go on vacation in Hawaii by one group of friends and asked to go to Costa Rica by another group of friends. You can only choose one trip. Similarly, in the *avoidance-avoidance conflict,* there are two alternatives, but both are unattractive and you still must choose one; for example, take out the garbage or vacuum the rugs on cleaning day. The *approach-avoidance conflict* states that there are attractive and unattractive parts to both sides. For example, you might want a vacation home in the Bahamas, but you do not want to pay for someone to take care of it while you are not there. All of these conflicts will motivate behavior in some direction.

EMOTION

Emotion is a topic that is easy to identify, but very difficult to describe. Emotions, which can range from how we feel about a certain topic to survival mechanisms, are complex and have the following elements: physiological responses, cognitive responses, sensory input, and behavioral correlates. In addition, emotions can be temporary and be either good or bad, and are passive in nature (since we do not choose how we feel). Since experience and learning guide emotions, to define them we have to incorporate all of the preceding factors. Thus, emotions can be defined as states that occur spontaneously and are accompanied by physiological changes in arousal. When our emotions last for a period of time that is not fleeting, we call this a *mood.*

Theories of Emotion

There are four major theories of emotion: the James-Lange theory, the Cannon-Bard theory, the Schachter-Singer theory, and Lazarus's appraisal theory.

The James-Lange theory was created by William James (1842–1910) and physiologist Carl Lange (1834–1900). Their theory holds that a visceral experience (gut reaction) is called an *emotional state.* James and Lange believed that we have autonomic reactions to stimuli. We observe these physical sensations and then assign feelings to them. They further believed that our emotional reaction is dependent on how we interpret responses to these physical reactions. William James said, "My thesis on the contrary is that bodily changes follow directly the PERCEPTION of the exciting fact, and that our feeling of the same changes as they occur IS the emotion." A classic example is if you are walking in the woods and you see a grizzly bear. You will tremble and your heart may race. The James-Lange theory holds that you will interpret your physical reactions and conclude that you are frightened (James, 1884).

This theory has a lot of great points, but it has been criticized as well. For example, one major criticism is that the visceral response may not occur quickly enough to account for sudden emotions. Some visceral responses are not even interpreted as emotions. Emotions seem to be much broader than gut reactions.

The Cannon-Bard theory, proposed by Walter Cannon (1871–1945) and Philip Bard (1898–1977), stated that when presented with a stimulus, the thalamus activates a physiological reaction and an emotional response. The theory also states that the thalamus simultaneously signals the autonomic nervous system and the cerebral cortex. However, psychologists now know that the rest of the limbic system plays a role in emotional responses as well. Another issue with this theory is that physiological responses and emotional reactions may not be simultaneous.

The Schachter-Singer theory was proposed by Stanley Schachter (1922–1997) and Jerome E. Singer. Their two-factor theory, or cognitive arousal theory, holds that a stimulus causes physiological arousal. The arousal is then interpreted as an emotional state based on the cues. This means that the environment is used to explain the physiological state. Individuals' emotional responses are triggered by events that are significant to their own well-being. Most of the research on the Schachter-Singer model has not upheld their theories. For example, subsequent research has shown that emotions can occur without physiological arousal, and physiological factors alone can cause emotions.

Lazarus's appraisal theory, an extension of the Schachter-Singer theory, was proposed by Richard S. Lazarus (1922–2002). It states that cognitive appraisal of a situation is of primary importance in emotional states. Lazarus went on to amend his theory and worked with other researchers to continue his thought processes. Appraisal processes were found to play an important part in emotional reactions to stimuli. Some critics' arguments are that the term *appraisal* is a very vague term and that this view ignores the social context of emotional experiences.

Nonverbal Expression of Emotions

Since emotions are often difficult to explain, we look for the subtle, nonverbal cues that are offered instead. Individuals can express themselves very effectively without using words, through facial expressions, eye movements and eye contact, and posture. People can also change the tone of their voice and make sounds without words to express themselves well. Research by Paul Ekman (1934–present) shows that expressions tend to be innate. He postulated that people in all cultures show six basic emotions in their faces: fear, anger, disgust, sadness, surprise, and happiness. Psychologists and researchers today widely accept Ekman's conclusions about the universality of basic expressions of emotions.

SUMMARY

Human motivations and emotions are complex entities that require a lot of consideration. Many theories offer explanations of both phenomena, but as scientific aspects are further explored, these issues become better understood. Motivation and emotions are at the cornerstone of behavior and influence us regardless of whether or not we are consciously aware of them.

CASE STUDY #1 HOW QUICKLY CAN DATE NIGHT HAPPEN?

Wok Inn was clearly one of the most favored eating places in town. Between six and eight in the evening you could count on having to wait for about 45 minutes to be seated. The wait was always worth it since the food was so delectable. The lunch rush, however, was considerably less of a wait. Taking advantage of this, Ruth and David moved their "date nights" to lunchtime and met at Wok Innfrequently for lunch. In fact, David was spending so much time and money there this semester that he started working 25 hours a week (up from 20 hours a week) at a part-time job on campus.

Today, David showed up at Wok Inn at 11 in the morning, a solid hour before he was meeting Ruth. His goal was to finish a chemistry homework assignment that was due at two that afternoon. He assumed that an hour would be plenty of time. However, at 11:45 David still had two fairly complicated problems left. Worried about not finishing in time, he worked diligently, and by ten minutes past noon he had finished his assignment. Ruth arrived five minutes later.

1. How would instinct theory explain why people eat? How was this explanation modified by the drive-reduction theory?
2. How would incentive theory differ from these earlier theories?
3. According to drive-reduction theory, what are primary drives? What are secondary drives? Which drive motivated David to add five hours to his workweek?
4. How does the arousal theory of motivation differ from the drive-reduction theory? What prediction would arousal theory make about the quality of David's homework assignment (assuming his chemistry assignment is a complicated task)? Did his performance improve or decline on the last two problems?
5. How might instinct theory explain why people like David and Ruth date each other? Contrast this explanation with that offered by drive-reduction theory and arousal theory. In your opinion, which theory provides the best explanation of this phenomenon?

CASE STUDY #2 RETIREMENT LIFE

At age 50, Ryan Stone is on top of his world. After receiving his MBA 25 years ago, Ryan borrowed $20,000 from his father to open a small business in Chicago. In 10 years he was operating a small chain of 10 stores. In 10 more years his company had doubled in size. Last summer Ryan sold it for $5 million, bought a home in Florida, and with his wife and son moved south.

Not sure what to do next, the family is working on retirement life. Ryan's wife is taking drawing and painting classes. Ryan and his son are taking waterskiing lessons at a nearby aquatic center. Their ski instructor, Gus, is very good at his job. Gus grew up waterskiing and still loves it. At times, Ryan wonders if selling out was the right thing to do. However, these doubts grow smaller each day spent in the sun with his family.

1. Most people find waterskiing to be somewhat frightening the first time they try it. Why would someone ski if they were frightened?
2. How would Maslow's humanistic theory of motivation explain Ryan's decision to sell a business that he had worked hard to create? How would cognitive theories explain his decision to sell?
3. What motivates a person to express one's self-creativity through art? At what level of Maslow's hierarchy would artistic motives reside?
4. According to cognitive theories, there are two basic types of emotions. What are they? Which of these motives drove Gus to ski as a child? Which motive led him to become an instructor?
5. Gus appears to love skiing as much today as he did growing up. Would this statement surprise a cognitive motivation theorist? Why or why not?

CASE STUDY #3 I BET I CAN BEAT YOU!

Seth and Justin have been best friends since elementary school. In high school and college they played the same sports (baseball and football), took many of the same electives, and belonged to the same clubs. Now, they have graduated and work in the same jobs at similar companies (information technology). This evening they are playing video games together.

"Man, you are good," said Seth, shaking his head. "I guess it's clear who the better gamer is."

"Funny thing about video games, you play long enough and you get pretty good at it," joked Justin. "You up for one more game? I'll spot you some extra time."

"Actually, I should take off," Seth replied. "I'm going to a neighborhood watch meeting. It starts in 15 minutes and I want to get there early. . . . Oh, what the heck, I'll play one more game with you, but I don't want any extra time from you!"

Justin laughed, "You're on."

1. What do psychologists mean by the need for affiliation? How would you judge both Seth and Justin in their level of need for affiliation? What level is typical for high school students? What level is typical for adults out of school?
2. How would you judge both men's need for achievement? Using examples from the story, explain your answer.
3. How is the fear of failure related to the need for achievement? Which participant is more fearful of losing this final video game?
4. Which video game player exhibits characteristics of being high in the need for power? How do men and women who are high in the need for power behave?
5. Of the three motives discussed above, which seem to be strongly tied to biological drives? Which seem to be more tied to motives that are learned through a culture?

CASE STUDY #4 HOW QUICKLY THINGS CAN CHANGE

The changing leaves signaled the return of autumn to Pennsylvania. Although Laura had planned to spend this Saturday studying for her psychology midterm, today was just too beautiful to be indoors. Donning her new jacket and hiking boots (which were a little too tight, but not too painful), Laura started the half-mile walk to a wooded conservation area near her home.

If someone had asked her how she felt as she followed a trail into the woods, it would have been hard for her to answer. It was a mix of awe and peacefulness, of inspiration and restlessness. Suddenly, Laura's daydreaming was broken with a jump and a start when a three-foot snake slithered in front of her. Turning around and walking quickly made this particular snake easy to avoid. However, Laura could not shake the fear of running into another snake and was finally forced to head back to the street. What a disappointing end to a beautiful afternoon.

1. Most theories believe that emotions have both a cognitive and a physiological component. Are the two always mixed together or can an emotion be solely one or the other? Consider Laura's fright at seeing a snake and her sense of peacefulness upon entering the woods.
2. According to the James-Lange theory of emotion, what are the stages that led to Laura's experiencing fear of the snake? How does this process differ from that proposed by Cannon and Bard?
3. Laura continued to be frightened even after she successfully avoided the snake. How would Schachter and Singer's theory of emotion explain this? In what way does their explanation differ from James and Lange's theory?
4. Some psychologists attempt to explain emotions in terms of the functions they serve. How would a functionalist theory of emotion explain Laura's lingering fear after avoiding the snake? How would it explain the sense of peaceful feelings of being in a beautiful place?
5. The English language has more than 500 words that describe different shades of emotions. Does this mean that we can experience over 500 different types of emotions?

CASE STUDY #5 ROAD RAGE

Brandon wasn't sure what he wanted to do this evening, so when his friend Heather called and invited him to go see a foreign film, he immediately agreed.

"What's the name of this movie we're going to see?" he asked. Just at that moment a black car coming the other way swerved to make a left turn, forcing Heather to hit her brakes to avoid a collision.

"Did you see that, Brandon?" Heather's face tightened with anger. "Some people think they're the only car on the road! Anyway, what was your question?"

"I was asking about this movie we're going to see. It's in Spanish, right? I hope it's not too hard to follow. Did you ever notice that the emotions in foreign films never seem to be quite right? Sometimes I find myself wondering what a character is really feeling."

Heather laughed at Brandon's unexpected diatribe on foreign films. "Really, Brandon, sometimes I find myself wondering the same thing about you!"

1. Brandon is concerned with not being able to understand what emotions the characters in foreign films are experiencing. According to research on the facial expressions of emotion, how valid is his concern? Explain your answer.
2. Some acting techniques stress the importance of actually feeling the emotions that one is acting out. How do you propose actors can accomplish this feat?
3. Why is Heather angry at being cut off while driving to the movie?
4. Why might laughing make people feel better?
5. How many different emotions are evident in this story? Why is this important? Explain your answer.

ACTIVITY #1 GOAL SETTING AND ACHIEVEMENT

1. Write down a list of your current goals.
2. Rank these goals in order of importance.
3. Explain how you will achieve each of these goals in detail.
4. What might get in the way of you achieving your goals?
5. What will help you to achieve your goals?
6. If you imagine that you are accomplishing each one of these goals, how does each one make you feel? Be specific.

ACTIVITY #2 COGNITIVE DISSONANCE

Cognitive dissonance appears in virtually all judgments and decisions and is the core mechanism by which we experience new differences in the world. When we see other people behave differently from our images of them, when we hold any conflicting thoughts, we experience dissonance. Give examples of what causes you cognitive dissonance and how you try to resolve each one. Make sure you list at least five examples and solutions.

ACTIVITY #3 WHAT MOTIVATES US TO EAT?

Psychologists do not believe that one theory of motivation can explain behavior. Motivation is affected by several factors that include biological, behavioral, cognitive, and social components. Explain the motivation to eat using all of these areas.

ACTIVITY #4 WHERE AM I GOING?

You may have previously written your autobiography, entitled "Who Am I?", in Chapter 1. Now, you are being asked to write an essay about where you are going. This paper, once again, is about you. Your paper should be at least four pages, double spaced. Some of the questions you may want to answer are as follows:

1. Where do you see yourself in 5 years? In 10 years?
2. What motivates you to achieve your goals?
3. What motivates you in the future?
4. What career will make you happy?
5. Will you go on for further education?
6. What does your life look like?

REFERENCES

Festinger, L. (1957). *A theory of cognitive dissonance.* Stanford, CA: Stanford University Press.

James, W. (1884). What is an emotion? *Mind, 9,* 188–205.

Kleinginna, P., Jr., & Kleinginna, A. (1981). A categorized list of motivation definitions, with suggestions for a consensual definition. *Motivation and Emotion, 5,* 263–291.

Maslow, A. (1970). *Motivation and personality* (rev. ed.). New York: Harper & Row.

CHAPTER 8

Development

LEARNING ASSETS

Case Study #1 Who Knows More?

Case Study #2 Developmental Effects on Personality

Case Study #3 What, No Sleepover?

Case Study #4 Let's Make Applesauce

Case Study #5 Time Does Not Stand Still

Case Study #6 Wedded Bliss

Case Study #7 Grandma's Playing Video Games?

Activity #1 What's in a Name?

Activity #2 Lifespan Development Paper: Part I

Activity #3 Lifespan Development Paper: Part II

Activity #4 How Old Am I?

Activity #5 Freud Versus Erikson

NATURE VIA NURTURE

Human development is a topic that is studied greatly in terms of biology, anatomy and physiology, cognitive processes, conditioning and learning, states of consciousness, motivation and emotions, and psychosocial factors. Development is the cornerstone of existence. We need to know the processes that make us who we are, and we need to know how we can change anything that is not acceptable. In the past there was a grand debate about nature and nurture and which one contributed more to development. This was known as the *nature versus nurture debate.* More recent theory has changed the thinking to center around the notion of *nature via nurture.*

There were two schools of thought when it came to nature (biology) and nurture (environment). The proponents of the nature argument felt that biology and genetics were more influential in the development of a person. The proponents of the nurture argument felt that environmental factors were more influential in the development of a person. The current trend applies both aspects as being equally influential in a person's development. For example, if someone is an artist and can create incredibly beautiful works of art, is it nature or nurture that allowed this to occur? If you break down the pieces, you can see that the person has an equally talented mother who encouraged drawing and painting from an early age. So, could this be a combination of both nature and nurture? The current thinking is yes, it could. The mother may have passed the genetic capabilities to the child and provided the environmental influence necessary to foster these skills.

HUMAN DEVELOPMENT FROM CONCEPTION TO BIRTH

Human life begins as a single cell that is created when the father's sperm fertilizes the mother's egg. Fertilization typically takes place in the fallopian tube, which connects the uterus with the ovary. The uterus, which is made up of muscle, is the size and shape of a large pear. It stretches to allow the baby to grow throughout the pregnancy. A woman typically has two tubes and two ovaries. Every month one of the ovaries releases an egg, which passes along the tube toward the womb cavity. If the egg is not fertilized within 12 hours of being released, it will die. However, if the woman has sexual intercourse during the days of this monthly cycle just before or at the time when an egg has been released, then the many sperm cells released may travel to the fallopian tube and one may fertilize the egg. When fertilization is completed and the nuclei of an egg and sperm have combined, then the potential for a new being comes into existence and may continue to develop (Society for the Protection of Unborn Children, 2009).

The one-celled structure formed from the fertilized egg and sperm is known as a *zygote.* The zygote moves from the fallopian tube to the uterus, where it attaches itself to the uterine wall. Mitosis then occurs, which is the process of cell division. Mitosis allows the zygote to reproduce itself several times; thus, two cells become four cells, four cells become eight cells, and so on. On the fifth day, the zygote contains one hundred cells (Moore, 1989). The cell division continues throughout the pregnancy until the baby is born with billions of created cells. The major organs are created from the second week of pregnancy until the eighth week of pregnancy when the zygote is then called an embryo. Not all zygotes become embryos. The uterus can reject the zygote and cause the woman to miscarry.

GENETICS

The zygote contains genetic material that will direct development. All human cells, except for the egg and the sperm, contain 46 chromosomes, which are arranged in pairs of 23 each. One member of each pair belongs to each of the parents of the zygote. These chromosomes are the basic building blocks of inherited genes. Genes can be defined as hereditary material that inhabits the chromosomes and offers information about the form and function of each cell. The 46 chromosomes have numerous genes, but only several thousand have been identified to date (Holliday, 2007). Deoxyribonucleic acid (DNA) is the chemical name for the genetic material in the nucleus of each cell. Chromosomes are considered large segments of DNA and explain the individual development of each individual.

The term *genetics* derives from ancient Greek and falls within the discipline of biology. Genetics has always sought to understand the process of inheritance. The work of Gregor Mendel (1822–1884) observed that organisms inherit traits via discrete units of inheritance, which are now called genes (Griffiths, Miller, Suzuki, Lewontin, & Gelbart, 2000). Mendel's work is still viable today, which is a rare feat in the advancement of science. During Mendel's time it was believed that the traits observed in a child were a combination of the two parents' characteristics. However, his work on cross-pollination revealed that the traits are not just a combination of the two parents. Mendel found that genes can be either dominant or recessive, and this also played into inheritance.

Another important concept in the study of genetics is meiosis. Meiosis is a type of cell division that results in a reduction of the amount of genetic material in each of the resulting cells, which is how sex cells are formed. When meiosis is complete, the cells only have half of the 46 chromosomes that were present before cell reduction. That is how the sperm and the egg contribute 23 pairs each to the newly formed zygote. This leads us to the conception of twins. There are monozygotic twins, who are identical, and dizygotic twins, who are fraternal. Monozygotic twins are created when a single egg is fertilized to form one zygote that divides into two separate embryos. Dizygotic twins are created when two fertilized eggs are implanted into the uterine wall at the same time. Dizygotic twins are genetically similar to any other siblings born to the same parents at different times. However, identical twins share nearly identical DNA. The similarities and differences between siblings and twins can be brought back to the nature and nurture theories that help to explain behavior.

How is the sex of the baby determined from a genetic standpoint? It is the contribution of the genetic material from the father that determines whether a child is male or female. The 23rd pair of chromosomes is responsible for the sex characteristics. The sex chromosomes in females are the same. They are labeled XX. The egg always contributes an X chromosome; however, in males there is an X and a Y chromosome. So, the father can contribute the X, making the child a girl, or a Y, making the child a boy.

As we have been discussing, the fertilized egg becomes a zygote, then an embryo, and then a fetus. At the end of the 8th week after fertilization, the embryo is considered a fetus. By week 12, the fetus fills the entire uterus. By the 14th week, the sex of the baby can be identified. By weeks 16 through 20 the woman can feel the fetus moving. By about week 24 the chance of survival outside of the uterus is possible. The lungs mature throughout the term of the pregnancy, and the brain accumulates new cells until after the first year of life.

During the early months of pregnancy, the placenta grows more rapidly than the fetus. The placenta is responsible for distributing nutrients and oxygen to the child. The placenta is also responsible for filtering out harmful substances that can affect a growing fetus. The mother's blood vessels intertwine with the child's through the umbilical cord. Three blood vessels connect the placenta to the fetus. Two provide nutrients and oxygen and the third removes waste. The amniotic sac, which is the pouch that holds the fetus, is filled with fluid to help with cushioning so that the fetus can move without the walls of the uterus being too tight against its body.

The development of a fetus can be interrupted by many environmental factors. Teratogens can cause birth defects. These may be something that the mother is exposed to during pregnancy, such as a prescription medication, a street drug, alcohol, or a disease that the mother has. Some periods of time during the pregnancy are considered critical periods where certain events may cause damage or harm or be fatal to the fetus.

INFANCY

Newborn babies are not known for their coordination or motor behavior. However, they do possess certain innate reflexes that help them with survival. The first one is known as the *rooting reflex,* and it is present at birth. The rooting reflex assists in breastfeeding and disappears around 4 months of age. During the time when the rooting reflex is present, infants will turn their head toward anything that strokes their cheek or mouth. They will search for this object until it is found.

The next reflex is known as the *palmar (grasping) reflex*. During the time when the palmar reflex is present, babies will grasp anything that you put in their palm, often with great force. This reflex is also seen at birth and lasts until 5 or 6 months of age. If you stroke the back of their hand, then babies will open their fingers instead of gripping them.

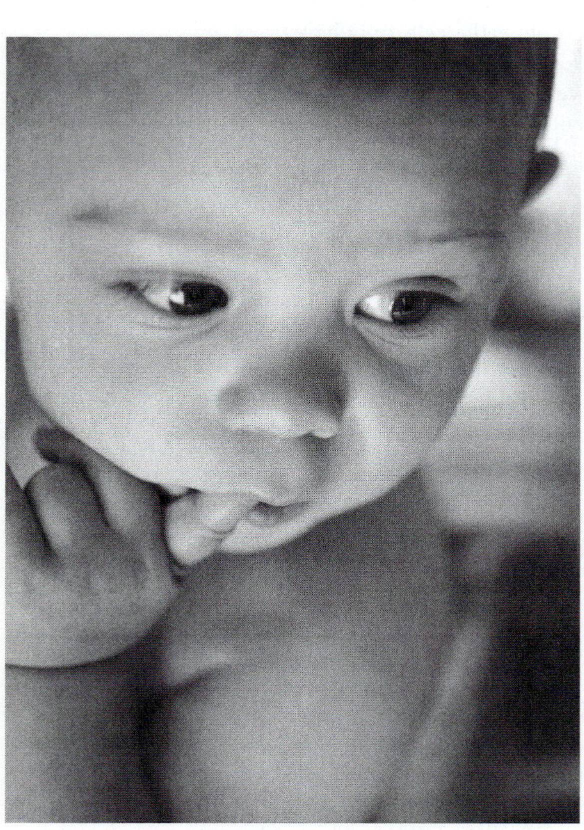

Next is the *Moro reflex,* which is also known as the *startle reflex*. The Moro reflex is also present at birth and begins to disappear around 2 months of age; however, it can last up to 6 months of age depending on the child. If babies are startled for some reason, such as by a loud noise or an abrupt temperature change, or if their head suddenly shifts position, the legs and head will extend while the arms jerk up and out with the palms up and the thumbs flexed.

Another reflex is the *Babinski reflex,* which is also present at birth and disappears at around the first year. This reflex occurs when the side of the foot is stroked and the toes fan out and the hallux (big toe) extends. The Babinski reflex is caused by a lack of myelination in the corticospinal tract in young children. It is a sign of a neurological abnormality.

Finally, there is the *sucking reflex,* which is also present at birth. The sucking reflex, associated with the rooting reflex and breastfeeding, causes infants to instinctively suck on anything that touches the roof of their mouth (Schott & Rossor, 2003).

The sensory abilities of newborns are quite fascinating. Although they rely on others for their ultimate survival, they possess several abilities that are often taken for granted. The first week of life offers limited vision to the newborn. They can focus best on objects that are only 7 to 12 inches away from their eyes. Within weeks this range will greatly expand.

Newborns are able to distinguish various patterns and shapes, with faces being their preference. In the first weeks of life, the newborn cannot distinguish colors other than black and white contrasts. Babies can track movement for only a short distance when they are first born and only if the object moves very slowly. There is no sense of what is known as object permanence at this stage. If something is out of sight, it is gone for the newborn!

Newborns typically have very sensitive hearing and pay attention to the sounds in their world. Researchers recommend that people speak softly to newborns so that they are not frightened. Newborns can also track sounds, just like they can track motion; if you are talking, the baby will try to find the source of the sound.

A newborn will also have an active sense of taste and smell in the first few days and weeks of being born. Research has shown that newborns who are exposed to more than just breast milk or formula will actually show preferences to specific tastes. The sense of smell remains a bit elusive since we often associate the sense of smell with the sense of taste. As mentioned with the reflexes, newborns are extremely sensitive to touch; and they show preferences to objects that feel good to them.

MATURATION

Maturation is the ongoing process of development that occurs throughout the lifespan. In early development, researchers specifically look at the motor and nervous system maturational development as well as the physical development that is occurring rapidly. From birth to age 3, the physical development that is occurring is phenomenal. After birth, newborns quickly double in height, quadruple in weight, and learn many complex motor actions.

Genetics and environment, nature and nurture, play an important role in the development of children. The height of a child is a good example. Genetics plays a role, but so does the environment when it comes to how tall a person might be. That is, your genetics has a limit for your height potential, but if you are not fed well as an infant, you may not grow and thrive. Therefore, you may be much shorter, if you are able to survive, than you would be if fed properly. Culture also plays a role in the development of skills. For example, some cultures work with their children from an early age to get them to sit up and walk and talk. These children typically hit these milestones at a much earlier rate than others.

PSYCHOSOCIAL DEVELOPMENT

So far we have been looking at early childhood development in terms of biological and physiological mechanisms. Now we turn to psychosocial components, which focus on psychology and cognitive aspects as well as social or environmental aspects of development. How much does environment affect individuals' development? We learn to interact with others from birth, and the interactions become more and more complex as we develop.

One of the areas that is highly regarded in psychosocial development is that of temperament. There are many different definitions of temperament, but the one by psychiatrists Alexander Thomas and Stella Chess (1980) is the most often studied, replicated, and pondered. They defined temperament "... as a general term referring to the 'how' of behavior. It differs from ability, which is concerned with the 'what' and 'how well' of behaving, and from motivation, which accounts for 'why' a person does what he is doing." Thomas and Chess identified nine different dimensions of temperament based on their research studies. This is how they classified temperament in children:

- *Easy children* comprise about 40 percent of the population and behave in consistent ways, approach new situations in a positive manner, and are highly adaptable to change. Their moods are mild to moderate and predominantly positive.
- *Slow-to-warm-up children* display a combination of intense, negative responses to new stimuli with slower adaptability and make up about 15 percent of the population.
- *Difficult children* comprise about 10 percent of the population, do not behave in consistent ways, have difficulty adapting, and are characterized by a negative mood.

Obviously, this only accounts for about 65 percent of the population. This means that many children do not fall into any of these groups. Some children show signs of all three groups depending on the circumstances. Much of the research shows that temperament remains relatively stable throughout development.

Stage Theories of Development

The first stage theories of development were created by Sigmund Freud (1856–1939). Freud called his stage theory the *psychosexual stages of development*. This theory was not well received during Freud's time due to the terminology and references that he made in his theory. However, his work set the tone for all of the theorists after him. Many theorists follow this concept of development occurring in stages. Freud's psychosexual stages of development are as follows:

Oral Stage	Birth to 18 months	During the oral stage, the child is focused on oral pleasures (sucking). Too much or too little oral pleasure during this stage can result in an oral fixation. People with an oral fixation may have a strong tendency to smoke, drink alcohol, overeat, or bite their nails. These people may become overly dependent upon others, gullible, and perpetual followers. On the other hand, they may also fight these urges and develop pessimism and aggression toward others.
Anal Stage	18 months to 3 years	The child's erogenous pleasure in this stage is on eliminating and retaining feces. The child has to learn to control anal functioning. If this stage is not successfully completed, then an anal fixation can occur and will create an obsession with cleanliness, perfection, and control (anal retentive). On the opposite end of the spectrum, they may become messy and disorganized (anal expulsive).
Phallic Stage	3 to 6 years	The erogenous zone switches to the genitals.
Latency Stage	6 years to Puberty	During this stage, sexual urges remain repressed and children interact and play mostly with same-sex peers.
Genital Stage	Puberty	The final stage begins at the start of puberty when sexual urges are awakened. Adolescents direct their sexual urges onto opposite-sex peers where the primary focus of pleasure is the genitals.

In the 1950s Erik Erikson (1902–1994) took Freud's psychosexual stages of development and revamped them. His stage theory of development is called the *psychosocial stages of development*. They are as follows:

Stage (age)	Psychosocial Crisis	Significant Relations	Psychosocial Modalities	Psychosocial Virtues	Maladaptations and Malignancies
I (0–1)—infant	Trust vs. Mistrust	Mother	To get, to give in return	Hope, faith	Sensory distortion—withdrawal
II (2–3)—toddler	Autonomy vs. Shame and Doubt	Parents	To hold on, to let go	Will, determination	Impulsivity—compulsion
III (3–6)—preschooler	Initiative vs. Guilt	Family	To go after, to play	Purpose, courage	Ruthlessness—inhibition
IV (7–12 or so)—school-age child	Industry vs. Inferiority	Neighborhood and school	To complete, to make things together	Competence	Narrow virtuosity—inertia
V (12–18 or so)—adolescence	Ego Identity vs. Role Confusion	Peer groups, role models	To be oneself, to share oneself	Fidelity, loyalty	Fanaticism—repudiation
VI (the 20s)—young adult	Intimacy vs. Isolation	Partners, friends	To lose and find oneself in another	Love	Promiscuity—exclusivity
VII (late 20s to 50s)—middle adult	Generativity vs. Self-absorption	Household, workmates	To make, to take care of	Care	Overextension—rejectivity
VIII (50s and beyond)—old adult	Integrity vs. Despair	Humankind or "my kind"	To be, through having been, to face not being	Wisdom	Presumption—despair

Chart adapted from Erikson, 1959.

Social Bonds and Attachment

Attachment theory was created by psychiatrist John Bowlby (1907–1990) and provides a framework for understanding interpersonal relationships. The premise is that children have a need for a secure relationship with their caregivers and that, without this relationship, normal social and emotional development will not occur.

Bowlby's ethological theory of attachment stresses the adaptiveness between infants and caregivers. Bowlby (1951) postulated that attachment progresses through the following four stages:

1. Stage 1: *Preattachment* occurs from birth to 6 weeks of age. Babies do not form attachments at this stage and do not mind being left with unfamiliar adults.
2. Stage 2: Beginning of *attachment* occurs at approximately 6 weeks of age and lasts until 7 months. Infants in this stage respond to familiar adults but do not mind when they are separated from caregivers.
3. Stage 3: Attachment begins at approximately 7 months and lasts until 21 months. Babies form a secure attachment to a familiar caregiver. *Separation anxiety* begins to occur at approximately 7 months and increases until 15 months, cross-culturally.
4. Stage 4: *Reciprocal relationships* occur at approximately 21 months. As language develops, separation anxiety decreases and the child begins to understand that the caregiver will return. It is the development of language skills that allows a child to make reciprocal bargains with the caregiver.

One of the first experimental studies done on attachment was conducted by Harry Harlow (1905–1981) beginning in 1959. Harlow used rhesus monkeys for his attachment experiments. Approximately eight hours after birth, the monkeys were separated from their mothers and raised in experimental chambers where they were exposed to an inanimate object that served as a surrogate caregiver. Some of the surrogates were made of harsh wire cylinders, and others were covered with terry cloth. When the surrogates were equipped with bottles, the baby monkeys could be fed by these surrogate mothers. Some of the baby monkeys were exposed to both types of surrogate mothers, and some were not. The baby monkeys showed a strong preference for the terry-cloth surrogate. The researchers came to this conclusion after watching the behavior of the baby monkeys when the investigators made a sudden, startling noise. The monkeys would run to the terry-cloth "mother" for comfort. This was even true if they were just fed by the wire "mothers" as opposed to the terry-cloth surrogate. Harlow concluded that contact comfort, a preference for holding soft objects, yields physical comfort and warmth.

The long-term effects of this study were also studied to see how this contact affected social behavior. The finding was that these baby monkeys did not adapt well to change. They avoided contact, fled from touch, curled up and rocked, or tried to attack the biggest, most dominant monkey of the group. These findings led Harlow (1959) to believe that although attachment is important, its existence does not ensure normal social development.

COGNITIVE DEVELOPMENT

A very important concept in developmental psychology is that of cognitive development. Cognitions refer to processing thoughts, perceiving, thinking, learning, and analyzing. Jean Piaget (1896–1980) was one of the earliest pioneers in cognitive development processes in children. Piaget's work has been so influential that it is still used in American school systems to this day. Piaget was mainly interested in the biological influences on "how we come to know." He felt that what separates humans from other animals is our ability to do "abstract symbolic reasoning."

Piaget at work with a study subject

Piaget's Theory of Development

Piaget's theory has two major components: the process of coming to know, and the stages humans move through as they gradually acquire this ability. Piaget's (1972) stages of cognitive development are as follows:

1. *Sensorimotor stage* (Infancy). In this period (which has six substages), intelligence is demonstrated through motor activity without the use of symbols. Knowledge of the world is limited (but developing) because it is based on physical interactions/experiences. Children acquire object permanence at about 7 months of age (memory). Physical development (mobility) allows the child to begin developing new intellectual abilities. Some symbolic (language) abilities are developed at the end of this stage.
2. *Preoperational stage* (Toddler and Early Childhood). In this period (which has two substages), intelligence is demonstrated through the use of symbols, language use matures, and memory and imagination are developed, but thinking is done in a nonlogical, nonreversible manner. Egocentric thinking predominates.
3. *Concrete Operational stage* (Elementary and Early Adolescence). In this stage (characterized by seven types of conservation: number, length, liquid, mass, weight, area, volume), intelligence is demonstrated through logical and systematic manipulation of symbols related to concrete objects. Operational thinking develops (mental actions that are reversible). Egocentric thought diminishes.
4. *Formal Operational stage* (Adolescence and Adulthood). In this stage, intelligence is demonstrated through the logical use of symbols related to abstract concepts. Early in the period there is a return to egocentric thought. Only 35 percent of high school graduates in industrialized countries obtain formal operations; many people do not think formally during adulthood.

Vygotsky's Theory of Sociocultural Development

One of the biggest challenges to Piaget's work was put forth by Lev Vygotsky (1896–1934). Vygotsky proposed the theory of sociocultural development, which emphasized the external forces that impact development, such as society and culture. Vygotsky believed that, through social interaction, children learn to perform skills that are beyond their initial capabilities. Vygotsky's work has left a great impact on education and educational psychology. His work is studied in great detail in the field of education.

The Development of Language

Language acquisition is the process of cognitively interpreting and learning language. Language allows for new concepts to be taught and learned. It is a means for expressing oneself. The development of language begins with a child using phonemes, which is Greek for "sounds"; phonemes, then, are the most basic sounds in language. In the English language there are 44 phonemes, but only 26 letters in the alphabet. An example of a phoneme can be seen with the letter *k*. If you pronounce the word *kit* as opposed to the word *skill,* you see the difference. Phonemes do not have meaning alone; there needs to be a combination of phonemes to have meaning.

A morpheme is the smallest unit of sound that actually has meaning. For example, the word *dogs* has two morphemes. The *dog* and the *s* are two separate morphemes. The letter *s* is known as an inflectional morpheme since it modifies a word's tense, number, and aspect without creating a new word. When words are organized into meaningful phrases and sentences, this is known as *syntax.*

Children's language development follows a rather predictable path based on age, and it defies culture. Babies make the same sounds, regardless of culture, at around the same time. They typically start to coo at around 2 months old; cooing includes squeals, gurgles, or vowel sounds. When babies are around 6 months to 8 months old, they start to babble, which consists of one-syllable sounds that contain both vowels and consonants. By 9 months to 18 months, babies typically start to say their first words that have actual meaning. By 18 months to 24 months, they are constructing minisentences with simple meaning. The development of language continues rather quickly from this point forward.

Within the first five years of life, children develop an impressive mastery of complex language skills. This does not mean that they have a mastery of the language, but rather have learned the basics in order to express language in a meaningful manner. The use of language is an important skill to possess and a difficult one as well. Sometimes there are issues with acquisition of language skills, and several language and speech disorders can arise during this process.

MORAL DEVELOPMENT

The concept of moral development became an interest for Lawrence Kohlberg (1927–1987). Kohlberg was a Piagetian thinker and maintained this frame of reference in his work. Piaget studied moral judgment, but his work fit into a two-stage theory. He believed that children younger than 10 or 11 years old think about moral development one way; older children consider it differently (Crain, 1985, pp. 118–136).

Kohlberg interviewed children and adolescents about moral dilemmas and found that there was much more to Piaget's findings. By creating three levels with two stages at each level, Kohlberg created a six-stage platform of moral development. It is considered rare to regress backward in stages, and stages cannot be skipped. Here are Kohlberg's stages of moral development (Kohlberg, 1973):

Level 1. Preconventional Morality

- Stage 1—Obedience and Punishment: At this stage, children see rules as fixed and absolute. Obeying the rules is important because it is a means to avoid punishment.
- Stage 2—Individualism and Exchange: At this stage of moral development, children account for individual points of view and judge actions based on how they serve individual needs.

Level 2. Conventional Morality

- Stage 3—Interpersonal Relationships: Often referred to as the "good boy–good girl" orientation, this stage of moral development is focused on living

up to social expectations and roles. There is an emphasis on conformity, being "nice," and consideration of how choices influence relationships.
- Stage 4—Maintaining Social Order: At this stage of moral development, people begin to consider society as a whole when making judgments. The focus is on maintaining law and order by following the rules, doing one's duty, and respecting authority.

Level 3. Postconventional Morality
- Stage 5—Social Contract and Individual Rights: At this stage, people begin to account for the differing values, opinions, and beliefs of other people. Rules of law are important for maintaining a society, but members of the society should agree upon these standards.
- Stage 6—Universal Principles: The final level of moral reasoning is based upon universal ethical principles and abstract reasoning. At this stage, people follow these internalized principles of justice, even if they conflict with laws and rules.

Kohlberg's moral stages of development have remained quite popular; however, there has been much criticism of this work as well. Some of the criticisms include the fact that Kohlberg conducted his research on young boys, but applied his findings to girls as well. Another criticism is that the moral stages are not culturally neutral; that is, they are considered biased to specific cultures. Many alternative theories have been proposed to address some of these concerns.

ADOLESCENCE TO ADULTHOOD

Puberty is the process of rapid change of physical development in boys and girls. It typically starts at age 11 for girls and age 13 for boys. However, due to a number of factors, puberty is starting earlier and earlier. This transition period allows an adolescent to become a fully physiologically mature adult. During this stage, the sex organs mature, and secondary sex characteristics appear. Boys experience a broadening of the shoulders, and girls experience their hips widening. Boys typically experience more large muscle growth, which gives them strength advantage over girls for the first time. The hands and feet of both sexes grow even more rapidly than their bodies, and their lips, nose, and ears grow more quickly than their heads. This can be an awkward time for many boys and girls. There are also hormonal changes that both sexes go through that are quite complex. Males produce androgens and females produce estrogen. This creates the fully mature male and female.

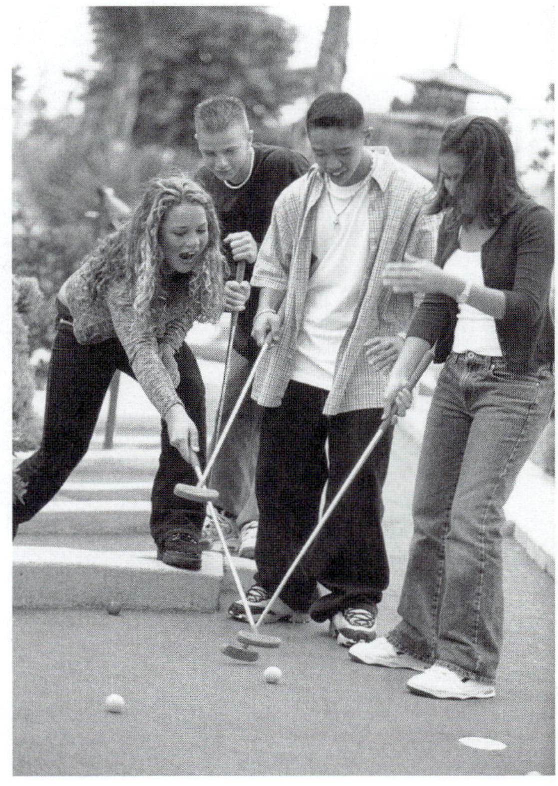

Variations in development occur between males and females as well as between individuals. Research has reported that girls who develop and mature early and males who develop and mature late have the most difficult time adjusting to their new roles.

The next transition is into adulthood. Early adulthood is thought to begin around the age of 20, although that is hotly debated by many, and to last until the age of 40. This is the time when young adults are working, starting families, and engaging in responsible activities.

Middle adulthood is thought to occur between the ages of 40 to about 65. Again, these ages are often debated. The body starts to decline at this time unless measures are taken to maintain good health. The psychological consequences of middle adulthood may be problematic for some and may even create what has been termed a *midlife crisis.* This can occur at an earlier age as well; it is often associated with a lack of coping mechanisms that create feelings of uneasiness with the changes that are taking place both physically and psychologically.

Finally, there is late adulthood, which is postulated to occur from age 65 and up. Again, the psychological aspects of late adulthood are enormous. Likewise, many physical changes are occurring, and some people handle them better than others. Individuals in late adulthood also are grappling with the issues of mortality that accompany this stage of development. People look back on their lives and wonder whether or not they accomplished what they wanted to accomplish. There can be joy or remorse based on these thoughts.

DEMENTIA AND ALZHEIMER'S DISEASE

Dementia and Alzheimer's disease are typically thought of as an older person's issues. However, the statistics show that there can be early onset of these conditions. Typically, people do not show signs of dementia or Alzheimer's until after 65 years old. Dementia incorporates memory loss, language difficulties, personality changes, and impaired cognitive functioning due to trauma or disease. These changes are not part of the normal aging process and impact daily life functions. Alzheimer's disease is a brain disorder that is the most common form of dementia. It is a progressive fatal brain disease that does not have a cure.

SUMMARY

In this chapter, we have looked at development throughout the lifespan. The physical, cognitive, and psychological changes that occur are significant in every stage of development. In our quest to figure out who we are, and what we are all about, these developmental aspects are quite significant.

CASE STUDY #1 WHO KNOWS MORE?

Dina, a fifth-grade teacher at Highland Elementary School, was among the first to notice that the vice principal was exhibiting odd new behavior. It began with her giving up smoking and drinking after 20 years. When the book *Expecting Twins?* was found on her desk, the odd behavior mystery was solved. Shortly thereafter, the vice principal went on maternity leave.

Much to her surprise, Dina found herself promoted to acting vice principal.

This could be my chance to make a difference and get a permanent promotion, she thought. Dina considered herself the right person in the right position. All she needed was a platform to work on. During her usual walking tour of the building, she wondered what her platform would be.

As she walked past a display of essays written by fourth and fifth graders, it occurred to her that the fifth graders' essays were far superior to those of the fourth graders. She wondered if the fourth-grade teachers were getting sluggish in teaching writing skills.

Needing more evidence before she took any action, Dina mandated a vocabulary test of the fourth and fifth grades. The fifth graders clearly outperformed the fourth graders, which further supported Dina's idea that the fourth-grade teachers needed some motivation training.

1. What problem was the vice principal trying to avoid by not drinking alcohol while she was pregnant? Why did she give up smoking? Is there a period during which these concerns are especially important?
2. According to the stage theories that we have discussed, do we know which stage of development the vice principal's baby is in?
3. Explain the differences between Freud's stages of development and Erikson's stages of development for typical fourth-grade students.
4. Is the development for fourth-grade students significantly different than the development for fifth-grade students? Explain.
5. How would Piaget explain the developmental differences between the fourth- and fifth-grade students and their abilities?

CASE STUDY #2 DEVELOPMENTAL EFFECTS ON PERSONALITY

After his sizable Thanksgiving dinner, Jonah lay down, reclining across the living room rug. It was time for the family's annual post-Thanksgiving dinner discussion of family history. As always, the conversation quickly turned to Jonah and his identical twin brother, Jack.

"Mom practiced piano almost every day while she was pregnant with Jack and me," Jonah said to the ceiling. "That explains our talent for Chopin."

"Don't get me wrong," his sister Alexandra interrupted, "but I always thought the prenatal music lessons were hogwash. It seems to me that talent is inherited, just like personality."

"Well, then Jack and I sure inherited different personalities," said Jonah. "For example, where is he now? I can't believe that his social calendar is so full that he forgot his family!"

"He always has been outgoing," observed Alexandra. "Just like you were always shy."

"Actually," replied Jonah, "Jack realized he actually liked all that attention in the third grade. The teacher forced him to play Thomas Jefferson in the school play, just because he was inventive." Jonah's voice dropped slightly, as he said, "I, however, was out with the flu that week."

1. Jonah thinks his mother introduced him to the music of Chopin before he was born. What scientific evidence, if any, suggests that such prenatal learning is possible?
2. Jonah and Jake differ in their level of shyness. Considering that they are identical twins, do you find this surprising? Defend your answer. Is there any evidence to support Alexandra's contention that shyness is inherited?
3. What does it mean when someone refers to the nature-nurture debate? How does maturation relate to this debate?
4. Why is the nature-nurture issue so important? What are its roots? Where do most people who study this phenomenon stand on this issue today?
5. List three physical, three intellectual, and three emotional characteristics that are heavily influenced by genetics. List some characteristics that are less influenced by genetics.

CASE STUDY #3 WHAT, NO SLEEPOVER?

Every Friday Tabitha and Gary sit down and work out a weekend schedule. As the parents of two daughters and one son, there are a lot of plans constantly being made. After agreeing that Tabitha would help the kids with their homework tomorrow morning, and that Gary would take them to soccer practice tomorrow afternoon, they turned to whether or not they should allow Daisy to spend the night at her friend Dana's house tomorrow night, even though she was supposed to be restricted for not keeping her room clean.

As usual, Gary pleaded Daisy's case. Tabitha always accuses him of allowing Daisy to walk all over him. He doted on her right from the start, taking charge of all aspects of her upbringing. He even convinced Tabitha not to breast-feed, wanting to help bottle-feed Daisy himself in order to build that special bond usually reserved for mothers and children.

"Gary, it is for Daisy's own good that she stays home from the sleepover. Children need to know what limitations and rules are, and that actions have consequences. The best environment for child rearing is where they know exactly what is expected, and that any deviation will be punished. We can't let her go to the sleepover."

1. How would you describe Gary and Tabitha's parenting style?
2. In general, Gary is in charge of setting and enforcing rules for Daisy, and Tabitha is in charge of Daisy's sister and brother. In what ways would Daisy and her siblings differ as a result of different parenting styles?
3. Define the concept "attachment" as it is used by psychologists to describe parent-infant relationships.
4. What is the role of breastfeeding in the development of attachment? Was Gary correct in thinking that the type of attachment brought on by breastfeeding is unique?
5. What roles do fathers traditionally play in raising children? How have these roles changed over the years?
6. Consider how Tabitha and Gary are dividing their time with their children on Saturday. Is this typical of most families today? Why or why not?

CASE STUDY #4 LET'S MAKE APPLESAUCE

"Daddy, can I have two apples in my lunch tomorrow?" asked 10-year-old Shelby. Shelby, with her father and little sister Nora, had spent the better part of a chilly October morning picking apples at Woodbury Farms.

"Honey, with all the apples that we picked yesterday, you may have as many apples as you want in your lunch. First, you have to help me cut and peel these apples for the applesauce that we said we were going to make."

"I'm going to eat three apples!" shouted Nora.

As they waited for the apples to cook, the three played games in the family room. However, after a long morning, the girls were both irritable. When they played hide-and-seek, they argued over where to hide. When they colored with crayons, they fought over the colors.

Four hours later the apples were cooked and mashed into sauce. Shelby and Nora watched excitedly as their father poured applesauce from the big bowl into the smaller storage bowls. As they watched their father, the girls divided up the bowls between themselves. Surprisingly, there was almost no arguing over which bowls belonged to whom.

1. According to Piaget, through what four stages of cognitive development do children progress? At what ages do these stages typically occur? At age 10, in which stage is Shelby most likely to be?
2. Nora is not very good at hide-and-seek. Often she will throw a blanket over herself to hide but not realize that her leg or half her body is uncovered. How would Piaget's theory explain this? At what stage of cognitive development is she?
3. When choosing which containers of applesauce they want, Shelby tends to pick short fat bowls, while Nora picks tall skinny bowls that don't hold as much. Assuming that they both love applesauce, why do the girls tend to choose these different types of bowls?
4. According to Kohlberg's theory of moral development, what stages are Shelby and Nora in currently?
5. According to Piaget's theory, children progress through distinct stages of cognitive development. How has this stage view been questioned? Do children simply wake up one morning understanding the principles of conservation, which were confusing before?

CASE STUDY #5 TIME DOES NOT STAND STILL

Walking through the doors of Springs High for the first time in five years was a strange feeling for Robert. It seemed like only a few months ago he and his friends had roamed these halls like they owned the place. In a way it still felt like that, like the halls had been waiting for him to return. Well, here he was, back in Springs—as the newest math teacher at Springs High.

Robert's sense that time had stood still at Springs High shattered after his first day. Time at Springs High had not stood still, it had accelerated. These kids were a whole new generation of students. Not only did they look as if they should still be in junior high (was he that small in high school?), but they acted like it as well. They seemed to have no sense of what was appropriate and what was not, of what was right and wrong. When a particular student gave him grief during lunch, Robert actually caught himself taking comfort in the fact that, like all adolescents, this kid was probably going through some very rough times. Robert was quickly developing a feeling that, unlike each of the past five years, this year was going to be a long one.

1. In the morning, Robert teaches a freshman course made up of 14-year-olds. What are the major physical developments that these students are going through?
2. According to Kohlberg's theory of moral reasoning, at what stage are most of Robert's students? Are Robert and his students at different stages? Defend your answer.
3. What does Eriksonian psychosocial theory say is these students' biggest social task during adolescence? What would constitute a successful resolution of this task? What would constitute an unsuccessful resolution?
4. As a young adult, what does Eriksonian theory view as Robert's primary social task? Describe a successful and an unsuccessful resolution of this task.
5. Is Robert correct in assuming that for most people adolescence is a difficult time? What are the major problems experienced by teenagers today? How have these problems changed over the years?

CASE STUDY #6 WEDDED BLISS

Tyler and Denise have been dating for seven years, but surprisingly they are not married yet. Meeting in the fall of their second year at college, they moved in together after graduation. Denise put her finance degree to work at an accounting firm, and Tyler began taking graduate courses in hospitality management.

Tyler and Denise wanted to get their careers in order before they got married, so they decided to wait until Tyler was done with graduate school. However, these plans had to be changed when Denise decided that she wanted to go back to school to get her MBA. So, after two years of being the breadwinner, Denise switched roles with Tyler; now he has the full-time job and she is a student.

This May Denise will have her MBA, and their financial future seems to be heading in the right direction (she has already received several impressive offers). Denise and Tyler cannot wait any longer to be married, and arrangements are being made for a June ceremony.

1. In what ways is Denise and Tyler's relationship characteristic of modern times? In what ways was their parents' dating history likely to be different? How about their grandparents' dating history?
2. Denise, more than Tyler, wants to have children soon. What biological factors make having children sooner less complicated than later? Can men or women have children later in life?
3. At what age do physical strength and reflexes reach their peak? At age 26, are Denise and Tyler's physical abilities increasing or decreasing?
4. How do most husbands and wives divide household chores today? Does this trend differ for couples such as Denise and Tyler in which the woman is the primary provider?
5. Denise is confident that their marriage will stand the test of time. What are the odds that this marriage will end in divorce? What are the chances that Denise will raise a child as a single parent?

CASE STUDY #7 GRANDMA'S PLAYING VIDEO GAMES?

Nine-year-old Junie handed the joystick to her grandmother Bernice. "Your turn, Gram. I got up to the fourth level, so I am just about to beat you!" The two were playing video games; it was a regular pastime on the days that Bernice watched Junie.

"Well, you'd better watch out because I am about to beat my high score. I'm having a good day today!"

Just as the game ended, Junie's father came home from work. "Who won today?" he asked, grabbing Junie in a big hug.

"Grandma did. Again! Maybe when I am a little older, I will be able to beat her. Is Gram staying for dinner?" Junie asked her father.

"Sorry, sweetheart, but I've got to run. I've got to go play cards with my card buddies. Afterwards we are all going to get some dessert. Maybe next week I will be able to stay."

Bernice pushed herself out of the chair in front of the video monitor and began to get her coat.

"I'm going to practice nonstop until then, Gram!" Junie challenged.

1. Think about the kinds of motor skills it takes to play a video game well. As they both get older, who do you suppose will get better at the game, Junie, Bernice, or both? Support your answer?
2. How do older adults acquire new skills?
3. Bernice seems to lead a pretty active life. What do you think research would say about older adults like her?
4. What does Erikson's theory say about Bernice's stage of development?
5. Bernice is likely to forget appointments unless she writes them down on a calendar. Is Bernice's forgetfulness typical of older adults? What types of memory loss (e.g., short-term, long-term, semantic, or implicit) are most common in old age? What types are not vulnerable to aging?

ACTIVITY #1 WHAT'S IN A NAME?

ADHD, ADD, ODD, bipolar disorder . . . the list can go on and on. Children are often labeled and grouped into these various categories when their behavior is erratic or different than other kids'. For this assignment, look up one of these childhood disorders and collect research and information about that disorder. Be prepared to partake in a debate about whether or not children should be diagnosed and labeled early in life. Does this create a self-fulfilling prophecy? Are labels necessary or harmful? Keep these concepts in mind as you are collecting your research for this debate.

ACTIVITY #2 LIFESPAN DEVELOPMENT PAPER: PART I

Directions: For this assignment you will need to focus on your early childhood development. You may want to ask your older siblings, parents, caregivers, or other relatives for some of the information for this paper. Answer the following questions using your personal information as well as support from the text, including theories that match relevant questions.

1. When were you born? How old were your parents when you were born? Were there any special circumstances surrounding your birth? Were there any complications? How long did labor last? How much did you weigh, how big were you?
2. Did you have any older siblings? If so, how did they take your arrival? How did your parents plan for your arrival?
3. What type of physical development was taking place from birth through puberty? What type of cognitive development was taking place from birth through puberty? What type of moral development was taking place from birth through puberty?
4. How did you do in school through puberty? Was there anything significant about this time?

ACTIVITY #3 LIFESPAN DEVELOPMENT PAPER: PART II

Directions: For this assignment you will need to focus on your middle childhood through adult development. You may want to ask your older siblings, parents, caregivers, or other relatives for some of the information for this paper. Answer the following questions using your personal information as well as support from the text, including theories that match relevant questions.

1. What type of physical development was taking place from puberty through adulthood? What type of cognitive development was taking place from puberty through adulthood? What type of moral development was taking place from puberty through adulthood?
2. How did you do in school after puberty? Was there anything significant about this time?
3. What was the transition like from puberty to adulthood? How did you know when you were an adult?
4. How has adulthood been difficult? How has it been easy?
5. Explain how you will continue to develop as you get older.
6. What do you think your life will be like in five years? Ten years? Twenty years?

ACTIVITY #4 HOW OLD AM I?

Directions: For this project you will research what it is like to get older for some people. Research the potential ailments and loss of functioning that can occur with age. How can you combat some of these issues while you are young? What more can we do to help our older citizens? What do you think you will be like as you get older? How old is old to you? Be prepared to discuss this information in class.

ACTIVITY #5 FREUD VERSUS ERIKSON

Directions: Compare and contrast Freud's psychosexual stages of development with Erik Erikson's psychosocial stages of development. How are they alike? How are they different? Which one do you like better? Make sure you substantiate your answers.

REFERENCES

Bowlby, J. (1951). *Maternal care and mental health.* World Health Organization. No. 14.

Crain, W. C. (1985). *Theories of development.* NY: Prentice-Hall.

Erikson, E. H. (1959). *Identity and the Life Cycle* (Psychological Issues Series, Vol. 1, No. 1). New York: International Universities Press.

Griffiths, A. J. F., Miller, J., Suzuki, D., Lewontin, R., & Gelbart, W. (2000). *An introduction to genetic analysis.* New York: W. H. Freeman.

Harlow, H. F. (1959, June). Love in infant monkeys. *Scientific American, 200,* 68, 70, 72–73, 74.

Holliday, R. (2007). *Aging: The paradox of life.* Netherlands: Springer.

Kohlberg, L. (1973). The claim to moral adequacy of a highest stage of moral judgment. *Journal of Philosophy, 70,* 630–646.

Moore, K. L. (1989). *Before we are born: Basic embryology and birth defects* (3rd ed.). Philadelphia: Saunders.

Piaget, J. (1972). *The psychology of the child.* New York: Basic Books.

Schott, J. M., & Rossor, M. N. (2003). The grasp and other primitive reflexes. *Neurosurgical Psychiatry, 74*(5), 558–560.

Society for the Protection of Unborn Children. (2009, January 1). London. Retrieved from http://www.spuc.org.uk/ethics/abortion/humandevelopment.

Thomas, A., & Chess, S. (1980). *The dynamics of psychological development.* New York: Brunner: Mazel.

CHAPTER 9

Personality

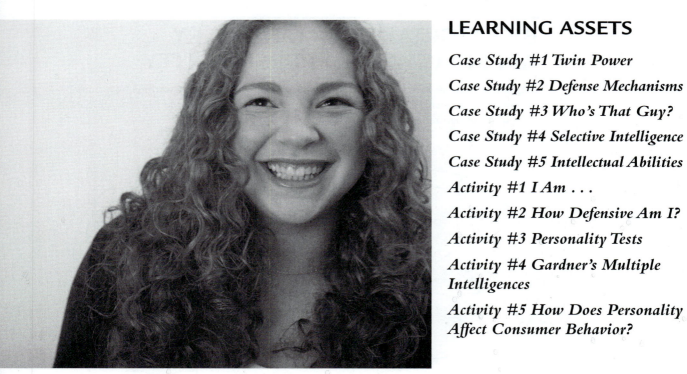

LEARNING ASSETS

Case Study #1 Twin Power

Case Study #2 Defense Mechanisms

Case Study #3 Who's That Guy?

Case Study #4 Selective Intelligence

Case Study #5 Intellectual Abilities

Activity #1 I Am . . .

Activity #2 How Defensive Am I?

Activity #3 Personality Tests

Activity #4 Gardner's Multiple Intelligences

Activity #5 How Does Personality Affect Consumer Behavior?

WHAT IS PERSONALITY?

How do you describe your personality? The term *personality* means many different things to many different people. The trick is to define the term in an acceptable manner that has meaning. Since the word *personality* comes from the Latin word *persona,* which means "mask," we can look at the study of personality as the study of the masks that people wear. These masks often belie the true personality underneath the surface. Psychologists and other practitioners concern themselves with the cognitions (thinking), emotions (feeling), and behaving (outward behavior) that others exhibit as a true definition of their personalities. The reason that the study of personality is so intriguing and widespread is due to two main factors. First, personalities are rather consistent throughout the lifespan. Second, our personalities make us unique.

BIOLOGICAL/EVOLUTIONARY APPROACHES TO PERSONALITY

Philosophers and scientists throughout the ages have been trying to determine how humans' personalities are formed. They have looked at every aspect imaginable to come up with a plausible explanation for why we are the way we are.

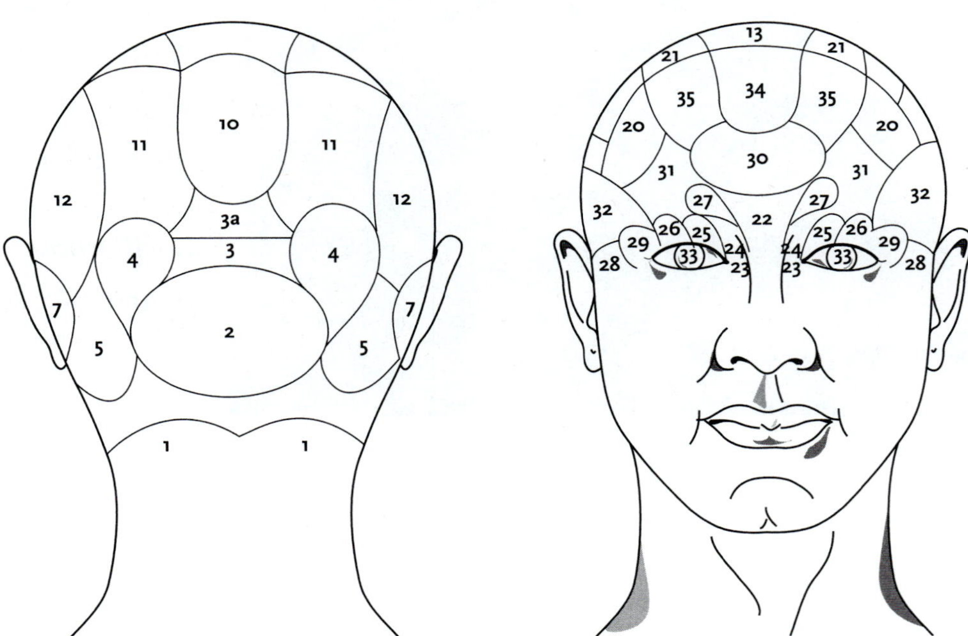

Phrenology by Franz Joseph Gall

1 Amativeness; 2 Philoprogenitiveness; 3 Concentrativeness; 3 *a* Inhabitiveness; 4 Adhesiveness; 5 Combativeness; 7 Secretiveness; 10 Self-esteem; 11 Love of Approbation; 12 Cautiousness; 13 Benevolence; 20 Wit; 21 Imitation; 22 Individuality; 23 Form; 24 Size; 25 Weight; 26 Coloring; 27 Locality; 28 Number; 29 Order; 30 Eventuality; 31 Time; 32 Tune; 33 Language; 34 Comparison; 35 Causality.

The Greek physician Hippocrates named what he considered the four temperaments. These temperaments have endured the test of time and have been built upon for centuries. His four temperaments are as follows: melancholic, sanguine, choleric, and phlegmatic. These were named for the human bodily fluids that Hippocrates believed influenced personality. The bodily-fluids-and-personality theory turned out to be a dead end, but the notion of various human temperaments was accurate.

Phrenology was the main school of thought in regard to personality development in the 1800s. The word *phrenology* can be broken down into *phren,* meaning "mind" in Greek, and *logos,* meaning "knowledge." Now considered a pseudoscience, phrenology was developed by Franz Joseph Gall (1758–1828) in 1796 and is based on the concept that the brain can be analyzed through the bumps and indentations on the skull. The bumps are then linked to personality characteristics within the individual. Gall compared the brain to a muscle and believed that, by finding well-developed parts of the brain, various characteristics could be found.

PSYCHODYNAMIC APPROACHES TO PERSONALITY

The work of Sigmund Freud (1856–1939) has been discussed throughout various sections of this textbook. In chapter 8, we looked at Freud's psychosexual stages of development and how they contributed to personality development. Here his contributions to the theories of personality are considered, and his structure-of-the-mind concept as it relates to personality development is examined.

Freud discussed three levels of awareness based on different components of the mind. He called these the *conscious mind,* the *preconscious mind,* and the *unconscious mind.* The conscious mind consists of the part of our mind that we are aware of. It includes thoughts and activities that are part of the present. The preconscious mind is the part of personality that we may not be thinking about or currently aware of, but we can easily remember the information. Examples may be what clothes you wore yesterday or what you ate for dinner. Again, anything that is easily remembered is included in the preconscious mind. The unconscious mind is a bit trickier. The unconscious mind includes all aspects of our personality that we are not aware of. The unconscious mind, according to Freud, is the largest part of our personality structure.

Freud believed that the unconscious mind includes evil thoughts, immoral wishes, as well as every horrible memory a person has endured as a part of his or her life experience. Freud felt that an individual's unconscious mind is always trying to surface, but since these thoughts are potentially stressful, people tend to censor the information. The censor works to ensure that unpleasant thoughts that do surface are turned into bland, harmless information. Freud also maintained that the unconscious tries to reveal itself through dreams. He felt that individuals' dreams were the road to their unconscious. He asserted that nightmares could be explained by a reaction to unconscious material that was not filtered properly by the censors.

According to Freud, the structure of the mind is further broken down into three controlling parts of personality. These are known as the *id, ego,* and *superego.* These are Latin roots that Freud translated into German. The id in German is *das Es,* which means "the it." The ego in German, *das Ich,* means "the I." The superego in German is *das Über-ich,* which means "the above I."

The id is also known as the *pleasure principle,* and it wants you to do whatever is pleasurable with no regard to the consequences. In addition, the id wants this satisfaction immediately. It is like the little devil that sits on your shoulder telling you to "Do it, do it!" The superego works on the idealistic principle and is like the little angel on the other side of your shoulder. The superego tells you "Don't do it." This is the moral component of your personality and works in contrast with the demands of the id. The ego works off the reality principle and is considered the decision maker. It hears the demands of both the id and the superego and is in touch with the real world.

Freud postulated that the ego experiences different kinds of anxiety due to the demands of the id, the superego, and the ego. He called these *reality anxiety,* due to the demands of the external world; *moral anxiety,* when the ego is threatened by the demands of the superego; and *neurotic anxiety,* which occurs when the id threatens to overwhelm the ego and force the person to do something unacceptable. To explain how people protect themselves from these anxieties, Freud wrote about various defense mechanisms. Here is a list of the defense mechanisms that Freud stated we use when we need help with these anxieties:

Denial—Believing that what is true is actually false

Displacement—Redirecting emotions to a substitute, more suitable, target

Intellectualization—Focusing on intellectual components of a situation rather than dealing with the feelings associated with it

Projection—Denying feelings and attributing them to others

Rationalization—Realizing that one's actions are not acceptable so creating a false justification

Reaction formation—Overacting in the opposite manner to unacceptable feelings or thoughts

Regression—Acting like a child to protect the conscious mind

Repression—Pushing unwelcome thoughts into the unconscious

Sublimation—Redirecting improper urges into socially acceptable actions

BEYOND FREUD . . . NEO-FREUDIANS

Many theorists expanded Freud's work, or changed some of the key elements, but still maintained the integrity of his personality structures. One of the most well-known neo-Freudians is Carl Jung (1875–1961). Jung created what he called the *collective unconscious,* which was more in-depth than what Freud proposed. Jung felt that the unconscious mind is capable of accessing all of human memory. He asserted that the psyche consists of all human possibilities—past, present, and future—through archetypes in the collective unconscious. Jung looked at the collective unconscious in terms of layers.

Another classic neo-Freudian is Karen Danielsen Horney (1885–1952; pronounced HORN-eye). Horney's work is called *psychosocial analysis* because she placed emphasis on the emotional relations between parent and child in early childhood. Horney's distinction is due to radical differences of opinion with Freud. Freud viewed neuroses in terms of universal instinctual conflicts. Horney, however, felt that neuroses were due to cultural factors that are indigenous to the region in which a person lives. In the psychosexual stages of development that Freud created, he offered the notion of *penis envy.* Horney did not agree with penis envy, but rather offered a new concept called *womb envy.* She said that men are envious that women are able to carry babies and they will therefore overcompensate for this envy by developing a neurotic focus on career success.

Karen Horney

Another neo-Freudian, considered to be the first to break off from Freud, is Alfred Adler (1870–1937). Adler created individual psychology, with an emphasis on interpsychic (interpersonal) phenomena; this was different from the intrapsychic (within the psyche) theory of Freud. Although Adler was not considered to be a follower or student of Freud, Freud heard about Adler's work and invited him to participate in one of his roundtable discussions. Adler later became the president and coeditor of one of Freud's journals. As Adler developed his own theories, however, and they were radically different from those of Freud, Adler resigned and took nine associates with him.

TRAIT APPROACHES TO PERSONALITY

Trait approaches to personality focus on descriptive traits that can be identified and summed up to create an accurate picture of someone's personality. A trait is an adjective that describes a person. A pioneer in the field of personality research was Gordon Allport (1897–1967), who believed in individuality and that people have consistent personalities across time. Allport thought that each person had various traits that can be categorized into the following:

Individual traits—Traits possessed by one person

Common traits—Traits possessed by many people

Cardinal traits—One trait that dominates a person

Central traits—Important traits that affect many different behaviors

Secondary traits—Many consistent traits that are not often shown

Motivational traits—Strongly felt traits that guide behavior

Stylistic traits—Less strongly felt traits that guide behavior

Another key trait theory figure was Raymond Cattell (1905–1998), who developed questionnaires and tests to determine personality characteristics. Cattell worked in the area of intelligence as well and realized the importance of offering solid scientific research to explain his work. Thus, he created a statistical technique that allowed him to analyze data

TABLE 9.1 CATTELL'S 16 PERSONALITY FACTORS

Factor	Range	Factor	Range
Abstractedness	imaginative vs. practical	Reasoning	abstract vs. concrete
Apprehension	insecure vs. complacent	Rule Consciousness	moralistic vs. freethinking
Dominance	aggressive vs. passive	Self-Reliance	leading vs. following
Emotional Stability	calm and stable vs. high-strung and changeable	Sensitivity	sensitive vs. tough-minded
Liveliness	enthusiastic vs. serious	Social Boldness	uninhibited vs. timid
Openness to Change	liberal vs. traditional	Tension	driven and tense vs. relaxed and easygoing
Perfectionism	compulsive and controlled vs. indifferent	Vigilance	suspicious vs. accepting
Privateness	pretentious vs. unpretentious	Warmth	open and warmhearted vs. aloof and critical

from various sources to determine personality characteristics. He suggested that human personality traits could be summed up by 16 personality factors (PFs) or main traits. He felt that everyone has some of each of these traits and that tests would determine how much of each trait a person has (Cattell, Eber, & Tatsuoka, 1970). Table 9.1 shows a list of Cattell's 16 personality factors and their ranges.

Hans Eysenck (1916–1997) was another psychologist who helped shape the trait approach to personality. Eysenck believed that the way to deal with the large numbers of personality traits was to organize them into narrowly defined categories. Thus, he suggested that personality consists of three basic traits: extraversion, neuroticism, and psychoticism (Eysenck & Eysenck, 1985). Extraversion involves relating to other people and the environment while the opposite, introversion, involves directing attention inward. Neuroticism, or emotional stability, consists of moodiness versus being even-tempered. This refers to the tendency to become upset or emotional or the tendency to remain emotionally constant. Psychoticism was added later to his list after Eysenck studied people with mental illness. This category includes people who have difficulty dealing with reality and who may have other illnesses as well.

As a result of Cattell's and Eysenck's work, the five-factor theory of personality was created. Some theorists believe that Cattell focused on too many traits and Eysenck focused on too few traits. The five-factor theory holds that five core traits—extraversion, agreeableness, conscientiousness, neuroticism, and openness—interact to form the human personality.

BEHAVIORIST PERSPECTIVES OF PERSONALITY

Behavioral psychology began with John B. Watson (1878–1958) and looks at personality development as largely resting with the individual's environment. Since each person experiences different situations in his or her life, then each acquires his or her personality differently as well. Another famous behaviorist is B. F. Skinner (1904–1990), who looked at punishment and reinforcement within the individual as paramount to shaping personality.

One behaviorist, Julian Rotter (1916–), left his roots to create a new approach to the development of personality, the social learning theory of personality. Rotter feels that reinforcement does not automatically stamp in behavior. He believes that most of the reinforcers that people strive to obtain are social and that most learning occurs in social situations (Rotter, 1990). Therefore, Rotter's social learning theory of personality incorporates cognitive factors into reinforcement principles. He states that behavior is a function of expectancies, and he defines this phenomenon with the term *locus of control*. Thus, Rotter suggests that individuals who have an internal locus of control believe that they can influence their own reinforcers via their skill and ability. Those who have an external locus of control believe that desired outcomes or results that have already occurred happen because of forces beyond their control (Rotter, 1990). Many psychological tests have been conducted to assess locus of control and personality factors.

Another behaviorist who left his roots to follow the social learning theory perspective is Albert Bandura (1925–). The social learning theory that Bandura created emphasizes the importance of observing and modeling the behaviors, attitudes, and emotional reactions of others (Bandura, 1977). Bandura stated, "Learning would be exceedingly laborious, not to mention hazardous, if people had to rely solely on the effects of their own actions to inform them what to do. Fortunately, most human behavior is learned observationally through modeling: from observing others one forms an idea of how new behaviors are performed, and on later occasions this coded information serves as a guide for action" (1977, p. 22).

According to Bandura, social learning theory explains human behavior in terms of continuous reciprocal interaction between cognitive, behavioral, and environmental influences. The component processes underlying observational learning include the following: (1) *attention,* including modeled events (distinctiveness, affective valence, complexity, prevalence, functional value) and observer characteristics (sensory capacities, arousal level, perceptual set, past reinforcement); (2) *retention,* including symbolic coding, cognitive organization, symbolic rehearsal, and motor rehearsal; (3) *motor reproduction,* including physical capabilities, self-observation of reproduction, and accuracy of feedback; and (4) *motivation,* including external and vicarious reinforcement and self-reinforcement.

THE HUMANISTIC APPROACH TO PERSONALITY

The humanistic approach to personality is unparalleled from the psychodynamic and behaviorist perspectives. This perspective puts forth the idea that in order to understand human behavior, psychologists, researchers, and other practitioners must first look at unique human aspects and qualities. Humanistic theorists believe that the perception of each individual is more important than the actual events or the opinions of the therapists working with these issues. This theory stresses the importance of personal growth and freedom to make choices.

Two of the most identified theorists within humanistic, or phenomenological, psychology are Carl Rogers (1902–1987) and Abraham Maslow (1908–1970). Rogers felt that we all need unconditional positive regard, which is the opposite of what most of us believe. Conditional positive regard is based on the notion that we are given love only if we behave in ways that are deemed appropriate by the people with whom we are seeking attention. If we receive unconditional positive regard, that is, love and acceptance, regardless of societal definitions, then our self-concept is enhanced and we are more productive. Maslow created a hierarchy of needs that has self-actualization as the top tier and the most important component of personality development (Maslow's hierarchy is discussed in more detail in Chapter 7).

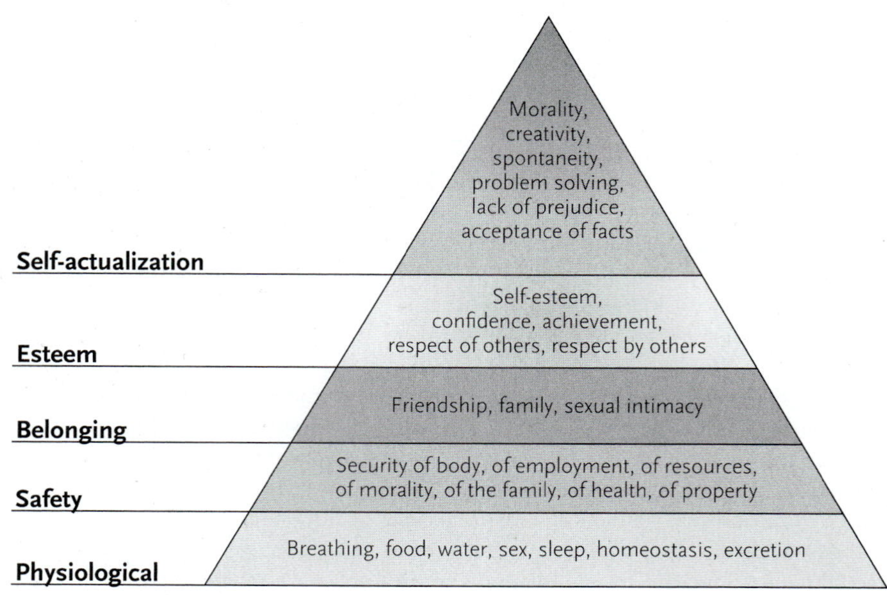

Maslow's Hierarchy of Needs.

HOW DO WE ASSESS PERSONALITY?

As we have seen, numerous approaches can be used to assess personality. How is this information collected? Who is right? These questions have plagued personality research throughout its inception. For theories to be considered fact based, they need to include a certain level of scientific measurement. Therefore, the range of personality assessments goes from self-reports (not very scientific) to case studies, naturalistic observation, laboratory experiments, and psychological tests that have been created with scientific standards implemented. Some of the most widely used tests that psychologists use to measure personality are self-report personality inventories and projective tests.

A *self-report inventory,* which is widely used to determine personality characteristics, is typically a yes/no or true/false test that asks questions about symptoms, behaviors, and personality traits associated with mental disorders or personality types (Aiken, 2002). The tests are typically geared toward a certain perspective, and many of them can be taken in about 15 minutes. However, the most scientifically sound personality test is the Minnesota Multiphasic Personality Inventory-2 (MMPI-2). This 567-question test can take up to three hours to complete; the MMPI-2-RF (second edition, restructured form) is a 338-question test that can also take that long to fully complete. One of the main criticisms of the MMPI test is that people can exaggerate their symptoms to try to look as though they have serious pathology.

Projective tests, which are personality tests designed to let a person respond to ambiguous items, are administered by trained psychologists. The premise here is that the ambiguity in the tests will lead to hidden cognitions, emotions, and behaviors. The responses offered to these types of tests are analyzed for content, and themes are the central focus. The two most common projective tests are the Rorschach Inkblot Test and the Thematic Apperception Test (TAT). The Rorschach Inkblot Test examines the answers that a person gives to prepared inkblot cards. The answers are then analyzed for content and themes. The Thematic Apperception Test has 30 cards with pictures, which are also aimed at projections from the test taker. The TAT is ambiguous in nature and allows for multiple interpretations.

The criticisms of projective tests are that they are open for interpretation and may only be as good as the person interpreting them.

A distinction needs to be made about the different types of tests and how they are utilized. Standardized tests are administered and scored in a consistent manner for anyone who takes them. Achievement tests measure the level of acquired knowledge that has been taught based on a specific criterion. Aptitude tests test how much an individual knows. These differences in tests, although potentially slight, make a big difference in the scoring and interpretation of results.

INTELLIGENCE

Intelligence is an evasive concept that is highly debated in the psychological community. Many definitions of intelligence include being able to perform school-related tasks well. However, many people contend that "street smarts" are not accounted for in this definition. It is important to look at the origins of intelligence testing and the intent that was outlined for its uses.

Francis Galton (1822–1911), an inventor and an explorer who was first cousins with Charles Darwin, was one of the first scientists to study intelligence. He was interested in the heredity of intellect and believed that genetics contributed greatly to the outcome. Since Galton was a scientist, he looked at the family trees of many different artists, judges, poets, scientists, and military commanders and found that they came from prominent family members as well. He concluded that intelligence and creativity runs in families. However, the actual scientific research revealed that prominent people did not perceive the world any better than anyone else did (Galton, 1869).

Alfred Binet (1857–1911), a self-taught French psychologist, spent many years trying to find the best way to measure intelligence. Binet had been commissioned by the French government to create a test to determine which children needed extra help with their studies. This was due to an 1881 mandate in France that all children needed to attend school. Prior to this date the French schools were not required to teach children with various abilities. They focused on average to above-average children only. So it was up to Binet to pinpoint the average to above-average students as well as single out those who were below average. In 1905 Alfred Binet and Théodore Simon (1873–1961) set out to find a way to assess children's abilities. Their theory was that intelligence could not be assessed based on testing simple functions like sensory discrimination. They felt that you had to test higher-order functions like reasoning, memory, and spatial abilities. Therefore, the initial test they designed asked children to define common words, name objects seen in pictures, draw designs from memory, and repeat strings of digits. The mental age of each child was determined by the number of items that the child was able to complete correctly. The mental age was often different from the chronological age of the child and was significant to the test results.

In 1906 Lewis Terman (1877–1956), an American psychologist, revised the Binet-Simon scale for American populations. The Stanford Revision of the Binet-Simon Scale eventually became known as the Stanford-Binet. After hearing some recommendations from the psychologist William Stern (1871–1938), Terman changed some of the issues with the calculations of the mental age and created what is now called the intelligence quotient, or IQ. The Stanford-Binet has undergone several revisions since its inception, but it remains in use today. Subsequently, there have been several other versions of intelligence tests that also follow these initial variables. Although the test was broadened to include testing of adults, the mental age did not work for adults, so that was altered during its transformation.

A major criticism of intelligence tests is that they are broad and do not take culture into consideration. Binet had actually recommended against using these tests for any purpose other than to identify children with learning needs. However, intelligence tests are used for many different purposes today other than to test children.

VARIED INTELLIGENCES

Since we have discussed that there is no single definition of intelligence and it is primarily used for purposes other than the original intent, we have to look at some of the alternative theories and types that have been created since the inception of the concept of intelligence. First is the theory proffered by British psychologist Charles Spearman (1863–1945), who described intelligence in terms of a *g* factor. The *g* represents a general intelligence and another factor, the *s,* represents specific abilities (Spearman, 1904). Spearman contended that people who performed well on one cognitive test tended to score well on the other, and those who scored badly on one would also likely score badly on the other. Therefore, Spearman (1904) concluded that intelligence is a general cognitive ability that could be measured and numerically expressed.

Robert Sternberg (1949–), a Yale psychologist, believes that intelligence tests do not always indicate how successful a person may be in adapting to real-life situations (Sternberg, 1985). He created a triarchic theory of intelligence, which incorporates analytical intelligence, creative intelligence, and practical intelligence. Analytical intelligence is the ability to break a problem into workable components. Creative intelligence is the ability to cope with novel stimuli and solve problems using critical thinking. Finally, practical intelligence is common sense. Sternberg believes that the third component is primarily missing from all other intelligence tests and is very important in society.

Harvard psychologist Howard Gardner (1943–) created a recent and popular model of intelligence known as *multiple intelligences.* Gardner believes that intelligence consists of more than mathematical or verbal abilities and that each person has certain strengths and weaknesses that need to be identified. Additionally, Gardner (1983) looks at culture as a factor that greatly influences the strengths and weaknesses of each individual.

The eight intelligences Gardner described are as follows:

Visual-spatial intelligence—The ability to grasp how objects orient in space

Verbal-linguistic intelligence—Skill in using language and words

Bodily-kinesthetic intelligence—The ability to control movement and body motion and handle objects skillfully

Logical-mathematical intelligence—The ability to think logically with mathematical calculations

Interpersonal intelligence—The ability to understand others

Musical intelligence—The ability to compose and perform music

Intrapersonal intelligence—The ability to understand others

Naturalistic intelligence—The ability to see patterns in the way things are organized

SUMMARY

Personality is an interesting concept that has spawned entire fields within psychology. Psychologists seek answers and need to find methods that are acceptable to create these answers. Abilities come in all forms, and psychologists and other professionals continue to strive to find the ultimate guide to the human psyche.

CASE STUDY #1 TWIN POWER

Ellen and her twin brother, Evan, just turned five. For their birthday party their parents are taking them to a favorite dinner place, a pizza restaurant filled with games for kids, including an enclosed area two feet deep in plastic balls where children can jump around. When they get to the restaurant, Ellen grabs her father's hand and pulls him toward the door. Evan does the same with his mother.

Although Ellen and Evan are twins, their behavior at the restaurant could not have been more different. As always, Ellen is neat and polite, watching out for younger children as she plays. Evan, on the other hand, yells and makes a lot of noise and tends to be messy. One of his favorite games is with the plastic swords, when he runs around pretending to cut off other children's arms and legs. Ellen also enjoys playing with swords, but she is not nearly as aggressive with them.

1. What significance would Freud see in the children's wanting to hold their opposite-sex parent's hand while crossing the parking lot? What might this signify about their state of psychosexual development?
2. What personality traits would you expect Evan and Ellen to share since they are twins? What personality traits would be different?
3. How do the id, ego, and superego factor into children's play? How does this apply to Evan and Ellen?
4. How would humanistic theory explain the differences between Evan and Ellen?
5. What are twin studies and how are they used to assess behavior?

CASE STUDY #2 DEFENSE MECHANISMS

Mimi is having a bad week. The first of her final exams is tomorrow, and the pressure is really on her this time. Her parents were not at all happy about her grades last term and threatened to take her car away if she doesn't improve her grades this term. Although she is doing well so far, next week's finals could make or break her grade point average for the semester.

As she sits in the library, her worry turns to anger.

Where do they get off threatening me? she thinks to herself. *I should fail all of my finals. That would show them!*

Now, too upset to concentrate, Mimi decides to go for a jog to let off steam. There will be time to study tomorrow morning before the exam. However, Mimi does not believe her friend who took the class last semester and told her that the final exam is really tough. How could the final for an introductory class be that hard? Besides, her friend was probably nervous about having to get a good grade and choked under the pressure.

1. Explain the Freudian defense mechanism displacement. Is there any evidence in this story of Mimi using this defense mechanism? Consider her thoughts about her friend who took the course as well as her thoughts about her parents.
2. When she got too upset to study, Mimi decided to go jogging. This is an example of what type of defense mechanism? Did Freud consider this to be healthy behavior? Do you?
3. What is projection? What behavior of Mimi's could be viewed as projection? What does this behavior tell us about how Mimi really feels about her upcoming test?
4. Failing a test to make a point seems a very childish thing to do. How would Freudian theory view this behavior? What name did Freud give it?
5. A common method for coping with stress is through denial. How does Mimi use denial to reduce her own level of stress? What are the costs and benefits of this strategy?

CASE STUDY #3 WHO'S THAT GUY?

"Lauren! Wait up. Where are you headed?" yelled Eden to her friend as she was leaving the library.

"I have to be at work in thirty minutes," Eden told Lauren when she caught up.

"Ahhh, the video game store. How is life in the video game world? By the way, did a guy named Dylan start working there?" Lauren asked.

"Yeah, he did," said Eden. "Do you know him? He's a pretty nice guy and is really fun to work with. He cracks jokes and does funny stuff."

"Really? Are we talking about the same Dylan? Dylan Jonesteen?" asked Lauren. "Dylan's usually pretty quiet and shy. I mean he's nice, but just not that friendly."

"Well, I've only worked with him a couple of times, but he's not shy at work. He's the first one to talk to customers who come in. Plus he knows a lot about video games. He has an amazing memory. People are always surprised when he knows the game they are describing when they can't remember the titles."

"I don't know," puzzled Lauren. "That sure doesn't sound like the Dylan Jonesteen I know."

1. How would trait theories of personality evaluate Dylan? How would these theories deal with the differences in his behavior in different situations?
2. How would learning theories of personality account for the variation in Dylan's behavior in different situations? How does this approach differ from trait theory approaches?
3. According to humanistic theories of personality, why might Dylan be outgoing and confident sometimes, and shy at other times? According to humanistic theory, which woman has seen the "real" Dylan, Lauren or Eden?
4. Compare how each of these theories treat situational factors when describing Dylan's personality. Which theories believe that situations can control people's behavior? Do these theories view situational control over behavior as a positive or negative thing?
5. How sociable is Dylan? Discuss this question from a trait, social learning, and humanistic viewpoint.

CASE STUDY #4 SELECTIVE INTELLIGENCE

Professor Jenner quickly handed back the French quizzes that her students had taken two days before. Nigel, looking over his test with a grimace that expressed disappointment, turned to Chloe. "Hey, Chloe, how did you do?" he asked.

"Pretty well," she said. "For some reason I usually do on these things. I should have majored in foreign languages. I'm getting an A in here, and I will probably fail my engineering class."

"I don't know why I can't get the hang of this class," Nigel complained. "I'm thinking of dropping it and trying Spanish next semester. I lived in California for a few years while I was training for the Olympic swim team so I know a few words already."

"That's right," said Chloe. "I forgot that you competed in the Olympics before you came here. Why did you ever leave?"

"I didn't do very well there," Nigel said. "I was used to winning first place in everything I did and coming in third just didn't cut it for me. I guess I just decided that it wasn't worth it for me. It's not like I could do it forever."

"I guess not," said Chloe. Hearing Professor Jenner begin the lecture, Chloe opened her book while Nigel searched through his bag for a pen.

1. What contemporary theories can better explain Chloe's performance in French class versus her engineering class?
2. Which type of intelligence is Chloe using when taking her French vocabulary quizzes?
3. Describe the concept of creative intelligence. How would Nigel score on a test of this type of intelligence?
4. What is the distinction between achievement tests and aptitude tests? To which category do intelligence tests belong? To which category do French vocabulary quizzes belong?
5. Despite his failing French, Nigel is an excellent athlete. Although traditional intelligence tests would ignore this fact when discussing Nigel's intelligence, some contemporary tests would not. Do you think that athletic ability should be considered to be a form of "intelligence"? Defend your answer.

CASE STUDY #5 INTELLECTUAL ABILITIES

Among the budget cuts that the city council is considering is a 5 percent reduction in funds for secondary education. As the principal of one of the junior high schools that could be affected, Stella is worried. Such a reduction would almost certainly mean teacher layoffs and fewer teachers teaching more students.

Currently the school offers basic math and English courses for students on three levels: average, below average, and above average. However, a smaller budget may require offering only two levels next year. One possibility that Stella is considering is dropping the accelerated courses. After all, the bright kids would do well no matter what. On the other hand, dropping courses designed for below-average students would mean that those children would not get the extra attention that they need. Stella thinks that if push comes to shove, it's the honors programs that will have to go.

1. What solution would you offer if you were Stella and there were budget cuts in your school?
2. Is Stella right that bright kids will do well no matter what? Explain your answer.
3. At what age is intelligence set? Is there anything you can do to improve your intelligence score on an IQ test?
4. Is it possible for gifted students to perform poorly on IQ tests? Explain.
5. Should gifted students and below-average students be integrated into the same classes? Explain.

ACTIVITY #1 I AM . . .

Directions: Complete the following statements about yourself. Then decide if these statements are truthful about how you perceive your own personality.

When I am happy I am ______________________.

When I am sad I am ______________________.

I am mostly ______________________.

Most people say that I am ______________________.

I am lonely when ______________________.

I enjoy being with people when I am ______________________.

I do not enjoy being with people when I am ______________________.

I am proud of ______________________.

I am least proud of ______________________.

My biggest goal is ______________________.

ACTIVITY #2 HOW DEFENSIVE AM I?

Directions: Look up the Freudian defense mechanisms and read the definitions of each. In the following spaces write a personal example of how you have used each defense mechanism in the past and why.

Denial: ______________________________

Displacement: ______________________________

Intellectualization: ______________________________

Projection: ______________________________

Rationalization: ______________________________

Reaction Formation: ______________________________

Regression: ______________________________

Repression: ______________________________

Sublimation: ______________________________

ACTIVITY #3 PERSONALITY TESTS

Directions: Go to the following website and take the Jung Typology test: http://www.humanmetrics.com/cgi-win/JTypes2.asp.

Next, go to the following website: http://www.similarminds.com. Take the following personality tests:

- Big 5/Global 5/SLOAN Tests—Big 45 Test (225 questions)
- Right Left Brain Tests—Any
- Maslow Inventory Test
- Locus of Control Test
- Freudian Inventory Test
- Eysenck Personality Test
- Cattell 16 Factor Test
- Intelligence Tests—All

Save your results for a discussion on the process of taking these tests. Keep in mind whether or not these tests match what you perceive about your own personality!

ACTIVITY #4 GARDNER'S MULTIPLE INTELLIGENCES

Directions: Research the concept of multiple intelligences. Print out information regarding what multiple intelligence is all about and be able to explain the whole theory. Find out who created this theory and why it was created. How does it compare with the traditional concept of intelligence? How does it differ from the traditional concept of intelligence?

ACTIVITY #5 HOW DOES PERSONALITY AFFECT CONSUMER BEHAVIOR?

Directions: Write an essay explaining how personality affects consumer behavior. Make sure to include at least three different theories of behavior and how they would change the outcome of consumerism. You may want to do some research on consumer behavior and psychology before you take on this venture.

REFERENCES

Aiken, L. R. (2002). *Psychological testing and assessment.* New York: Allyn & Bacon.

Bandura, A. (1973). *Aggression: A social learning analysis.* Englewood Cliffs, NJ: Prentice-Hall.

Bandura, A. (1977). *Social learning theory.* New York: General Learning Press.

Cattell, R. B., Eber, H. W., & Tatsuoka, M. M. (1970). *Handbook for the sixteen personality factor questionnaire (16PF).* Champaign, IL: Institute for Personality and Ability Testing.

Eysenck, H. J., & Eysenck, M. W. (1985). *Personality and individual differences.* New York: Plenum.

Fancher, R. (1985) *The intelligence men: Makers of the IQ controversy.* New York: Norton.

Freud, S. (1940). *An outline of psychoanalysis. The standard edition of the complete psychological works of Sigmund Freud* (Vol. 23). London: The Hogarth Press and the Institute of Psychoanalysis.

Galton, F. (1869). *Hereditary genius: An inquiry into its laws and consequences.* New York: Macmillan.

Gardner, H. (1983). *Frames of mind: The theory of multiple intelligences.* New York: Basic Books.

Rotter, J. B. (1990). Internal versus external control of reinforcement. *American Psychologist, 45,* 489–493.

Spearman, C. (1904). General intelligence: Objectively determined and measured. *American Journal of Psychology, 15,* 201–293.

Sternberg, R. J. (1985). *Beyond IQ: A triarchic theory of intelligence.* Cambridge, MA: Cambridge University Press.

CHAPTER 10

Health Psychology

LEARNING ASSETS

Case Study #1 Exhaustion Hurts

Case Study #2 Jog It Out

Case Study #3 Type A Personality, Who Me?

Case Study #4 Smoke Up

Case Study #5 Would I Lie to You?

Activity #1 Freudian Defense Mechanisms

Activity #2 Can You See the Forest Through the Trees?

Activity #3 Stress Workbook

HEALTH PSYCHOLOGY, THE BIOPSYCHOSOCIAL MODEL

Throughout this book we have discussed the physiological and cognitive components to health. Now we are going to examine the conscious decisions that we make that contribute to our well-being, or lack thereof. Health psychology focuses on the cognitive effects of stress and disease on the body. This field is also known as medical psychology and behavioral medicine. Much of the focus of health psychology is based on prevention.

Health psychology came into existence as a result of the research that has been conducted on causes of death. Since health psychologists now know that stress can cause serious illness and even death, they strive to look at how individuals' emotional reactions, social influences, and behavior affect their health. Because of these emphases, this model is often labeled the biopsychosocial model. The biological factors include genetic predispositions; behavioral factors include lifestyle, stress, and health beliefs; and the social conditions include culture, family relationships, and social support systems.

THE EFFECTS OF STRESS

What is stress? What causes stress? These are common questions without common answers. Stress is a term that means different things to different people. So where did the notion of stress come from originally? The word *stress* was coined by Hans Selye (1907–1982) in 1936. He defined stress as "the non-specific response of the body to any demand for change." Selye was working on lab experiments with animals that were subjected to nocuous physical and emotional stimuli. When these lab animals were exposed, they responded in a most peculiar way. After much exposure some of the lab animals had stomach ulcerations, shrinkage of lymphoid tissue, and enlargement of the adrenal glands. Selye revealed that with repeated exposure these animals would show signs of heart attacks, strokes, kidney disease, and rheumatoid arthritis. Before he conducted these experiments, the notion was that pathogens created each of these ailments. Selye had to invent the word *stressor* to apply to anything that causes an organism to adjust and display the nonspecific stress response. He also postulated that stress can be a motivator if applied properly in just the right doses. The word *stress* became a very popular catchphrase after Selye's experiment results were reported.

Hans Selye

Selye (1946, 1952) created what he called the *general adaptation syndrome* to explain the nervous and endocrine systems' response to stressors. The three stages of response are the alarm stage, the resistance stage, and the exhaustion stage. In the alarm stage of response, we have an immediate physical reaction to surprises or threats. This is often called the *fight-or-flight reaction,* and it prepares the body for anything life-threatening. The body focuses on the immediate muscular and emotional needs that will help to sustain life if necessary. This leads to the immune system being depressed, which in turn, makes us more susceptible to disease. In the resistance stage of response, we see that we are becoming more used to the increased stress levels, which makes us more resistant to disease, initially. Hence, we believe that we can easily adapt to stressful situations that come our way. However, the immune system is working at abnormally high levels and can only take this for so long. In the exhaustion stage of response, reality kicks in and our bodies give up on maintaining these high levels of stress. Then parts of the body break down and we will become ill. If this continues without relief, we will eventually die.

THE SOURCES OF STRESS

To determine the sources of stress, psychologists and other practitioners must look at each person individually. However, there are some common universal sources of stress. General categories of stress include things such as major life changes, daily routine issues, unrealistic self-expectations, and interpersonal relationships. Some common stressors include:

- Family issues
- Mental illness
- Issues with child care
- Issues with elder care
- Financial problems
- Legal problems
- Grief
- Communication errors
- Work-related problems
- Addiction issues
- General health concerns
- Issues with balancing work and family
- Time-management issues
- Issues regarding life changes
- Anger-management problems

One of the issues concerning stress is that the stressor needs to be properly identified in order for any progress to take place. If the stressor is not properly identified and dealt with, it can lead to posttraumatic stress disorder (PTSD). According to the *Diagnostic and Statistical Manual of Mental Disorders* (American Psychiatric Association, 2000), PTSD is an anxiety disorder that can develop after exposure to a single terrifying event or multiple ordeals in which grave physical harm occurred or was threatened. PTSD can be triggered by accidents, catastrophes, military combat, rape, or any number of traumatic events. Signs and symptoms of PTSD include having persistent frightening thoughts of the ordeal, feeling emotionally numb, having sleep problems, and being easily startled.

STRESS AND ILLNESS

"My head hurts every single day." "My back feels like it is broken, but the doctor can't find anything wrong." "I know that there is something wrong with my stomach, but no one can see it." Have you ever heard people utter these statements and think to yourself that they were just making it up? Well, you are not alone. In the past, people who offered these psychosomatic complaints were just dismissed. The word *psychosomatic* stems from the core word *psyche,* which means "the mind," and *soma,* which means "the body." In the past when individuals were told that their illnesses were psychosomatic, all in their head, the thought was that there was no physiological component to match the complaint. Current trends in psychology are to use the term *psychophysiological*, since psychologists, practitioners, and researchers now know that these complaints have true physiological origins. Don't get this confused with someone who is a hypochondriac. A hypochondriac is someone who is constantly complaining about being ill with no root causes.

Thousands of studies that have been conducted over the last 25 years have shown that stress is a significant contributor to all major illnesses. The number one cause of death in the United States is cardiovascular disease, and stress has been shown to be a contributing factor. The immune system can also be directly impacted by stressors. The immune system works to determine which cells and substances do not belong in our bodies and to eliminate them. Antigens, substances that trigger an immune reaction, consist of bacteria, parasites, fungus, and viruses. There are two specialized cells that work to rid the body of these antigens. They are lymphocytes, small white cells produced in the bone marrow, and phagocytes, larger white cells that engulf foreign particles such as viruses. However, stressors can reduce the effectiveness of the immune system and thus leave a person more susceptible to antigens.

STRESS AND COPING SKILLS

Coping skills seem to be greatly varied among individuals, and people's bodies have their own unique ways of coping with stress. Is this something we learn? Is it innate? Why do some people cope with hassles better than others? One explanation that has been offered is that some people release higher levels of stress hormones during the alarm stage of the general adaptation syndrome (Selye, 1956). The notion of social support is also directly linked to stress and methods for coping (Bolger & Eckenrole, 1991).

Personality characteristics likewise have played a major role in coping skills. For example, researchers have created a label for a personality type known as Type A. People who fit this category are generally seen as competitive, impatient, and hostile, and they are often victims of coronary heart disease (Rosenman, 1978). Type B personalities are known to be the opposite of Type A and do not seem to encounter as many stress-related issues. Eysenck coined the term Type C personality to represent people who are what he calls *repressors* and more prone to cancer (Eysenck, Grossarth-Maticek, & Everitt, 1988).

Another theory identified the term *hardiness* to be a personality characteristic that seems to relate to how well a person copes with stress as opposed to others who are not able to withstand the pressure and succumb to illness. Hardiness is psychological in nature and consists of commitment to self, work, and family; belief in a sense of control over one's life; and the ability to view change as a challenge rather than a threat (Kobasa, 1979). If one of these thoughts is not present, then the person is more likely to succumb to stress and pressure. Eventually, illness will exist if the person is unable or unwilling to learn the tools necessary for better insights.

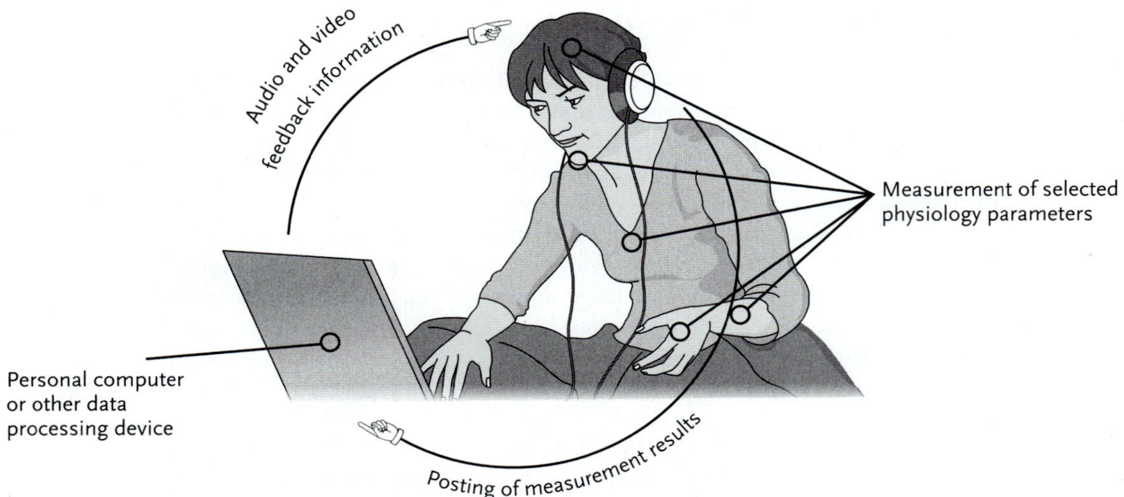

Biofeedback measures stress responses.

STRESS REDUCTION AND RELAXATION

How do you deal with stress? Many of our self-imposed methods for dealing with stress are actually counterproductive. We often turn to drugs, pain medicines, smoking, eating, and other high-risk behaviors to help us cope more effectively. Unfortunately, these methods will not counteract the stress that we are feeling and may even add new stressors into our lives. More effective treatments for stress include regular exercise, meditation, relaxation techniques, structured time-outs, diaphragmatic breathing, progressive muscle relaxation, therapy, guided imagery, yoga, biofeedback, or any other stress-management techniques. A person's willingness to make the necessary changes for a healthy lifestyle is the cornerstone of these approaches. Quite frankly, people do not like change. People will often stick with something that is unhealthy rather than change toward the unknown, thinking that the unknown is scary and may be worse than the current reality. You might be asking yourself why people don't consider that the unknown could be better. Once again, people are afraid of change and will do anything to avoid it.

Let's take a look at some of the methodologies identified for increasing coping skills and decreasing stress responses.

- Diaphragmatic breathing is also called abdominal breathing. Stress can cause our breathing to be shallow, which will actually cause physiological stress because it puts less oxygen in the bloodstream and increases muscle tension. Diaphragmatic breathing helps you slow down your breathing so that you can maintain a good balance and decrease your stress.
- Progressive muscle relaxation (PMR) is a gradual exercise that helps you reduce anxiety and stress. First you create tension in certain muscle groups and then you allow yourself to totally relax them. The focus on various muscle groups makes you aware of their existence and how the tension feels to your body. This allows you to relax a particular group and notice if you are tensing during stress situations.

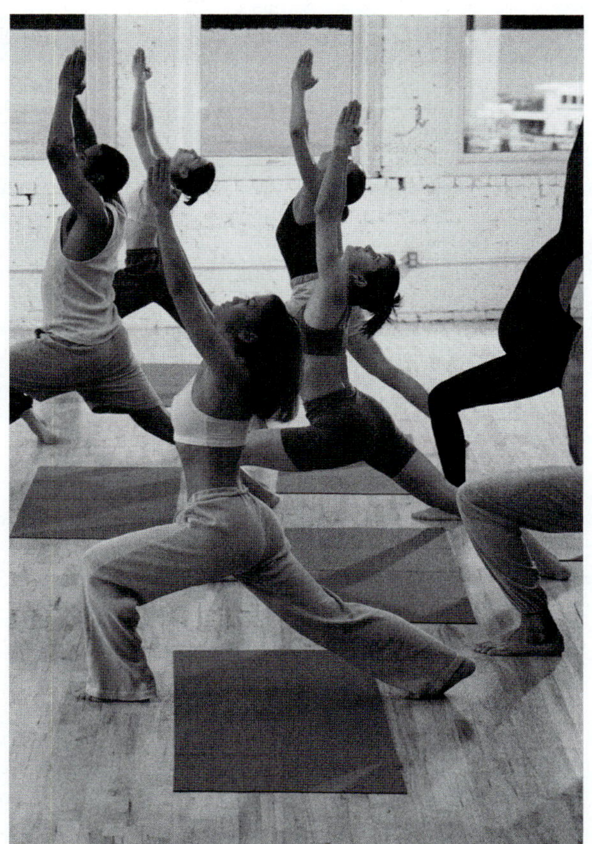

- Meditation is a practice that quiets the mind. It allows you to engage in exercises that help you focus on your breathing, an object, body sensations, and so on. The goal of meditation, regardless of which type you practice (there are many different kinds), is to relax the mind, body, and spirit.
- Yoga is also used as a form of relaxation, and people practice many different kinds of yoga. It involves combining physical movements with meditative mental states to create a less stressful, more relaxed sense of awareness.
- Guided imagery, or visualization, is the language that the body listens to in order to have a reaction. This technique allows you to use your imagination to conjure mental images to produce relaxation and encourage healing.
- Biofeedback is a method that allows people to improve their health by identifying and using signals from their own bodies. It is used for many different purposes, but it is also highly effective in helping people who are tense to relax. Biofeedback machines act as a thermometer would if you thought you had a fever. For example, if you think you have a fever, you take your temperature to confirm that you do indeed have a fever; if it is confirmed, you know that you need to work on eliminating the fever. For stress, the biofeedback machine can detect the stress response when it seems to be occurring and point out what triggers it; you are then left with the information you need to eliminate or work on your responses to these stressors.

There are many additional methodologies for reducing or coping with stress reactions. The key is to find one that suits you and get to work!

SUMMARY

This chapter has focused on the interconnectedness of psychology and physiology. We looked at stress, stressors, and coping mechanisms. Health psychology is an area that is ever changing and ever growing. It is a major connection between the psychological community and the medical community.

CASE STUDY #1 EXHAUSTION HURTS

Although most doctors her age seem to be accustomed to working under such stressful conditions, Amanda feels that she may be growing less able to cope with the pressure. During one month, while working in the emergency rooms at County Hospital, Amanda treated more gunshot wounds than in six years working for the U.S. Army.

Now on her way home from a particularly exhausting day, Amanda would normally think about her husband, Phil, and daughter, Kim, waiting for her at home. Tonight, however, she will be coming home to an empty house. Phil and Kim are spending the weekend at a father-daughter retreat.

Even when she feels physically exhausted, Amanda often finds it difficult to fall asleep until she can unwind from the tensions of the day. On days like this, Phil usually is able to help by massaging her muscles while she describes the events of her day. Without that back rub, Amanda knows that it is going to be a couple of hours until she can get any sleep.

1. Why does Amanda find relief from her stress in back rubs? In what way might this help her?
2. After stressful days, Phil can be a great source of comfort for Amanda. In what ways does having social support help people deal with stress?
3. What are three categories of stressors? Which types has Amanda experienced recently?
4. When Amanda does manage to fall asleep, it is a restless sleep. In her dreams she once again relives an experience that occurred during the war, which occurred more than three years ago. She sees a missile explode less than 50 yards from her quarters. Describe the phenomenon that Amanda is experiencing.
5. Although many war veterans experience problems such as Amanda's, many more do not. Discuss this in terms of the psychological nature of stress. What difficulties does this pose for stress theorists who assign fixed stress values to events when determining a person's level of stress?

CASE STUDY #2 JOG IT OUT

Halfway through her finals week, Barbara is exhausted. This morning she woke up at 6:30 a.m. to study for a morning exam, skipping breakfast and disrupting her sleep schedule. Returning from her exam, Barbara passed out on the couch, waking up an hour later feeling only slightly more rested. Half asleep, Barbara put on an exercise outfit and jogging shoes. "By the end of this week I will have run 100 miles!" she mutters to herself.

The jogging helps. Returning home, she feels more awake and less stressed about the test. Despite her last-minute efforts this morning, though, the test went badly. Feeling hungry for the first time since yesterday afternoon is a good sign, she decides and wonders what she should do about a late lunch. Barbara has another exam scheduled in the morning. The idea of studying is not at all appealing to her. Since the studying she did in the morning did not help, why should she bother now? So Barbara heads out to rent a movie, something to take her mind off her tests.

1. Efforts to cope with stress can be either emotion focused or problem focused. Explain this distinction, using illustrations from Barbara's behavior.
2. At what stage of Selye's general adaptation syndrome model is Barbara? During this story, has her stress changed stages? Explain.
3. Can Barbara's recent loss of appetite be attributed to stress? What does it mean to say that an illness is psychosomatic?
4. Barbara felt much better after jogging. In what ways does exercise help reduce levels of stress?
5. Is Barbara using stress reduction tactics that are effective? What else can she do to eliminate her stress?

CASE STUDY #3 TYPE A PERSONALITY, WHO ME?

In recent years, medical knowledge and technologies have grown tremendously. As a consequence, more people today live longer with conditions they know may ultimately be fatal. Unfortunately, living with a potentially terminal disease can be very difficult psychologically. In response to this, a number of support groups have sprung up to offer counseling for the terminally ill. The groups not only improve psychological functioning, but they have actually improved the prognosis of many forms of cancer and other diseases.

Also in recent years, doctors have begun to notice a surprising similarity among patients suffering from various heart ailments. These patients tend to be highly ambitious, competitive, and preoccupied with deadlines. This personality trait is now known as Type A personality, and over the past 30 years much literature and research supports its association with increased incidents of heart disease.

What do these two findings have in common? They demonstrate that psychological health is important for physiological health, and that understanding emotions and attitudes is important for medical doctors as well as psychologists.

1. What type of attitude is associated with increased cancer survival rates? How do survival rates of people who deny they have cancer at all compare with those people who accept that they have cancer, but not that it will kill them?
2. Nestor, a 33-year-old project manager, reports being extremely self-confident and very happy with his life. What is the association between this pattern and heart disease? What is the association between this pattern and surviving cancer? Explain your answers.
3. Philosophers have long believed the mind and the body to be distinct and discrete entities. How do psychologists explain that mental processes can affect physiological health specifically?
4. Type As are more likely to suffer a heart attack than Type Bs. Does this mean that being a Type A increases your chance of having a heart attack?
5. Some psychologists believe that being a Type A does not promote heart disease, but rather being a Type B person helps prevent it. Discuss the merits of this argument. Consider that 100 years ago heart disease was relatively rare and today it accounts for one in three deaths in our society.

CASE STUDY #4 SMOKE UP

Naomi started smoking her freshman year of high school. It was not something she took to right away, but, rather, she smoked only with her friends in the beginning. In those early days, the best thing about smoking was the ritual, such as tapping the package to pack the tobacco and lighting another person's cigarette.

In time Naomi grew more and more comfortable with her new habit, and by her junior year she averaged two or three packs a week. However, even then she primarily smoked only on weekends. It wasn't until her senior year that she smoked alone and at home with any frequency. That is when her parents found out about her smoking habit.

Other smokers pleaded with Naomi to quit, saying that they would quit if they could. In fact, her mother and her father had, on separate occasions, tried unsuccessfully to stop. Both of her parents were furious that their daughter had adopted their habit.

1. In the preparation stage, future smokers develop ideas about the role of smoking in their culture. Where might Naomi have developed these ideas?
2. At what point does the initiation period end and the period of being a smoker begin? What important psychological event occurs causing this transition?
3. Smoking is both psychologically and physiologically addictive. Discuss how both addictions might have caused Naomi's parents' attempts to stop smoking to fail?
4. What role do rituals play in the formation and continuation of smoking?
5. Nicotine is physically addictive. Some psychologists now think that nicotine can become emotionally addictive as well. Describe this process and how it works.

CASE STUDY #5 WOULD I LIE TO YOU?

"Hi, Logan, how are things this morning?" asked Dr. Stern, closing the cloth curtain that sectioned off the examination room.

"Just fine, Dr. Stern. How's my cholesterol?" asked Logan, who suffered from an inherited condition that raised his cholesterol levels.

"Well, it's not as low as I expected," said Dr. Stern. "You have been taking your medication, haven't you?"

"Yes, I hardly ever forget," Logan lied. Actually he had a hard time getting used to taking medications and forgot as often as not.

"How about your diet? Have you been eating foods low in saturated fats and cholesterol? Are you doing your aerobic exercise?" asked Dr. Stern.

"I still work out and I think I am avoiding fats," said Logan.

"That's a good boy. I don't want you to eat nasty fats," mumbled the doctor to himself as he scribbled down Logan's answers, not hearing Logan's slight emphasis on the word *think*.

When the doctor finished writing, he got up to leave. "Well, Logan, keep up the good work and I'll see you in six months."

1. Logan lied about how often he forgets to take his medication. How might Dr. Stern's behavior have made Logan want to lie? What aspects of patient-physician relationships might make patients want to lie to their doctors?
2. How is communication between patients and physicians complicated by language? Is there any evidence that the level of language used by Dr. Stern is difficult for Logan to understand? Defend your answer with examples.
3. Dr. Stern's language becomes childlike near the end of his interview, referring to fats as "nasty." How does this affect the patient-physician relationship?
4. Imagine that you are to speak to incoming patients about how to get the most out of their health-care providers. What information would you give them?
5. Some people don't trust doctors or hospitals and are not likely to follow medical advice. What responsibilities does a physician have to these people? Describe some suggestions for how these issues may be resolved.

ACTIVITY #1 FREUDIAN DEFENSE MECHANISMS

Step 1: Freud created what he called ego defense mechanisms. Look up the defense mechanisms and write an outline of what they are, when they are applied (an example of each), and possible treatments for each one.

Step 2: The next step is to write about yourself again. Explain how these defense mechanisms apply to your own life. Do you use any of them? Would you know if you did? Which ones do you use and how do you use them? What can you do to stop using these defense mechanisms?

Step 3: Assess what you wrote and determine if this has been an eye opener for you. What are you going to do with this information in the future?

ACTIVITY #2 CAN YOU SEE THE FOREST THROUGH THE TREES?

Directions: Create a visualization or guided imagery scenario that would have someone trekking through the woods to the beach and then back home again. Explain why your visualization would help someone to relax. What is the point of this visualization? Be very specific in your details so that the person who would use this would gain maximum relaxation benefits from it.

ACTIVITY #3 STRESS WORKBOOK

Part I

Directions: During the course of one week you will need to keep track of your responses to stimuli; that is, you will keep a stress diary. In the diary record the day, date, time, and stressful event that occurred. Be honest and include *all* stressful events that happen over the course of this week.

Part II

Directions: Once the week is over and you have your stress diary complete, go through each occurrence and see what triggered a stress response. The second phase of this activity is to go through these events and think of effective coping mechanisms that you could have used to stop the stress reaction or deal with it more effectively.

REFERENCES

American Psychiatric Association. (2000). *Diagnostic and statistical manual of mental disorders* (4th ed., text rev.). Washington, DC: Author.

Bolger, N., & Eckenrole, J. (1991). Social relationships, personality, and anxiety during a major stressful event. *Journal of Personality and Social Psychology, 61,* 440–449.

Eysenck, H. J., Grossarth-Maticek, R., & Everitt, B. (1988). Personality and stress as causal factors in cancer and coronary heart disease. In M. P. Jaisse (Ed.), *Individual differences, stress, and health psychology* (pp. 309–322). New York: Springer-Verlag.

Kobasa, S. (1979). Stressful life events, personality and health: An inquiry into hardiness. *Journal of Personality and Social Psychology, 37,* 1–11.

Rosenman, R. H. (1978). The interview method of assessment of the coronary-prone behavior pattern. In T. M. Dembroski, S. M. Weiss, J. L. Shields, S. G. Haynes, & M. Feinleib (Eds.), *Coronary-prone behavior* (pp. 71–83). New York: Springer-Verlag.

Selye, H. (1936). A syndrome produced by diverse nocuous agents. *Journal of Neuropsychiatry and Clinical Neurosciences, 138,* 32.

Selye, H. (1946). The general adaptation syndrome and the diseases of adaptation. *Journal of Clinical Endocrinology, 6,* 117–230.

Selye, H. (1952). *The story of the adaptation syndrome.* Montreal, Quebec, Canada: Acta Inc.

Selye, H. (1956). *The stress of life.* New York: McGraw-Hill.

CHAPTER 11

Psychological Disorders and Treatment

LEARNING ASSETS

Case Study #1 What Is Abnormal?

Case Study #2 House Fright

Case Study #3 How Crazy Am I?

Case Study #4 Is This for Real?

Case Study #5 Moody Much?

Case Study #6 Mystery Solved!

Case Study #7 Heightened Anxiety

Case Study #8 Life Is Meaningless

Case Study #9 What Kind of Therapist Would I Be?

Case Study #10 Does Therapy Make You Self-Reliant?

Activity #1 Diagnoses

Activity #2 Mental Illness Defined

Activity #3 Personality Disorders

Activity #4 Psychopathology

DEFINING ABNORMAL BEHAVIOR

What is abnormal behavior? To define abnormal behavior, psychologists have to first look at what is considered normal behavior. "Normal" behavior is very subjective and consists of cultural definitions indigenous to specific cultures and regions. For example, is cannibalism considered normal behavior in most cultures? The answer, of course, is no. However, there are still tribes that practice cannibalism currently and it is accepted throughout those areas. Therefore, it is difficult to really offer a single definition of normal or abnormal behavior.

Contrary to what the media would have us believe, most behavior falls somewhere in the continuum of normal behavior. Statistically, more people than not do not murder others or practice other ritualistic behaviors that would be considered unacceptable in our culture. Thus, psychologists look at abnormal behavior in terms of whether or not it violates social norms or if individuals are impaired in an important aspect of their lives. This approach still does not lead to a complete understanding or even provide an appropriate definition of the term *abnormal,* but it does emphasize the most important point in assessing disorders: Abnormal behavior depends on many factors and each individual needs to be assessed separately.

The history of mental illness is quite fascinating and a bit horrifying. Throughout most of the 1600s medicine men and shamans were used to treat people who exhibited signs of what was considered mental illness. Their job was to use rituals to create purity and atonement for the individual in hopes that the illness would go away. In the late 1600s mental illness was considered a form of demonic possession and religious figures were called to exorcise demons. In the 1700s the first signs of physical descriptors as the cause of mental illness surfaced. Advocates for proper treatment of the mentally ill started to surface in the 1800s, and by the end of the century, medical doctors, physiologists, and researchers had started to focus on the biological and physiological causes of mental illness. Research, experimentation, and therapy finally emerged in the field of psychology. Two major models account for the descriptors of abnormal behavior. One is the medical model; the other is the psychological model. Each of these models has many aspects that are considered when looking at behavior.

MEDICAL MODEL

The medical model of abnormal behavior views abnormal behavior as a disease. This methodology began in the latter half of the nineteenth century and came about due to increasing awareness of illnesses and their causes. Physicians, who were tracking symptoms and then associating them with the causes, were increasingly becoming aware that if they treated the symptom, then they were also treating the illness. However, they also knew that treating the symptoms did not eradicate the disease. Many physicians in the late 1800s and early 1900s adopted this model to explain abnormal behaviors. The underlying causes were still a mystery for these early practitioners.

PSYCHOLOGICAL MODEL

The psychological model of abnormal behavior includes several different subcategories. These subcategories include: psychodynamic perspectives, behavioral perspectives, cognitive perspectives, humanistic perspectives, and sociocultural perspectives.

Psychodynamic perspectives focus on unconscious conflicts involving personality structures known as the id, ego, and superego. Psychodynamic therapy and treatment focus on resolving inner conflicts that reveal themselves in behavior or emotions. The idea is to conjure conflicting aspects of self into conscious awareness.

Behavioral perspectives look at abnormal behavior in terms of environmental influences and drives and focus on maladaptive learning through conditioning. Behaviorists tend to look at treatment in terms of changing prior learning through classical and operant conditioning. In addition, behaviorists think that the philosophical concept of free will is an illusion and that behavior is a combination of genetic factors and environmental factors that are gained through association or reinforcement. Therefore, behaviorists believe behavior can be changed by changing the conditions and reinforcers.

Cognitive perspectives focus on the human mind and how it processes information. The cognitive model is in contrast with the behavioral model in the sense that cognitive theorists believe the foundation for cognitions is maladaptive thinking, which causes abnormal behavior. Cognitive therapy focuses on changing the maladaptive thinking in order to make changes in the behavior.

Practitioners who follow *humanistic perspectives* focus on the human dimension in psychology. This view has its roots in existential philosophy, and treatment is centered on self-direction and -understanding of an individual's own development.

Finally, *sociocultural perspectives* focus on higher-order functions developing out of social interaction. A psychologist adhering to a sociocultural perspective focuses on the importance that the external social world has on the individual. Treatment focuses on the intrapsychic components that arise due to these external interactions.

THE CLASSIFICATION OF MENTAL DISORDERS

To create a unified diagnostic skill set, practitioners have created a manual that has the entire set of criteria specifically spelled out for each disorder. This is known as the *Diagnostic and Statistical Manual of Mental Disorders,* or the *DSM.* Currently, the *DSM* is in its fourth edition with a text revision (the *DSM-IV-TR*), and a fifth edition is currently being worked on. The *DSM* has undergone revisions to the disorders since its first edition in 1952. The *DSM* employs a five-level (axes) system to classify different components within a disorder or disability. The axes look like this:

Axis I: Clinical disorders, including major mental disorders, as well as developmental and learning disorders

Axis II: Underlying pervasive or personality disorders, including mental retardation

Axis III: Acute medical conditions and physical disorders

Axis IV: Psychosocial and environmental factors contributing to the disorder

Axis V: Global Assessment of Functioning or Children's Global Assessment Scale—a numeric scale from 0 to 100 for a subjective rating of social, occupational, and psychological functioning

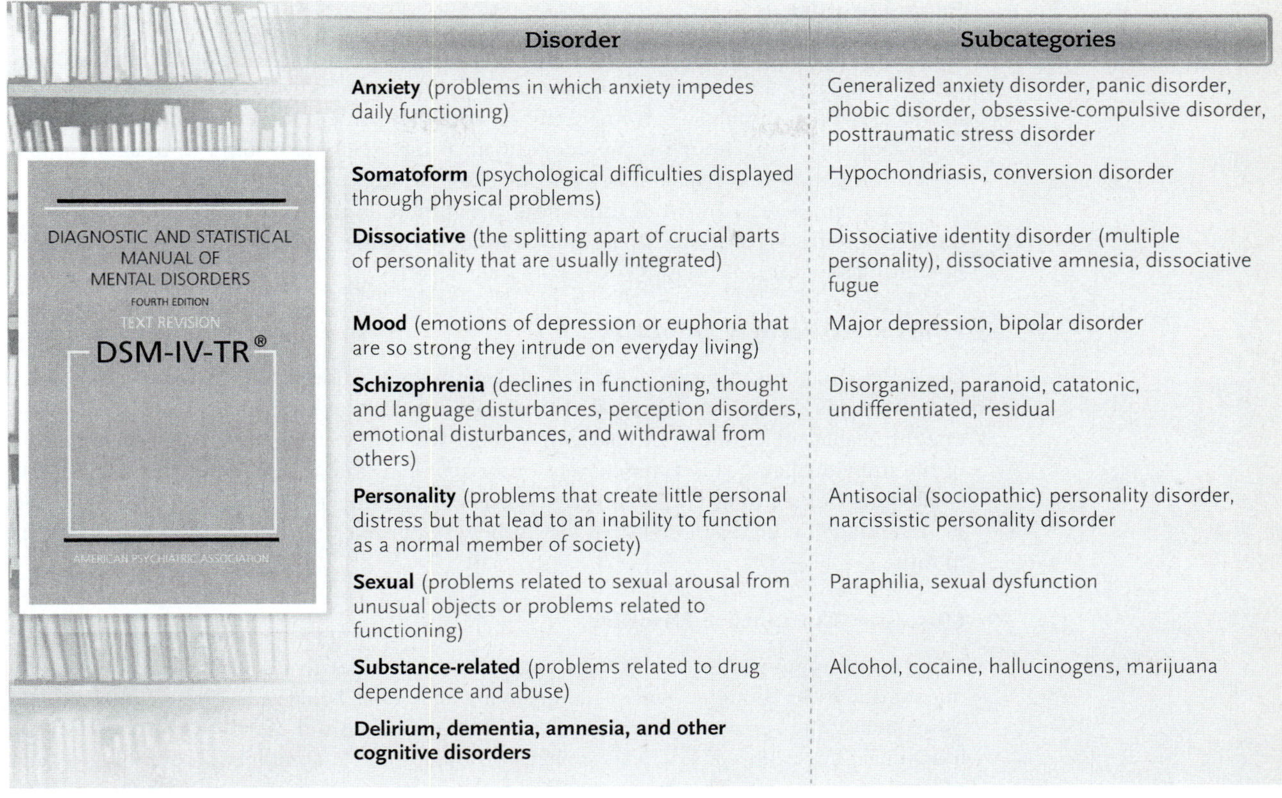

Disorder	Subcategories
Anxiety (problems in which anxiety impedes daily functioning)	Generalized anxiety disorder, panic disorder, phobic disorder, obsessive-compulsive disorder, posttraumatic stress disorder
Somatoform (psychological difficulties displayed through physical problems)	Hypochondriasis, conversion disorder
Dissociative (the splitting apart of crucial parts of personality that are usually integrated)	Dissociative identity disorder (multiple personality), dissociative amnesia, dissociative fugue
Mood (emotions of depression or euphoria that are so strong they intrude on everyday living)	Major depression, bipolar disorder
Schizophrenia (declines in functioning, thought and language disturbances, perception disorders, emotional disturbances, and withdrawal from others)	Disorganized, paranoid, catatonic, undifferentiated, residual
Personality (problems that create little personal distress but that lead to an inability to function as a normal member of society)	Antisocial (sociopathic) personality disorder, narcissistic personality disorder
Sexual (problems related to sexual arousal from unusual objects or problems related to functioning)	Paraphilia, sexual dysfunction
Substance-related (problems related to drug dependence and abuse)	Alcohol, cocaine, hallucinogens, marijuana
Delirium, dementia, amnesia, and other cognitive disorders	

The following sections describe the main types of disorders categorized in the *DSM-IV-TR*.

Anxiety Disorders

How do you know if you have regular anxiety or an abnormal amount of anxiety? This question plagues many people. Anxiety is an ever-growing, greatly researched phenomenon. Within the scope of anxiety are subcategories: phobias, panic disorder, generalized anxiety disorder, and obsessive-compulsive disorder.

Phobias

Phobias are highly irrational fears of objects, places, activities, or situations in which coping mechanisms are seemingly nonexistent. Within the *DSM-IV-TR* there are three classifications of phobias (American Psychiatric Association, 2000): agoraphobia, social phobia, and specific phobias. Agoraphobia is a general fear of leaving home or a more specialized safe place due to the fear of being humiliated in public, which may trigger or be caused by panic attacks. Social phobias typically focus on the fear of being around other people where scrutiny and judgment is likely to occur. Finally, specific phobias are a fear of a specific object. For example, you can be afraid of snakes, spiders, or rats.

Panic Disorder

Panic disorder is an anxiety disorder that manifests itself with panic attacks. People who suffer from panic disorder are often quite anxious about these panic attacks and worry that they will happen in public. It is important to note that panic disorder is not the same thing as agoraphobia, even though many people with panic attacks also suffer from agoraphobia. When someone is experiencing a panic attack, it is often mistaken for a heart attack. The heart rate can increase by 50 or more beats per minute in this state. Some additional common symptoms of panic attacks are perspiration, trembling, dizziness, hyperventilation, and uncontrollable fear.

Generalized Anxiety Disorder

Generalized anxiety disorder (GAD) is also an anxiety disorder, but it differs from phobias and panic disorder in the sense that it manifests itself as a general feeling of excessive, uncontrollable, and often irrational worry. This worry interferes with the daily functions of the individual and causes muscle tension or aches, insomnia, rashes, hot flashes, difficulty swallowing or breathing, fatigue, headaches, nausea, fidgeting, twitching, irritability, sweating, or trembling. To be diagnosed with GAD, these symptoms must be constant for at least six months.

Obsessive-Compulsive Disorder

Obsessive-compulsive disorder (OCD) is an anxiety disorder that is characterized by involuntary obtrusive thoughts with accompanying irrational behaviors. These thoughts, and subsequently the behaviors, interfere with daily functioning and often create distress for the individual. The causes of OCD are generally thought to be a combination of biological and psychological factors. This brings us back to the nature and nurture element again—that is, the degree of OCD varies depending on whether either the nature component or the nurture component is more involved in the OCD. Since there are biological components to OCD, some treatments rely on medications for assistance.

Somatoform Disorders

Somatoform disorders are quite unique in the sense that they perfectly mask disease or injury for which there is no biological or physiological cause. Quite often people are accused of faking these symptoms or illnesses, when in fact they are very real to the person experiencing them. This means that cognitive components are largely to blame for these physiological responses. The *DSM-IV-TR* recognizes several somatoform disorders. They include: hypochondriasis, somatization disorder, conversion disorder, body dysmorphic disorder, and pain disorder. Two other categories are reserved for unspecified symptoms: undifferentiated somatoform disorder, and somatoform disorder not otherwise specified.

Hypochondriasis

The word *hypochondriac* refers to someone who is preoccupied with having a serious illness; that is, he or she has hypochondriasis. If an illness is described to such individuals, then they believe that they may have it. Even after hypochondriacs have been assessed by a physician and told that no illness exists, they are skeptical. There is typically a central focus area for a hypochondriac, like the brain, stomach, lungs, and so on, and the worries typically stem from minor symptoms that have been inflated to become potentially deadly events to the person.

Somatization Disorder

Somatization disorder, originally called hysteria by Sigmund Freud (1856–1939), is formally diagnosed when physical symptoms that are reported have no physical origin. Freud postulated that internal psychological conflicts originate from unconsciously expressed physical symptoms. Individuals suffering from somatization disorder will typically visit many different doctors trying to get a handle on whatever it is that they think is causing these symptoms.

Conversion Disorder

Conversion disorder also stems from Freudian diagnoses. In this disorder, the person presents neurological symptoms such as numbness, fits, or different kinds of paralysis, but no physiological reasons are found. The symptoms are typically thought to stem from difficulties in the life of the person presenting these symptoms. Conversion comes from Freud's theory that anxiety can be converted into physical symptoms.

Body Dysmorphic Disorder

Body dysmorphic disorder is characterized by an excessive preoccupation with a perceived defect in physical features. For example, someone with body dysmorphic disorder may have a slightly crooked nose and think that he or she has a terrible hook nose that is invading his or her whole face. The individual's perception is an exaggeration of the feature, but it is very real to the person experiencing these feelings.

Pain Disorder

Pain disorder occurs when perceived pain in one or more areas is caused by psychological rather than physiological causes. The pain can be debilitating and can last anywhere from a few hours to years. This disorder seems to afflict women more than men, but that may change as times change. The perceived pain typically takes place after a real injury has actually healed.

Dissociative Disorders

Dissociative disorders are rather interesting and not nearly as prevalent as some movies would have you believe. They are called dissociative disorders because they are characterized by a dissociation or interference with a person's consciousness. Several dissociative disorders are classified in the *DSM-IV-TR*: depersonalization disorder, dissociative amnesia, dissociative fugue, and dissociative identity disorder.

Depersonalization Disorder

According to the *DSM-IV-TR,* depersonalization disorder is characterized by a period of detachment from one's self or surrounding; this period may be experienced as "unreal" even while the person retains awareness that this is only a feeling and not reality. Most people can relate to this disorder at some time or another. It is feeling far away from your current reality, but knowing that reality exists. The experience becomes problematic when it occurs so frequently that it interrupts normal functioning.

Dissociative Amnesia

According to the *DSM-IV-TR,* dissociative amnesia is a noticeable impairment of recall resulting from emotional trauma. This disorder causes the person to block out personal information that is of a traumatic or stressful manner. It is not a result of any other trauma. For example, a blow to the head that produces amnesia does not belong in this category.

Dissociative Fugue

According to the *DSM-IV-TR,* a dissociative fugue is a physical desertion of familiar surroundings and experience of impaired recall of the past. This may lead to confusion about actual identity and the assumption of a new identity. A very rare disorder, dissociative fugue will typically last for days or months if it occurs. Individuals who experience dissociative fugue will usually embark on some sort of journey, and they may travel thousands of miles.

Dissociative Identity Disorder

According to the *DSM-IV-TR,* dissociative identity disorder (formerly known as multiple personality disorder) is the alternation of two or more distinct personality states, with impaired recall among these personality states of important information. This is an extremely controversial diagnosis since many people do not think that it actually exists. The movie industry has presented several famous portrayals of people with dissociative identity disorder. However, if it exists at all, this is also considered quite rare.

Mood Disorders

Mood disorders have received a lot of attention because they affect many people in the population. Two of the most common, and potentially dangerous, mood disorders are depression and bipolar disorder.

Depression

Everyone experiences sadness at one point or another in their lives, but how do practitioners know if it has crossed the line into depression? The *DSM-IV-TR* goes into great detail about the criteria necessary for a depression diagnosis. However, a good measure to go by is the length of time that sadness persists; when sadness persists beyond a few weeks, it may be depression. Women seem to suffer from depression twice as often as men. A lot of research is conducted in the field of depression, and it still holds many mysteries. However, one of the research findings to date has identified two neurotransmitters that are affected by depression. These are serotonin and norepinephrine. Therefore, some treatments include medications to set these levels back to a normal level.

Depression manifests itself in different ways with different people. For example, you may notice depression symptoms by changes in appetite or sleeping patterns, feelings of hopelessness, worthlessness, guilt, anhedonia (loss of pleasure in previously important activities), lack of concentration, stomachaches, headaches, or suicidal thoughts or behaviors. The *DSM-IV-TR* classification requires the symptoms to be present continually for at least two weeks before a formal diagnosis can be given. An interesting subcategory within depression is called seasonal affective disorder (SAD). This disorder is characterized by depression

symptoms associated with the time changes in the amount of daylight; less daylight creates these sad feelings. Have you ever noticed how colorful most cold weather clothes are? That is not an accident!

Bipolar Disorder

Bipolar disorder is exhibited by extreme mood swings with periods of even temper. People with bipolar disorder experience depressive episodes, whose symptoms mask those outlined in the explanation of depression, but these individuals also have periods of mania. Mania encompasses periods of elevated moods. Bipolar disorder typically runs in families, begins in the mid-20s, and continues throughout the lifespan once diagnosed. Symptoms of mania include increased energy, racing thoughts, poor judgment, feelings of being invulnerable, heightened sex drive, decreased need for sleep, irritable mood, inflated self-esteem, and an overwhelming denial that there is anything wrong with them. As mentioned, the depression symptoms are the same as those outlined in the depression category. Many people say that bipolar disorder is a chemical imbalance in the brain; there aren't any tests that can prove that fact.

Schizophrenia

Schizophrenia is a mental illness that is chronic, severe, and potentially disabling. This brain disorder only affects approximately 1 percent of the population. The term *schizophrenia* literally means "split mind" and was coined by Swiss psychiatrist Eugen Bleuler (1857–1939). People with schizophrenia typically require hospitalization and medication to deal with the symptoms. The onset of schizophrenia typically manifests in the late teens or early 20s, although lack of focus and emotional response may be seen in childhood. Severe social impairment is typically a cornerstone of schizophrenia.

The symptoms of schizophrenia fall into three broad categories: positive symptoms, negative symptoms, and cognitive symptoms. The positive symptoms are typically denoted by unusual thoughts or perceptions, including hallucinations (seeing something that no one else can see), delusions (false beliefs that do not change), thought disorders (disorganized thinking), and disorders of movement (clumsiness). Negative symptoms are typically denoted by a decrease in the ability to initiate plans, speak, express emotion, or find pleasure in everyday life. Cognitive symptoms are denoted by lack of attention, memory issues, and the inability to plan and organize.

Personality Disorders

Personality disorders are unique in the sense that they are classified in the *DSM-IV-TR,* but they are not considered mental illnesses. They seem to reveal a pervasive pattern of maladaptive behavior that begins in adolescence and persists throughout the lifespan. Ten personality disorders have been categorized in the *DSM-IV-TR,* and they are as follows:

Cluster A: Odd or Eccentric Disorders

Paranoid personality disorder: Characterized by irrational suspicions and mistrust of others

Schizoid personality disorder: Lack of interest in social relationships, seeing no point in sharing time with others

Schizotypal personality disorder: Characterized by odd behavior or thinking

Cluster B: Dramatic, Emotional, or Erratic Disorders

Antisocial personality disorder: Pervasive disregard for the law and the rights of others

Borderline personality disorder: Extreme "black-and-white" thinking; instability in relationships, self-image, identity, and behavior

Histrionic personality disorder: Pervasive attention-seeking behavior including inappropriate sexual seductiveness and shallow or exaggerated emotions

Narcissistic personality disorder: A pervasive pattern of grandiosity, need for admiration, and lack of empathy

Cluster C: Anxious or Fearful Disorders

Avoidant personality disorder: Social inhibition, feelings of inadequacy, extreme sensitivity to negative evaluation, and avoidance of social interaction

Dependent personality disorder: Pervasive psychological dependence on other people

Obsessive-compulsive personality disorder: Characterized by rigid conformity to rules, moral codes, and excessive orderliness (this is not the same as obsessive-compulsive disorder)

Childhood Disorders

Numerous childhood disorders are classified in the *DSM-IV-TR*. However, the focus here is on the main childhood disorders that are often referred to as *developmental disorders*. The two covered here are attention deficit disorder (ADD) or attention deficit hyperactivity disorder (ADHD) and autistic disorder.

Attention Deficit Disorder (ADD) and Attention Deficit Hyperactivity Disorder (ADHD)

Many children are being diagnosed with either attention deficit disorder (ADD) or attention-deficit hyperactivity disorder (ADHD). These are tricky diagnoses and should be paid special attention in each of the stages and treatment phases. Both are characterized by inattention or hyperactivity that is significantly more pronounced in children who have these disorders than peers of the same age. Inattention may consist of failing to pay close attention to details, not paying attention in tasks or play activities, not listening when being addressed, not following through on tasks, having difficulty organizing tasks, not participating in tasks that require mental effort, losing items frequently, being forgetful, or being easily distracted. Hyperactivity is characterized by fidgeting, running around when expectations are to sit still, talking excessively, and being unable to engage in leisure activities quietly. Signs of impulsivity in children with ADD or ADHD need to be addressed as well; these impulsive behaviors include blurting out answers before a question is complete, not waiting for their turn, and interrupting others. Before a diagnosis can be made, the symptoms must be present for at least six months and must occur in two separate settings, like the classroom and the home.

Autistic Disorder

According to the *DSM-IV-TR,* autistic disorder consists of impairments in social interaction and communication, and participation in restrictive and repetitive patterns of behavior, interests, and activities. The age of onset for autism is prior to 3 years old, and the cause is not yet clear. One type of autism, known as Asperger's disorder, is marked by impairment in social interaction and restricted repetitive and stereotyped patterns of behavior, interests, and activities. However, Asperger's is separate from autistic disorder because it does not cause a delay in language or cognitive functioning. Psychologists and other professionals continue to debate the causes of, as well as the treatments for, autism.

THERAPIES

Several forms of therapy have been discussed throughout this chapter. Each school of thought comes with a complete therapy schedule that is followed to help treat the various disorders. A few forms of therapy that have not been mentioned thus far are group therapy (one or more therapists work with a small group of people on specific issues), family therapy (a counselor works with the family unit on family issues), couples therapy (a counselor works with a couple on intimate relationship issues), self-help groups (support groups for specific issues), and biomedical therapy (medication therapy with a physician). Each of these forms of therapy works to help people cope with their issues and disorders more effectively.

SUMMARY

This chapter has focused on the psychological disorders, therapies, and treatments that are contained within the *DSM-IV-TR*. Mental illness still has a social stigma regardless of prevalence or acceptability. The theories and practices have evolved over time and continue to show signs of evolution and change.

CASE STUDY #1 WHAT IS ABNORMAL?

Bruce works in an upper-level engineering position at his firm and is considered motivated, intelligent, and well respected by his co-workers. Since he is generally competent, Bruce's friends are often surprised to discover that he can be quite fearful under common circumstances. For instance, during thunderstorms he becomes exceedingly anxious in general, and particularly fearful of any electrical device, including his cell phone.

Bruce is also extremely afraid of airplanes and has never flown in one. When he attended a conference on the West Coast last year, traveling by train cost him an extra two days of travel time. Furthermore, an upcoming international conference being held in Spain seems out of the question. Perhaps the most perplexing is his superstitious fear of the number 13. He refuses to live or work on the 13th floor of a building. Although Bruce is aware that his fears are somewhat irrational, he has no desire to change himself. After all, no one is perfect.

1. Many people become somewhat anxious during thunderstorms, and many people are afraid of flying. However, the level of Bruce's anxiety during these events is uncommon. Discuss what might be causing his fear of flying and of thunderstorms.
2. A fear of the number 13 has considerable precedence in Western society. How would you explain this fear in terms of personality?
3. What is the definition of a phobia? How would you explain Bruce's phobias? How many phobias does he have? How would you treat his phobias?
4. Although Bruce's fears are costly in terms of travel and missed opportunities, overall his life is a successful one. How could his abnormalities cause him to lose this success in the future?
5. What conclusion would you offer about the "normality" of Bruce's behavior? What definitions do you consider most relevant in this case?

CASE STUDY #2 HOUSE FRIGHT

When her alarm clock sounded at seven in the morning, Paris groggily reached over to hit the snooze bar. Cracking her eyes open just enough to see her clock, she was suddenly startled by the image of a strange woman crouching at the side of her bed. Frightened, Paris tried to scream but found that she could not. Then, as suddenly as the vision had appeared, it disappeared.

These morning frights were becoming more and more common for Paris. After a dozen or so scares, she decided to visit a neighborhood counselor, who advertised "free initial consultations." While discussing these experiences with the counselor, Paris was confused when the conversation turned to the history of the house in which she lived. When she inquired about the tangent that they had taken, her counselor explained that he believed that Paris was completely psychologically healthy. The visions, he explained, were probably spirits visiting her from the afterlife. Paris quickly left, surprised at the counselor's bizarre explanation.

1. Are Paris's visions a sign of abnormality? Describe and defend your case.
2. What do you think is going on with Paris's counselor? Where is his opinion of her case coming from?
3. Paris was dissatisfied with her original counselor and went to two additional ones. One diagnosed her as suffering from a form of hallucinations that affects people when they awaken from a dream and images of the dream linger into the wakened state. What type of treatment might this counselor offer to Paris?
4. The third counselor suggested that Paris was probably seeing visions of people from her childhood, a sign that Paris is repressing some traumatic memory. He is fearful that these intrusive visions will become more severe over time. What type of treatment might this counselor offer to Paris?
5. Briefly consider the behavioral and humanistic models of abnormality. What would each suggest about the roots of Paris's visions?

CASE STUDY #3 HOW CRAZY AM I?

Patrick has always been what his parents described "a fearful person." Easily and overly upset by minor incidents, he was called a "crybaby" all throughout elementary school, a "loser" in high school, and "overemotional" by his college peers. Even when things are going well in life, Patrick complains of being unable to relax, as well as being fearful of losing control of his things.

Although Patrick has had these difficulties for as long as he can remember, he was able to deal with them in college. Since he attended a college in his hometown, his family and social network remained in place and helped him cope during these years. However, a tough job market led to his taking a job out of state, and his condition worsened. Although his parents have recently encouraged him to speak to a doctor or counselor about his problem, he has resisted their efforts.

"After all," he tells himself, "I am not crazy."

1. How would the *DSM-IV-TR* diagnose Patrick's condition? To what general type of disorder does this diagnosis belong? What other diagnoses fall under this class of disorders and how do they differ from Patrick's?
2. Patrick's younger brother suffers from the same types of symptoms. How would the medical model of abnormal behavior explain this fact? How would the sociocultural model explain this fact? How would the psychoanalytic model explain this fact?
3. In what sense is Patrick's behavior abnormal? Defend your answer.
4. Patrick is reluctant to get professional help in part because of the stigma of being classified as having a psychological disorder. Discuss how you think being labeled is harmful to a person.
5. What treatment approaches would you take with Patrick to try to help him with his issues?

CASE STUDY #4 IS THIS FOR REAL?

Niya played volleyball ever since she was a child. Her mother had been a standout player in college, and Niya was set to follow in her footsteps. Niya earned a scholarship to the same college where her mother had won respect 30 years earlier.

Although excited about her situation, Niya also experienced anxiety over the prospect of not living up to her mother's expectations. As the season grew nearer, her anxiety grew more acute. Then, while practicing her serve a week before their first match, Niya suddenly noticed that she had no feeling in her hand. The numbness persisted despite medical reports that showed no evidence of any neurological or other physical problems. It looked like Niya was going to miss the first match of her college career and possibly more. The team doctors would not allow her to play while the numbness persisted.

1. How would the *DSM-IV-TR* diagnose Niya's condition? To what general type of disorder does this diagnosis belong?
2. How might the psychoanalytic model of abnormal behavior explain Niya's particular type of paralysis?
3. How might the medical model explain Niya's paralysis? How might the humanistic and cognitive models explain the paralysis?
4. Imagine that you are a therapist and you are aware of Niya's condition. What type of treatment would you recommend to her?
5. Considering the impact on her life that the numbness could have, Niya seems relatively unconcerned about her condition. In what way is her calmness not surprising?

CASE STUDY #5 MOODY MUCH?

Angel is 20 years old and grew up in a middle-class suburban environment. She is the only daughter of second-generation Mexican American parents. Overall, Angel's life has been a happy one. However, when she moved across the country out of her parents' home she began to experience periods of extreme sadness. She missed her family and worried about having to make new friends.

Although Angel's "bad days," as she called them, were infrequent during her first year away from home, her second year was much more difficult. In her first year, her sadness over leaving home was tempered by the excitement of living in a new place. Now that the newness was wearing off, Angel's bad days were becoming more common. Fortunately, Angel's mother began to notice her daughter's symptoms, having gone through the same thing after she gave birth to Angel. She convinced Angel to see a counselor about her bad days.

1. How would the *DSM-IV-TR* diagnose Angel's condition? How does this condition differ from bipolar disorder?
2. The most widely used treatment for Angel's condition is through drug therapy. Does this imply that the root of her problem is biological?
3. Explain why some people become depressed? What evidence suggests a cognitive explanation of depression may be correct?
4. Do you think that Angel's bad days would disappear if she moved back home? Defend your answer.
5. What type of therapy would you recommend to Angel?

CASE STUDY #6 MYSTERY SOLVED!

In 1926 the celebrated English author Agatha Christie disappeared in what was suspected by many to be a kidnapping or murder. After a nationwide search took place, she was discovered staying at a spa in northern England under an assumed name. Many suspected that the whole affair had been a publicity stunt. Agatha Christie's only public explanation was that she could not remember how she came to be where she was.

Today we may be in a better position to understand what really happened to Ms. Christie. A few months before her disappearance, her mother passed away. When her husband refused to involve himself in the matter, she was forced to handle the complicated matter of settling her mother's affairs on her own. If these events were not difficult enough, Ms. Christie was in for a greater shock. Her husband of more than 20 years revealed that he had been having an affair and was leaving her. It was shortly after this revelation that Ms. Christie disappeared.

1. Do the events that preceded Agatha Christie's disappearance make her story about memory loss seem plausible? Why or why not?
2. Assuming that her explanation is correct, how would the *DSM-IV-TR* diagnose her condition? How does dissociative amnesia differ from dissociative fugue? Of the two, which one is more common?
3. How might each of the following models of abnormal behavior explain Agatha Christie's case: psychoanalytic, medical, sociocultural? Which explanation do you prefer? Defend your answer.
4. When asked about how she got to be where she was, Agatha Christie claimed not to remember. Is it common for people who suffer from this disorder to have no memory of such periods?
5. The name under which Agatha Christie registered at the spa was that of her husband's mistress. Is it unusual for people who suffer from this disorder to have memories of the events that triggered their episode?

CASE STUDY #7 HEIGHTENED ANXIETY

Ina has suffered from generalized anxiety disorder for several years. Although she is young, intelligent, and articulate, social settings have always made her uncomfortable. Six months ago she decided to get professional help and has been meeting with a therapist twice a week ever since.

At first she was apprehensive about talking to a stranger about personal issues, but that quickly passed. Ina's relationship with her therapist is as close today as with any friend whom she has ever had. During their sessions, she talks about important events in her life, and the therapist just listens. Then the therapist will ask her about recent dreams she has had, and they try to decode their meaning. For example, Ina frequently dreams of flying; she now realizes that this represents her desire to be financially independent. Ina values these sessions together and feels that she has made great progress in the time that she has been in therapy.

1. What orientation is Ina's therapist? How would you classify the approach that she is using to treat Ina's anxiety?
2. What is the manifest content of Ina's dream described in this story? What is the latent content of Ina's dream?
3. Is it unusual for patients to feel as close to their therapists as Ina does? How can this closeness be beneficial to a therapeutic relationship? In what way can this closeness be harmful?
4. Ina feels that her therapy has been a success. What evidence suggests that this therapy will indeed be successful? Consider both her condition and her personality.
5. How would Ina's therapist describe the cause of her problem? How does the type of therapy described in this story resolve the roots of her anxiety? What assumptions about generalized anxiety disorder is the therapist making?

CASE STUDY #8 LIFE IS MEANINGLESS

Shortly after her youngest daughter, Sage, moved away to college, Darcy began to experience long periods of loneliness and depression. *It's only natural,* she told herself. *It will go away.*

However, over the next few months her bouts of depression only became more frequent and more severe. That was when she decided to seek counseling.

At first her therapist wanted to prescribe an antidepressant medication, but Darcy was uncomfortable with the idea of taking drugs. They decided to take a different approach, and Darcy was instructed to keep a diary of the times that she felt the most depressed. From this diary, she and her therapist discovered that she was most depressed on Saturday and Sunday mornings. When Darcy thought about why this occurred, she realized that it was during this time that she and Sage had spent most of their quality time in recent years. Now these mornings only reminded her that she wasn't needed anymore and that her life was meaningless.

1. What type of therapist is Darcy seeing? Do you feel that therapy will be helpful to Darcy?
2. What approach has her therapist decided to take with Darcy?
3. Now that they have discovered why weekend mornings are so difficult for Darcy, what is the next step? How will her therapist help her overcome her weekend episodes of depression?
4. What type of recommendations would you offer to Darcy to help her with her issues?
5. How effective do you think therapy is in general? Explain your answer.

CASE STUDY #9 WHAT KIND OF THERAPIST WOULD I BE?

Now in his fourth year of graduate school in clinical psychology, Abe has been thinking about what area of the profession he will pursue after graduation. He has developed a strong background in cognitive and behavioral approaches, psychodynamic approaches, and humanistic approaches. However, when he begins his own practice, Abe wants to focus on only one of these approaches.

One issue that concerns Abe is how directive he could be as a therapist. Admittedly, he is not a very forceful person and would be more comfortable as a more nondirective therapist. A second concern is whether he should choose a long-term or short-term style of therapy. Although the idea of the steady, long-term client is appealing, Abe is afraid he might tire of seeing the same clients after a while. For this reason, he would prefer a therapeutic approach that could meet its objectives quickly.

1. On the basis of Abe's desire to practice a short-term, nondirective style of therapy, which of the approaches with which he is familiar should he choose and why?
2. Abe believes that people's behavior is heavily influenced by past experiences. For this reason he prefers a therapy that focuses on early experiences and less on the here and now. Considering this, which style of therapy should he choose? Defend your answer.
3. One of the areas with which Abe is interested in working is phobias. On the basis of your answer to question number one, is it likely that Abe will be able to help people with their simple phobias? If so, how? If not, why?
4. Some therapeutic approaches focus on changing the thoughts, or cognitions, of clients while others focus on changing concrete behaviors. On the basis of your answer to question number one, where will Abe's approach fall on this dimension?
5. Compared with other types of therapies, how effective is the type chosen by Abe (question number one)? What reasons make it hard to answer this question?

CASE STUDY #10 DOES THERAPY MAKE YOU SELF-RELIANT?

Phoebe has been smoking cigarettes since she was 15 years old. Now, at age 30, she would like to quit. After several attempts to quit smoking failed, she has decided to get help and enrolled in a therapy group for people trying to kick an addictive habit. Most people in the group are trying to stop drinking; a few others, smoking; and some, harder drugs.

In Phoebe's weekly meetings with the group, people usually take turns sharing experiences related to their addiction. However, Phoebe usually does not talk very much, feeling that the other group members who are having more difficulty than she is should get more of the group's attention. She does enjoy going regardless of how little she interacts. The therapist is very warm and seems to genuinely care about each member in the group. He tells them that people are responsible for their own behavior and that their addictions are caused by insecurities. By learning to trust themselves, the members are becoming more self-reliant and less dependent on smoking, drugs, and alcohol.

1. What approach is Phoebe's therapist taking? How helpful do you think therapy will be for Phoebe? Explain.
2. How effective do you think group therapy would be when treating addictive behaviors? Are there any drawbacks to this method? Would these drawbacks affect all group members equally?
3. Do you think that offering positive reinforcements is helpful in therapy? Explain.
4. What type of advice would you offer to Phoebe in particular since she is so quiet during all of the group sessions?
5. An important part of Phoebe's group members' therapy sessions every week is acting out the anger that has built up over the week by hitting pillows. Do you think this is an effective treatment?

ACTIVITY #1 DIAGNOSES

Directions: Find the criteria for each axis in the *DSM-IV-TR*. Write down what information you would put on each axis when you are classifying behavior.

Axis I—

Axis II—

Axis III—

Axis IV—

Axis V—

ACTIVITY #2 MENTAL ILLNESS DEFINED

Directions: Choose any four of the following mental illnesses and explain the specific culture, age, and gender features of each disorder. Explain the prevalence of the disorder, the course of the illness, the familial pattern of the illness, and the diagnostic features (symptoms) of each illness. What else could this disorder be (are there other diagnoses that could explain the symptoms)? Then, explain potential courses of treatment for each illness. Is there a cure?

a. Autistic disorder
b. Attention-deficit hyperactivity disorder
c. Dementia
d. Substance dependence
e. Schizophrenia
f. Schizophreniform disorder
g. Schizoaffective disorder
h. Shared psychotic disorder
i. Major depressive disorder
j. Dysthymic disorder
k. Bipolar I disorder
l. Bipolar II disorder
m. Cyclothymic disorder
n. Panic attack
o. Agoraphobia
p. Specific phobia
q. Obsessive-compulsive disorder
r. Posttraumatic stress disorder
s. Generalized anxiety disorder
t. Somatization disorder
u. Conversion disorder
v. Pain disorder
w. Hypochondriasis
x. Body dysmorphic disorder
y. Dissociative amnesia
z. Dissociative fugue
aa. Dissociative identity disorder (formerly multiple personality disorder)
bb. Paraphilias
cc. Gender identity disorders
dd. Intermittent explosive disorder

ACTIVITY #3 PERSONALITY DISORDERS

Directions: Choose any four of the following personality disorders and explain the specific culture, age, and gender features of each disorder. You will explain the prevalence of the disorder, the course of the disorder, the familial pattern of the disorder, and the diagnostic features (symptoms) of each disorder. What else could this disorder be (are there other diagnoses that could explain the symptoms)? Then, explain potential courses of treatment for each disorder. Is there a cure?

a. Paranoid personality disorder
b. Schizoid personality disorder
c. Schizotypal personality disorder
d. Antisocial personality disorder
e. Borderline personality disorder
f. Histrionic personality disorder
g. Narcissistic personality disorder
h. Avoidant personality disorder
i. Dependent personality disorder
j. Obsessive-compulsive personality disorder

ACTIVITY #4 PSYCHOPATHOLOGY

Directions: Choose any psychopathology and define the illness. Explain the symptoms, causes, and treatment of the illness. Also, find a case study of someone with the illness and be able to discuss it with the class. Finally, address whether there is a cure for the illness.

Examples of Some Mental Illnesses

- Schizophrenia
- Dissociative identity disorder
- Bipolar disorder
- Oppositional defiant disorder
- Major depressive disorder
- Alcohol dependence
- Hallucinogen dependence
- Acute stress disorder
- Cyclothymic disorder
- Panic disorder
- Posttraumatic stress disorder (PTSD)
- Brief psychotic disorder

REFERENCES

American Psychiatric Association. (2000). *Diagnostic and statistical manual of mental disorders* (4th ed., text rev.). Washington, DC: Author.

CHAPTER 12

Social Psychology

LEARNING ASSETS

Case Study #1 Advertising That Sells

Case Study #2 Stereotypes

Case Study #3 Dog Bites and Dating

Case Study #4 Call You Later

Case Study #5 Love at First Sight?

Case Study #6 Dating Changes Everything

Case Study #7 Why Is the News So Depressing?

Case Study #8 Who Will Help?

Activity #1 A Good Deed Does Not Go Undone

Activity #2 Culture and Society

WHY IS SOCIAL PSYCHOLOGY DIFFERENT?

Why is social psychology separate from the rest of psychology? It is often an area that is a bit misunderstood. A simplified way to remember the difference is that psychology looks at the individual's cognitions, behaviors, and emotions, whereas social psychology looks at the individual within the group setting, such as society as a whole. This perspective considers how people view others in society and examines real-life behaviors in social settings.

The first published social psychology experiment was conducted in 1898 by Norman Triplett (1861–1931), who was a psychologist at Indiana University. His experiment was centered on the *social facilitation effect* (Strube, 2005). Triplett, who was a bicycle enthusiast, noticed that cyclists tend to have faster times when riding in the presence of other cyclists than when riding alone. He concluded that the "bodily presence of another contestant participating simultaneously in the race serves to liberate latent energy not ordinarily available" (Triplett, 1898, pp. 507–533). This began the journey into social psychological phenomena.

Social psychology starts out with simple observable behaviors and emotions. For example, when you meet new people for the first time, you like some and dislike others. Thus, *impression formation* is a concept that refers to the process of developing your opinion about other people. We also assign *attributions,* why people do what they do, to other people. When two people meet, they are considered the actor and the perceiver in the meeting. The perceiver is the one who forms an impression about the actor. The perceiver brings previous knowledge, attitudes, and values to the meeting. Sometimes an individual (the perceiver) makes a snap judgment when he or she is drawn to or repelled by another person without any real insights into the person's personality.

When we meet people and form impressions, we bring preconceived ideas, stereotypes, prejudices, and personal values into every situation. *Stereotypes* are generalizations or assumptions that people make about the characteristics of all members of that group. These assumptions are based on an image, which is often wrong, about the group in question. *Prejudice* is an implied belief about a group of people that is often formed based on the stereotypes that individuals create. It is commonly seen in the areas of race, gender, age, and religion. Stereotypes and prejudice often lead to *discrimination,* which is the mistreatment of a person or group of people based on the perceived category rather than individual merit.

The *halo effect* is also a contributing factor in the impressions that people form of others. It is how we categorize people into general categories of either good or bad; this is considered a subjective bias about the traits of another person based on one perception of performance. The halo effect was first identified by E. L. Thorndike (1874–1949) and defined as "a problem that arises in data collection when there is carry-over from one judgment to another" (Thorndike, 1920).

ATTRIBUTION THEORY

Attribution theory focuses on the way people explain, or attribute, the behavior of others or themselves. In essence, this is the rationalization of behavior and its consequences. Attribution theory offers internal and external sources of these explanations. Internal attributes are factors within the person, such as intelligence, and external attributes are outside of the person, such as the weather (Heider, 1958).

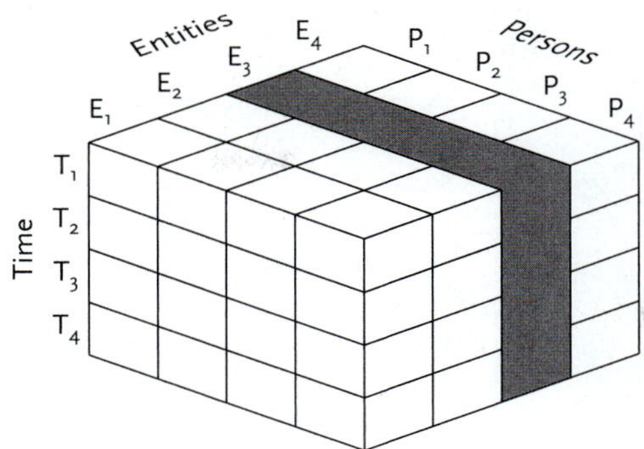

Harold Kelley's covariation model, to explain why people behave in a certain way.

Harold Kelley (1921–2003) created the covariation model, which is an attribution theory in which people make causal inferences to explain why they, as well as other people, behave in a certain way. Kelley (1973) postulated that it has to do with both social perception and self-perception. The covariation principle states that "an effect is attributed to the one of its possible causes with which, over time, it covaries" (Kelley, 1973, p. 108). This means that behavior is attributed to potential causes that appear at the same time.

Biases influence our cognitive processes in regard to internal or external attributes. The *fundamental attribution error,* which is also referred to as *correspondence bias* or *attribution effect,* is a theory that describes the cognitive tendency to overvalue dispositional or personality-based explanations for the observed behaviors of others, therefore undervaluing the potentiality of situational explanations for the behavioral motives of others (Heider, 1958). That is, people typically presume that the actions of others—rather than the kind of situations that motivate their behavior—reflect the kind of individuals they are. In regard to ourselves, we tend to prefer interpreting our own actions in terms of the situational variables accessible to our awareness. This discrepancy is called the *actor-observer bias* and is in direct opposition to the fundamental attribution error (Jones & Nisbett, 1971).

The *Pollyanna principle,* which is sometimes called *positivity bias,* is the tendency for people to agree with positive statements describing themselves. The research shows that our minds have a tendency, at an unconscious level, to focus on the optimistic, while at the conscious level we typically focus on the negative. This principle is based on the Pollyanna archetype, which is a young girl with infectious optimism (Matlin & Stang, 1978).

SOCIAL RELATIONSHIPS

Interpersonal relationships are at the heart of our existence. We form close bonds with some people while remaining mere acquaintances with others. These relationships take on many different forms and have very different meanings in our lives. The concept known as *interpersonal attraction* leads to friendships and romantic relationships, as well as to dislike and hatred of another person. Attraction is when we are drawn to a person, and many factors are at work to create this initial attraction.

For example, attraction can be based on proximity, which is how close two people live to each other. If a person is more accessible, then an individual is more likely to find a relationship attractive and seek a friendship or romance with that person. Attitudes are also

determining factors in attraction. People like other people with positive attitudes and try to avoid those with negative attitudes. However, it is possible for people to seek out others who closely resemble themselves. So, if someone has a poor attitude, then he or she may find comfort in another person with a similar attitude.

Romantic attractions become much more complicated. What is the definition of love? Depending on whom you ask, you will likely receive very different answers. Many people cannot even attempt to define love. Love also has many different forms. There is romantic love, friendship love, love of a pet, love of a relative, and so on. The list can go on and on, but are these types of love the same? Most people would say no.

Romantic love has many different components. The triangular theory of love proposed by Robert Sternberg (1949–) is based on intimacy, passion, and commitment. Sternberg postulates that love can consist of one component alone or any combination of the three parts. Intimacy, according to this theory, encompasses feelings of closeness, connectedness, and bondedness; passion consists of drives that lead to romance, physical attraction, and sexual consummation; commitment consists of the decision to remain with another, and the shared achievement and plans made with that other (Sternberg, 1986).

There are numerous theories on love and attraction. Quantitative and qualitative approaches to love exist as well. Quantitative approaches deal with numerical measurements; by contrast, qualitative approaches deal with how people understand their experiences. The scientific aspect has been applied to the elusive concept of love in order to make sense of it. Biological components as well as many other factors are recognized to determine the scope, degree, and intensity of love relationships.

PROSOCIAL BEHAVIOR

Prosocial behavior is caring about the well-being and rights of others, being concerned, having empathy, and acting in a way that benefits others (Santrock, 2007). Altruism, a type of prosocial behavior that has received a lot of attention, is an unselfish interest in helping another person or group of people. A criticism of altruistic acts is that it is often difficult to assess whether or not someone has something to gain by his or her actions. The gain may not be something that is obvious or immediate, but eventually reveals itself for the person who committed the supposed altruistic act.

Prosocial behavior has many different facets. For example, many people do not act in a prosocial manner on a daily basis, but they will offer something when they feel it is appropriate. A phenomenon that was researched in 1968 by John Darley (1938–) and Bibb Latané (1937–) is known as the *bystander effect*. The bystander effect refers to the circumstance where individuals are less likely to help in an emergency situation when other people are present. The greater the number of bystanders, the less likely it is that anyone will actually help the person in need. Some of the reasons for the bystander effect are the individual's perceived degree of danger, embarrassment, and a feeling of not being able to help the situation. In addition, a feeling of shared responsibility exists within a group. and many people think that someone else has taken the responsibility to help the person. Sadly, it is usually an erroneous thought process, and help is not forthcoming.

AGGRESSION

Aggression is an interesting phenomenon that can be defined as an inclination to engage in behaviors that cause intentional physical and emotional harm to others. Two broad types of aggression have been identified by social psychologists: hostile aggression and instrumental aggression. Hostile aggression presents itself as a direct result of rage or anger. Instrumental aggression occurs when a person has a certain goal in mind and the aggression helps the individual to achieve this goal. For example, instrumental aggression can be seen when someone is predatory and tries to take something away from his or her victim.

Aggression in humans is very culturally driven. Factors that contribute to the different aggression responses are culture, morals, and social situations. Each culture offers acceptable behaviors and posturing that may set it apart from another culture. Behaviors may be misinterpreted by one culture that are completely acceptable in another. There are also gender differences in regard to aggression. Males are typically more physically aggressive than females and commit higher incidences of murder. However, as times change, so do the statistics and incidences of aggression.

Sigmund Freud (1856–1939) created an instinct theory of aggression that has remained quite popular in this arena. As discussed in Chapter 7, Freud believed that humans were driven by conflicting central desires: the life instinct (Eros) and the death instinct (Thanatos). The life instinct, Eros, consists of such things as survival, hunger, thirst, sex, and propagation. The death instinct, Thanatos, consists of wishing to return to a state of calm or a dead state. Therefore, Freud proposed in his theory of aggression, given the existence of the preceding instincts, aggression is innate. In other words, according to Freud, it is natural and necessary for these instincts to exist and thrive, which leads to aggression. Since aggression cannot be eliminated, it must be controlled.

The frustration-aggression theory holds that frustration leads to aggressive behavior; that is, if a goal is unobtainable, then the aggressor becomes frustrated and will likely resort to aggressive behaviors. The target of the aggression may be displaced, but it occurs nonetheless.

However, frustration does not always lead to aggression. People who have learned solid coping mechanisms will not resort to aggressive acts. The original hypothesis of the frustration-aggression theory stated otherwise, but components of the social learning theory replaced that ideology. Social learning theory states that, within the social environment, people behave in the way that they have been taught to behave by observing others. So, if they have witnessed people who handle situations well, then they behave well, and if not, then they do not.

PERSUASION

Persuasion is a form of social influence. It is a means to guide people to adopt an idea, attitude, action, or reaction of another. Individuals are constantly being persuaded to do all sorts of things. For example, when you watch a commercial, you are being persuaded to buy something that you supposedly cannot live without.

Persuasion is a relatively simple process with four basic identified parts: the source or persuader, goals, messages, and an audience. The persuader wants something that he or she does not already have; goals are what persuaders seek to obtain; messages are directed to the audience to help achieve the goal of obtaining the object; and, finally, the audience is made up of people who can help the persuader obtain his or her goal. The role of persuasion is a process that must take place in order for it to be effective.

OBEDIENCE, CONFORMITY, AND COMPLIANCE

Another concept in social psychology that draws a lot of interest is that of obedience. Obedience is the act of carrying out commands and should not be confused with conformity (behavior intended to match that of the majority) or compliance (behavior influenced by peers). Two major experiments have outlined the nature and extent of obedience. The first is the Milgram experiment. Initially carried out in 1961, the Milgram experiment showed that, contrary to expectations, people would obey orders that involved harming another human being.

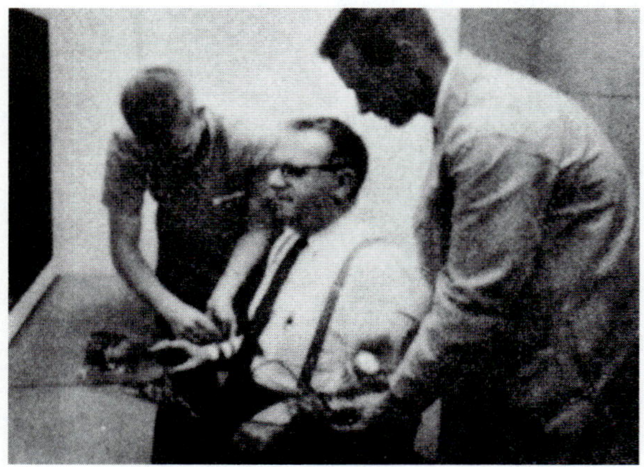

Stanley Milgram's famous experiment caused a lot of controversy regarding ethics in psychology.

The second experiment that demonstrated the concept of obedience is the Stanford Prison experiment, which was conducted in 1971 and led by psychology professor Philip Zimbardo (1933–). Twenty-four students were selected to play the roles of both guards and prisoners and live in a mock prison in the basement of the Stanford psychology building. The prisoners and guards adjusted to their new roles rather quickly, and the students playing guards exhibited sadistic tendencies while the students playing prisoners became emotionally traumatized.

GROUP PROCESSING

Group work is often a daunting task that is not enjoyed by individuals. Many people do not like having to rely on others for their work. However, in our society we have to depend on others for quite a bit of material. So working in groups and being a team player have become quite important in educational settings as well as career settings. Group work does have some pitfalls, however, which lends credence to the objections of those who do not like to work in groups. The phenomenon known as *groupthink* is one problematic concept that often interferes with progress. Groupthink, coined by William H. Whyte (1917–1999) in 1952 for a *Fortune* magazine article, is a type of thought exhibited by group members who try to reduce conflict and reach consensus without testing, analyzing, or evaluating ideas (Whyte, 1989). The group just tries to come to a conclusion without any real creativity or even proof of good research.

The process known as *brainstorming* has received a lot of attention as well in the career market. Brainstorming is a problem-solving technique that allows members of a group to express their ideas on a particular topic. This strategy may create a lot of solid ideas as well as many ideas that need to be scrapped. Once the brainstorming session is complete, then it is up to the group to go through the ideas and weed out the ones that are inconceivable and maintain the ideas that may lead to productivity.

SUMMARY

Social psychology is a large field that looks at the individual within the group setting. Many intricacies are involved in interpersonal relationships and endeavors. The key to social psychology is paying attention to the group interactions, dynamics, and behaviors that arise.

CASE STUDY #1 ADVERTISING THAT SELLS

After receiving her bachelor's degree in behavioral psychology last year, Melinda found employment in a small advertising firm in St. Louis. One of her first assignments was to come up with an idea for a television ad campaign for Softie, a new brand of fabric detergent. Although Softie is a new product, it does not contain any special quality that separates it from competing brands. The makers of Softie plan to price their product so that it is competitive with, but not substantially cheaper than, other major brands. Taking all of this into account, Melinda decides to design her campaign around a slogan that is catchy but relatively weak. Two of her ideas are: "There's clean and then there's Softie," or "When something is really clean, you call it Softie."

1. Which "route" to persuasion is Melinda attempting to use? What are the liabilities of using such an approach?
2. What characteristics will be most important in Melinda's ad?
3. Unfortunately, the amount of money that Softie is willing to spend on this campaign is limited. Due to this limited budget, Melinda decides to use an attractive but unknown model in her commercial. Is her decision a good one? Why or why not?
4. After further thought, Melinda changes her mind and decides to include strong statements about why Softie is superior to competing products. In addition, she is considering using a well-known spokesperson to deliver these arguments. Would changing spokespersons be a good idea? Defend your answer.
5. Is there any reason to believe that one of the two tentative slogans would work better than the other? Defend your answer.

CASE STUDY #2 STEREOTYPES

Parks, a Hispanic student at a private college, is enrolled in a large introductory psychology course taught by Dr. Emmett. When the last of four "critical thinking" papers was handed back, Parks was surprised and disappointed to find that he had received a B–. He had spent a fair amount of time and effort preparing his paper. After rereading the paper and the comments made by the professor, Parks still believed that the paper deserved an A. A friend who had taken the class before encouraged him to see his professor, explaining that Dr. Emmett was basically a warm and approachable person.

Parks met with his professor and began to explain why he believed that he deserved a higher grade. Almost immediately Dr. Emmett interrupted him and agreed to raise the grade to an A.

1. How might Parks's belief in Dr. Emmett's warm character have affected this particular interaction? Would Parks's impression of the interaction have been different had he expected Dr. Emmett to be a cold person? Defend your answer.
2. Dr. Emmett holds no negative stereotypes of Hispanics. Is it still possible that his grading of Parks's paper was discriminatory? Why or why not?
3. Why might Parks feel unsatisfied after having his grade raised? What negative consequences might result from his experience with Dr. Emmett?
4. Assume that Dr. Emmett believes that as a group Hispanics are less prepared for college-level work than Anglo students. Is it likely that interaction with well-prepared students such as Parks would change his negative belief? Explain.
5. How do stereotypes affect people's behavior? Give specific examples.

CASE STUDY #3 DOG BITES AND DATING

Carly would have been on time for her date, but Frank arrived early. The sound of the doorbell set off the usual series of sharp barks from her puppy, Snuffy. After calming Snuffy down, Carly went to get her jacket from her bedroom, but the jacket was not where she remembered putting it. This annoyance at not being able to find her jacket was heightened by a return of Snuffy's barks in the other room. With exaggerated steps Carly stamped back into the living room and began yelling for Snuffy to be quiet. To this day Carly is not sure whether the scene she walked in on was more funny or sad. Upon returning to the living room area, Carly was startled to find Frank holding Snuffy and biting her dog on the leg!

1. According to Kelley's attributional model, what questions would be running through Carly's mind?
2. Suppose that Carly recalls that Frank has done this before. According to Kelley's model, would this suggest a dispositional cause or a situational cause of Frank's behavior? Do you agree?
3. How might the Pollyanna effect influence Carly's attributions in this situation? Is the halo effect likely to factor into her decision?
4. According to the fundamental attribution bias, is Carly likely to blame Frank for this ugly incident? What explanations for the incident is Frank likely to give?
5. Imagine that this is Carly's first date with Frank and that she just purchased Snuffy that afternoon. What prediction would Kelley's model make about her attributions for this event? Do you view this prediction as a weakness in Kelley's model?

CASE STUDY #4 CALL YOU LATER

In addition to taking 12 hours of courses this semester, Steve is holding down a part-time job delivering pizzas on weekends and occasionally on weekday evenings. One recent Sunday evening, Steve arrived home after an exhausting eight hours at work. Steve checked his voice mail and found that he had three messages. Being very tired and not feeling like talking to anyone, Steve decided to listen to the messages but not return any calls until the morning unless they were important. The third message was from Eugene, a guy in Steve's math class that he only knew casually. Eugene was apparently having difficulty with an assignment that was due in the morning and was hoping to discuss it tonight. After turning the television on and flipping through a few channels, Steve fell asleep on the couch without returning any of his missed phone calls.

1. Based on your knowledge of attribution theory, what reasons would Steve give for his not returning Eugene's call? What reasons would Eugene postulate for Steve's behavior?
2. According to self-perception theory, how might this event affect Steve's friendship with Eugene?
3. Actually, Steve himself has not yet completed the assignment. Although math assignments usually require considerable time and effort, Steve believes that he will be able to finish it quickly in the morning. Is such overconfidence a sign of poor or good psychological health?
4. Imagine that Steve is a Japanese student. How might this cultural difference have contributed to his decision not to return Eugene's call?
5. In what way is self-perception theory in conflict with attribution theory in predicting how Steve will explain his own behavior? Can both theories be correct?

CASE STUDY #5 LOVE AT FIRST SIGHT?

Susan and Bo got married this summer. At the wedding Susan's father recalled aloud how often he had heard her say that a good man was hard to find, that the combination of qualities she was looking for just didn't seem to exist. Alas, along came Bo.

It was hardly love at first sight for Susan. She and two friends were moving out of their apartment and were looking for a fourth person to fill a four-bedroom house they had rented in the city. When Bo showed up to apply for the room, Susan hesitantly conceded that he would be an acceptable roommate. By the end of the first month in the house, Susan and Bo were happily dating, and two years later they were married.

1. Susan's father thought that it was ironic that, after looking everywhere for a perfect match, she met her future husband right in her own home. Would social psychologists find this so ironic? Why or why not?
2. When asked why she decided to marry Bo, Susan said that she just fell in love with the things that he did. She liked the way he always sang too loud in the shower, how he styled his hair, even his unique walk, which was the result of an old knee injury. Although she thought these qualities were slightly odd at first, now she couldn't imagine loving someone without them. What psychological phenomenon is operating here?
3. Bo never heard that Susan found him a barely acceptable roommate upon their first meeting until after they had been dating for nearly a year. If this had been revealed earlier, how might it have affected their relationship?
4. When Susan moved into the house, she moved in with her current roommate from the apartment and a friend of theirs who lived next door. Is her choice of housemates a coincidence or are some psychological factors at work here?
5. According to Bo, his decision to date Susan had less to do with how attractive she was and more to do with her personality. Susan just seemed like a really good person. Assuming that Bo is correct about his reasons, is it possible that her physical attractiveness still influenced his decision? Explain your answer.

CASE STUDY #6 DATING CHANGES EVERYTHING

Gary and Dawn met during a work conference on increasing performance in the workplace. Since they do not work for the same company or in the same city, they attend this workshop as a way to bring ideas back to their human resource department. When Gary and Dawn met the first year, they were both in committed relationships with other people. However, they became fast friends.

A year later both returned to the conference unattached. Although neither of them had thought about dating each other the previous year, they now experienced pangs of attraction for each other. Hesitant at first that dating might damage their valued friendship, they decided to give it a chance. They have been going out for over a year now.

1. Work-related conferences can be a very stressful experience. How might this have affected the attraction that Gary and Dawn felt for each other?
2. The first year Gary and Dawn knew each other, they told their friends that they liked each other very much. A year later, they told their friends that they loved each other. According to the dominant school of thought in love research, what had changed about their feelings for each other? Did their feelings change qualitatively or quantitatively?
3. According to Robert Sternberg's triangle theory of love, what component of love characterizes the liking that friends feel for each other?
4. When Gary and Dawn decided to commit themselves to a relationship, what component was added? What type of love did this create?
5. Consider a statement that Gary made about Dawn to a close friend: "Dawn has her share of faults, but overall they are pretty small compared to her strengths." Is this comment characteristic of a relationship that is just beginning, is mature and successful, or one that is mature and beginning to deteriorate? Explain your answer.

CASE STUDY #7 WHY IS THE NEWS SO DEPRESSING?

Olivia is considering giving up her subscription to the newspaper. All of the violence and tragedy in the world, and even in her community, is getting to be too depressing. For example, in today's edition there is a front-page article about terrorist attacks overseas detonating a car bomb near a night club frequented by local college students. The terrorists claim that the bombing is in response to a recent attack on their headquarters.

Closer to home, the city council has cut funds to schools in order to try to compensate for budget cuts. As a result, teachers will be fired and programs will be cut. Also slated for cutting is the animal shelter, which will no longer hold for adoption dogs or cats that are more than a year old. Older animals, which are not adopted as quickly, will be destroyed after being held one day.

1. Which of the acts mentioned above do you feel constitutes aggression?
2. Some psychologists define aggression as "intentionally hurting another person." According to this definition, which of the preceding acts described would constitute aggression?
3. Is there a difference between doing something in order to hurt someone and doing something that you are not sure will hurt someone but you do it anyway? How does this relate to the preceding scenarios?
4. According to the instinct theory of aggression, why are humans aggressive? If psychologists wanted to reduce the amount of violence in their community, what type of programs would instinct theory suggest they implement?
5. How do frustration-aggression theorists explain the situation that is going on overseas? What types of programs would psychologists from this school of thought implement to reduce the hostility overseas?

CASE STUDY #8 WHO WILL HELP?

The doctors told Mr. Saboa that he was a lucky man because for many people the first heart attack is their last. However, it was a little hard for him to feel lucky just now. Then again, he had to admit that things could have been much worse if it hadn't been for the assistance of two legal secretaries.

Mr. Saboa had been coming home from work much later than usual when he began to feel unusual sensations. His arms began to grow numb and he felt light-headed and dizzy, Mr. Saboa asked aloud if someone could help him. Taken aback, no one on the commuter train knew what to do. Becoming more forceful, Mr. Saboa pointed to a woman nearby and said, "You! Can you help me? I think I'm having a heart attack." She immediately came over to help, and someone else called 911.

1. At first no one knew how to react to Mr. Saboa's request for aid. What psychological phenomenon may have prevented these bystanders from taking action? How did Mr. Saboa's second request overcome this obstacle?
2. Although it was difficult to get the first person to help him, she was quickly followed by another person. How did the first helper's behavior influence that of the second?
3. To those who viewed Mr. Saboa's heart attack, two questions must have gone through their minds: *Does this man need help?* and *If so, should I be the one to help?* What psychological phenomena make these two questions difficult for the bystanders to answer?
4. According to learning theorists, would those who witnessed Mr. Saboa's heart attack, but did not help, be likely to give help if they were in this type of situation again?
5. What would moral reasoning theorists, such as Kohlberg, say about these inactive bystanders and the likelihood that they would help in other similar situations?

ACTIVITY #1 A GOOD DEED DOES NOT GO UNDONE

Directions: Your assignment is to perform an altruistic act for another person. Remember the definition of altruism before you complete this task. Next, you will need to write down your altruistic deed, the results, how it made you feel, and whether or not it was worth it to you after it was complete.

ACTIVITY #2 CULTURE AND SOCIETY

Directions: Research a culture that is not your own and write about the following customs:

1. Foods eaten
2. Rituals performed
3. Weddings
4. Funerals
5. Guests

REFERENCES

Darley, J. M., & Latané, B. (1968). Bystander intervention in emergencies: Diffusion of responsibility. *Journal of Personality and Social Psychology, 8,* 377–383.

Heider, Fritz. (1958). *The psychology of interpersonal relations.* New York: John Wiley & Sons.

Jones, E. E., & Nisbett, R. E. (1971). *The actor and the observer: Divergent perceptions of the causes of behavior.* New York: General Learning Press.

Kelley, H. H. (1973). The process of causal attribution. *American Psychologist, 28*(2), 107–128.

Matlin, M. W., & Stang, D. J. (1978). *The Pollyanna principle: Selectivity in language, memory, and thought.* New York: Schenkman.

Santrock, J. W. (2007). A *topical approach to life-span development.* New York: McGraw-Hill.

Sternberg, R. J. (1986). A triangular theory of love. *Psychological Review, 93*(2), 119–135.

Strube, M. J. (2005). What did Triplett really find? A contemporary analysis of the first experiment in social psychology. *American Journal of Psychology, 118,* 271–286.

Thorndike, E. L. (1920). A constant error on psychological rating. *Journal of Applied Psychology, 4,* 25–29.

Triplett, N. (1898). The dynamogenic factors in pacemaking and competition. *American Journal of Psychology, 9,* 507–533.

Whyte, G. (1989). Groupthink reconsidered. *The Academy of Management Review, 14*(1), 40–56.

GLOSSARY

A

abnormal behavior Behavior that causes people to experience distress (hardship) and prevents them from functioning in their daily lives

absolute threshold The smallest intensity (force) of a stimulus (see glossary definition) that must be present for the stimulus to be detected

achievement test A test designed to determine a person's level of knowledge in a given subject area

action potential An electric nerve impulse (stimulation) that travels through a neuron (see glossary definition) (nerve cell) when it is set off by a "trigger," changing the neuron's charge from negative to positive

activation-synthesis theory J. Allan Hobson's theory that the brain produces random (no pattern) electrical energy during REM (rapid eye movement) sleep that stimulates memories lodged in various portions of the brain

activity theory of aging A theory (proposition or idea) that suggests that the elderly who are more successful while aging are those who maintain the interests and activities they had during middle age

adaptation An adjustment in sensory capacity (space or room) after prolonged exposure to unchanging stimuli (see glossary definition)

addictive drugs Drugs that produce a biological or psychological dependence (reliance) in the user so that withdrawal from them leads to a craving for the drug that, in some cases, may be nearly irresistible

adolescence The developmental (growth) stage between childhood and adulthood

age of viability The point at which a fetus (see glossary definition) (developing human) can survive if born prematurely (early)

aggression The intentional (on purpose) injury of, or harm to, another person

algorithm A rule that, if applied appropriately (properly), guarantees a solution to a problem

all-or-none law The rule that neurons (see glossary definition) are either on or off

altruism Helping behavior that is beneficial to others but clearly requires self-sacrifice

Alzheimer's disease An illness characterized in part by severe memory problems; a progressive (advancing) brain disorder that leads to a gradual and irreversible (not reversible) decline in cognitive (thinking) abilities

amnesia Memory loss that occurs without other mental difficulties

anal stage According to Sigmund Freud, a stage from age 12–18 months to 3 years of age, in which a child's pleasure is centered on the anus

androgens Male sex hormones secreted by the testes (testicles)

anorexia nervosa A severe eating disorder in which people may refuse to eat while denying that their behavior and appearance—which can become skeleton-like—are unusual

anterograde amnesia Amnesia in which memory is lost for events that follow an injury

antianxiety drugs Drugs that reduce the level of anxiety (unease, nervousness) a person experiences, essentially (basically) by reducing excitability (the ability to be easily stimulated) and increasing feelings of well-being

antidepressant drugs Medications that improve a severely depressed patient's mood and feeling of well-being

antipsychotic drugs Drugs that temporarily reduce psychotic (loss of reality) symptoms such as agitation, hallucinations (false perception), and delusions (false belief)

antisocial personality disorder A disorder (illness) in which individuals show no regard for the moral and ethical rules of society or the rights of others

anxiety disorder The occurrence (happening) of anxiety (unease, nervousness) without an obvious external cause, affecting daily functioning

aptitude test A test designed to predict a person's ability in a particular area or line of work

archetypes According to Carl Jung, universal symbolic representations (images) of a particular person, object, or experience (such as good and evil)

archival research Research in which existing data (information), such as census documents, college records, and newspaper clippings, are examined to test a hypothesis

arousal approaches to motivation The belief that we try to maintain certain levels of stimulation and activity, increasing or reducing them as necessary

association areas One of the major regions of the cerebral cortex (see glossary definition); the site of the higher mental processes, such as thought, language, memory, and speech

assumed-similarity bias The tendency to think of people as being similar to oneself, even when meeting them for the first time

attachment The positive emotional bond that develops between a child and a particular individual

attention-deficit hyperactivity disorder (ADHD) A disorder (illness) marked by inattention, impulsiveness (acting on urges), a low tolerance for frustration, and a great deal of inappropriate (improper) activity

attitudes Evaluations of a particular person, behavior, belief, or concept

attribution theory The theory of personality (see glossary definition) that seeks to explain how we decide, on the basis of samples of an individual's behavior, what the specific causes of that person's behavior are

authoritarian parents Parents who are rigid and punitive (disciplinary) and value unquestioning obedience from their children

authoritative parents Parents who are firm, set clear limits, reason with their children, and explain things to them

autobiographical memories Our recollections of circumstances and episodes (events) from our own lives

autonomic division The part of the peripheral nervous system (see glossary definition) that controls involuntary movement of the heart, glands, lungs, and other organs

autonomy-versus-shame-and-doubt stage The period which, according to Erik Erikson, toddlers (ages 1½ to 3 years) develop independence and autonomy (self-rule) if exploration and freedom are encouraged, or shame and self-doubt if they are restricted and overprotected

aversive conditioning A form of therapy that reduces the frequency of undesired behavior by pairing an aversive (disliked), unpleasant stimulus (see glossary definition) with undesired behavior

axon The part of the neuron (see glossary definition) that carries messages destined for other neurons

B

babble Meaningless speechlike sounds made by children from around the age of 3 months through 1 year

background stressors ("daily hassles") Everyday annoyances, such as being stuck in traffic, that cause minor irritations and may have long-term ill effects if they continue or are compounded by other stressful events

basilar membrane A vibrating structure that runs through the center of the cochlea (see glossary definition), dividing it into an upper chamber and a lower chamber and containing sense receptors (receivers) for sound

behavior modification A formalized (formal) technique for promoting the frequency (occurrence) of desirable behaviors and decreasing the incidence (rate) of unwanted ones

behavioral assessment Direct measures of an individual's behavior used to describe personality (see glossary definition) characteristics

behavioral genetics The study of the effects of heredity (inherited traits) on behavior

behavioral neuroscientists (or biopsychologists) Psychologists who specialize in considering the ways in which the biological structures and functions of the body affect behavior

behavioral perspective The approach that suggests that observable, measurable behavior should be the focus of study

behavioral perspective on psychological disorders The perspective (view) that looks at the behavior itself as the problem

behavioral treatment approaches Treatment approaches that build on the basic processes of learning, such as reinforcement (see glossary definition) and extinction (see glossary definition) , and assume that normal and abnormal (unusual) behavior are both learned

biofeedback A procedure in which a person learns to control, through conscious thought, some internal physiological processes such as blood pressure, heart and respiration rate, skin temperature, sweating, and the constriction (tightening) of particular muscles

biological and evolutionary approaches to personality Theories that suggest that important components (parts) of personality (see glossary definition) are inherited

biomedical therapy Therapy that relies on drugs and other medical procedures to improve psychological functioning

biopsychologists *See* behavioral neuroscientists

bipolar disorder A disorder (illness) in which a person alternates between periods of euphoric (elated, joyous) feelings of mania (excitement, intensity) and periods of depression

bisexuals Persons who are sexually attracted to people of the same sex and the other sex

borderline personality disorder A disorder (illness) in which individuals have difficulty developing a secure sense of who they are

bottom-up processing A perception that consists of the progression of recognizing and processing information from individual components (parts) of a stimulus or stimuli and moving to the perception (see glossary definition) of the whole

bulimia An eating disorder (illness) in which a person binges (gorges) on incredibly (exceedingly) large quantities of food

C

Cannon-Bard theory of emotion The belief that both physiological arousal and emotional experience are produced simultaneously (at the same time) by the same nerve stimulus (see glossary definition)

case study An in-depth, intensive investigation of an individual or small group of people

cataclysmic events Strong stressors that occur suddenly, affecting many people at once (e.g., natural disasters)

catharsis The process of discharging built-up aggressive (hostile) energy

central core The "old brain," which controls basic functions such as eating and sleeping and is common to all vertebrates

central nervous system (CNS) The part of the nervous system that includes the brain and spinal cord

central route processing Message interpretation characterized by thoughtful consideration of the issues and arguments used to persuade

central traits The major traits considered in forming impressions of others

cerebellum The part of the brain that controls bodily balance

cerebral cortex The "new brain," responsible for the most sophisticated information processing in the brain; contains four lobes

chromosomes Rod-shaped structures that contain all basic hereditary (inherited) information

chunk A meaningful grouping of stimuli that can be stored as a unit in short-term memory

circadian rhythms Biological processes that occur regularly on approximately a 24-hour cycle

classical conditioning A type of learning in which a neutral stimulus (see glossary definition) comes to bring about a response after it is paired with a stimulus that naturally brings about that response

cochlea A coiled tube in the ear filled with fluid that vibrates in response to sound

cognitive approaches to motivation Theories suggesting that motivation is a product of people's thoughts and expectations—their cognitions

cognitive-behavioral approach A treatment approach that incorporates basic principles of learning to change the way people think

cognitive development The process by which a child's understanding of the world changes as a function (role) of age and experience

cognitive dissonance The conflict that occurs when a person holds two contradictory (different) attitudes or thoughts (referred to as *cognitions*)

cognitive learning theory An approach to the study of learning that focuses on the thought processes that underlie learning

cognitive perspective on psychological disorders The perspective (view) that suggests that people's thoughts and beliefs are a central component (part) of abnormal (irregular) behavior

cognitive psychology The branch of psychology that focuses on the study of higher mental processes, including thinking, language, memory, problem solving, knowing, reasoning, judging, and decision making

cognitive treatment approaches Treatment approaches that teach people to think in more adaptive (different) ways by changing their dysfunctional (improper) cognitions (thoughts) about the world and themselves

collective unconscious According to Carl Jung, a common set of ideas, feelings, images, and symbols that we inherit from our ancestors, the whole human race, and even nonhuman ancestors from the distant past

community psychology A branch of psychology that focuses on the prevention and minimization (making smaller) of psychological disorders (illnesses) in the community

companionate love The strong affection we have for those with whom our lives are deeply involved

compliance Behavior that occurs in response to direct social pressure

compulsion An irresistible urge to carry out some act that seems strange or unreasonable

concepts Categorizations (organization) of objects, events, or people that share common properties

concrete operational stage According to Jean Piaget, the period from 7 to 12 years of age that is characterized by logical (rational) thought and a loss of egocentrism (selfishness)

conditioned response (CR) A response (reaction) that, after conditioning, follows a previously (until that time) neutral stimulus (see glossary definition) (e.g., salivation at the ringing of a bell)

conditioned stimulus (CS) A once-neutral stimulus (see glossary definition) that has been paired with an unconditioned stimulus (see glossary definition) to bring about a response formerly caused only by the unconditioned stimulus

cones Cone-shaped, light-sensitive receptor (receiving) cells in the retina (see glossary definition) that are responsible for sharp focus and color perception (see glossary definition), particularly in bright light

confirmation bias The tendency to favor information that supports one's initial hypotheses (see glossary definition) and ignore contradictory (conflicting) information that supports alternative hypotheses or solutions

conformity A change in behavior or attitudes brought about by a desire to follow the beliefs or standards of other people

consciousness The awareness of sensations, thoughts, and feelings being experienced at a given moment

constructive processes Processes in which memories are influenced by the meaning we give to events

continuous reinforcement schedule Reinforcement (see glossary definition) of a behavior every time it occurs

control group A group participating in an experiment that receives no treatment

convergent thinking The ability to produce responses that are based primarily on knowledge and logic

conversion disorder A major somatoform disorder (see glossary definition) that involves an actual physical disturbance (trouble), such as the inability to use a sensory (sense) organ or the complete or partial inability to move an arm or a leg

coping The efforts to control, reduce, or learn to tolerate (handle) the threats that lead to stress

correlational research Research in which the relationship between two sets of variables is examined to determine whether they are associated, or "correlated"

creativity The ability to generate (create) original ideas or solve problems in novel ways

cross-sectional research A research method that compares people of different ages at the same point in time

crystallized intelligence The accumulation (gathering) of information, skills, and strategies that are learned through experience and can be applied in problem-solving situations

cue-dependent forgetting Forgetting that occurs when there are insufficient (not enough) retrieval (recovery) cues to rekindle information that is in memory

culture-fair IQ test A test that does not discriminate (show favoritism) against the members of any minority group

D

daily hassles *See* background stressors

daydreams Fantasies that people construct while awake

decay The loss of information in memory through its nonuse

declarative memory Memory for factual information: names, faces, dates, and the like

defense mechanisms In Freudian theory, unconscious (see glossary definition) strategies (plans or ideas) that people use to reduce anxiety (unease, nervousness) by concealing (hiding or masking) the source of the anxiety (see glossary definition) from themselves and others

deinstitutionalization The transfer of former mental patients from institutions (places of care, hospitals) to the community

dendrite A cluster of fibers at one end of a neuron (see glossary definition) that receive messages from other neurons

dependent variable The variable (see glossary definition) that is measured and is expected to change as a result of changes caused by the experimenter's manipulation (handling) of the independent variable

depressants Drugs that slow down the nervous system

depth perception The ability to view the world in three dimensions (lifelike aspects) and to perceive distance

descriptive research An approach to research designed to systematically (scientifically) investigate a person, group, or patterns of behavior

determinism The idea that people's behavior is produced primarily (mainly) by factors outside of their willful control

developmental psychology The branch of psychology that studies the patterns of growth and change that occur throughout life

Diagnostic and Statistical Manual of Mental Disorders, Fourth Edition, Text Revision (DSM-IV-TR) A system, devised (created) by the American Psychiatric Association, used by most professionals to diagnose and classify abnormal (unusual) behavior

dialectical behavior therapy A form of treatment in which the focus is on getting people to accept who they are, regardless of whether it matches their ideal

difference threshold (just noticeable difference) The smallest level of added or reduced stimulation (stimulus) required to sense that a change in stimulation has occurred

diffusion of responsibility The tendency for people to feel that responsibility for acting is shared, or diffused (spread), among those present

discrimination Behavior directed toward individuals on the basis of their membership in a particular group

disengagement theory of aging A theory that suggests that aging produces a gradual withdrawal from the world on physical, psychological, and social levels

dispositional causes (of behavior) Perceived (seeming) causes of behavior that are based on internal traits or personality (see glossary definition) factors

dissociative amnesia A disorder (illness) in which a significant (major) selective memory loss occurs

dissociative disorders Psychological dysfunctions (disturbances) characterized by the separation of critical personality (see glossary definition) facets that are normally integrated (combined), allowing stress avoidance through escape

dissociative fugue A form of amnesia in which the individual leaves home and sometimes assumes a new identity

dissociative identity disorder (or multiple personality disorder) A disorder (illness) in which a person displays (shows) characteristics (features) of two or more distinct (separate) personalities

divergent thinking The ability to generate unusual, yet nonetheless appropriate (proper), responses to problems or questions

double standard The view that premarital sex is permissible (acceptable) for males but not for females

dreams-for-survival theory The theory suggesting that dreams permit information that is critical for our daily survival to be reconsidered and reprocessed (rethought) during sleep

drive Motivational tension, or arousal, that energizes (activates) behavior to fulfill a need

drive-reduction approaches to motivation Theories suggesting that a lack of a basic biological requirement such as water produces a drive to obtain that requirement (in this case, the thirst drive)

drug therapy Control of psychological disorders (illnesses) through the use of drugs

E

eardrum The part of the ear that vibrates when sound hits it

eclectic approach to therapy An approach to therapy that uses techniques taken from a variety of treatment methods, rather than just one

ego The part of the personality (see glossary definition) that provides a buffer (cushion) between the id and the outside world

egocentric thought A way of thinking in which a child views the world entirely from his or her own perspective (point of view)

ego-integrity-versus-despair stage According to Erik Erikson, a period from late adulthood until death during which we review life's accomplishments and failures

electroconvulsive therapy (ECT) A procedure in which an electric current of 70 to 150 volts is briefly administered (applied) to a patient's head, causing a loss of consciousness and, often, seizures

embryo A developed zygote (see glossary definition) that has a heart, a brain, and other organs

emotional intelligence The set of skills that underlie the accurate assessment, evaluation, expression, and regulation of emotions

emotions Feelings that generally have both physiological (physical) and cognitive (thinking, processing) elements and that influence behavior

endocrine system A chemical communication network that sends messages throughout the body via the bloodstream

episodic memory Memory for events that occur in a particular time, place, or context

estrogens A class of female sex hormones

evolutionary psychology The branch of psychology that seeks to identify behavior patterns that are a result of our genetic inheritance from our ancestors

excitatory message A chemical message that makes it more likely that a receiving neuron (see glossary definition) will fire and an action potential will travel down its axon (see glossary definition)

experiment The investigation of the relationship between two (or more) variables (see glossary definition) by deliberately (on purpose) producing a change in one variable in a situation and observing the effects of that change on other aspects of the situation

experimental bias Factors that distort (alter) how the independent variable affects the dependent variable in an experiment

experimental group Any group participating in an experiment (see glossary definition) that receives a treatment

experimental manipulation The change that an experimenter deliberately (on purpose) produces in a situation

explicit memory Intentional or conscious recollection (remembering) of information

extinction A basic phenomenon (event, incident) of learning that occurs when a previously conditioned response (see glossary definition) decreases in frequency and eventually disappears

extramarital sex Sexual activity between a married person and someone who is not his or her spouse

F

familial retardation Mental retardation in which no apparent biological defect exists, but there is a history of retardation in the family

family therapy An approach that focuses on the family and its dynamics (relationships)

feature analysis An approach to perception (see glossary definition) suggesting that we perceive (see) a shape, pattern, object, or scene through the reaction of specific neurons (see glossary definition) to the individual elements that make up the stimulus (see glossary definition)

feature detection The activation (turn on) of neurons (see glossary definition) in the cortex by visual stimuli of specific shapes or patterns

fetal alcohol syndrome The most common cause of mental retardation in newborns, occurring (happening) when the mother uses alcohol during pregnancy

fetus A developing individual, from eight weeks after conception until birth

fixations Conflicts or concerns that persist (continue) beyond the developmental period in which they first occur

fixed-interval schedule A schedule that provides reinforcement (see glossary definition) for a response only if a fixed time period has elapsed, making overall rates of response relatively low

fixed-ratio schedule A schedule by which reinforcement (see glossary definition) is given only after a specific number of responses are made

flashbulb memories Memories centered on a specific, important, or surprising event that are so vivid it is as if they represented a snapshot of the event

fluid intelligence Intelligence that reflects information-processing capabilities, reasoning, and memory

formal operational stage According to Jean Piaget, the period from age 12 to adulthood that is characterized by abstract thought

free will The idea that behavior is caused primarily (mainly) by choices that are made freely by the individual

frequency theory of hearing The theory that the entire basilar membrane acts like a microphone, vibrating as a whole in response to sound

frustration The thwarting (prevention) or blocking of some ongoing, goal-directed behavior

functional fixedness The tendency (trend) to think of an object only in terms of its typical use

functionalism An early approach to psychology that concentrated on what the mind does—the functions of mental activity—and the role of behavior in allowing people to adapt (adjust) to their environments

fundamental attribution error A tendency to overattribute others' behavior to dispositional (personality, system) causes and the corresponding minimization of the importance of situational causes

G

g or g-factor The single, general factor for mental ability assumed to underlie intelligence in some early theories of intelligence

gate control theory of pain The theory that particular nerve receptors (receivers) lead to specific areas of the brain related to pain

general adaptation syndrome (GAS) A theory developed by Hans Selye that suggests that a person's response to a stressor (something that causes stress) consists of three stages: alarm and mobilization, resistance, and exhaustion

generalized anxiety disorder The experience of long-term, persistent (continuing) anxiety (unease, nervousness) and worry

generativity-versus-stagnation stage According to Erik Erikson, a period in middle adulthood during which we take stock of our contributions to family and society

genes The parts of the chromosomes (see glossary definition) through which genetic information is transmitted

genetic preprogramming theories of aging Theories that suggest that human cells have a built-in time limit to their reproduction, and that after a certain time they are no longer able to divide

genital stage According to Sigmund Freud, the period from puberty until death, marked by mature sexual behavior (that is, sexual intercourse)

genitals The male and female sex organs

gestalt laws of organization A series of principles that describe how we organize bits and pieces of information into meaningful wholes

Gestalt psychology An approach to psychology that focuses on the organization of perception (see glossary definition) and thinking in a "whole" sense rather than on the individual elements of perception

gestalt therapy A treatment approach in which people are led to examine their earlier experiences and complete any "unfinished business" from their past that may still affect and color present-day relationships

grammar The system of rules that determine how our thoughts can be expressed in written language

group therapy Therapy in which people meet with a therapist to discuss problems with a group

groupthink A type of thinking in which group members share such a strong motivation (see glossary definition) to achieve consensus (agreement) that they lost the ability to critically evaluate alternative (different) points of view

H

habituation The decrease in response to a stimulus (see glossary definition) that occurs after repeated presentations of the same stimulus

hair cells Tiny cells covering the basilar membrane (part of the inner ear) that, when bent by vibrations entering the cochlea (see glossary definition), transmit neural messages to the brain

hallucinogen A drug that is capable of producing hallucinations, or changes in the perceptual (perception, see glossary definition) process

halo effect A phenomenon (event) in which an initial understanding that a person has positive traits is used to infer other uniformly positive characteristics

hardiness A personality (see glossary definition) characteristic associated with a lower rate of stress-related illness, consisting of three components: commitment, challenge, and control

health psychology The branch of psychology that investigates the psychological factors (issues) related to wellness and illness, including the prevention, diagnosis, and treatment of medical problems

hemispheres The symmetrical (balanced, proportioned) left and right halves of the brain that control the side of the body opposite to their location

heritability A measure of the degree to which a characteristic (defined feature) is related to genetic (inherited) factors

heterosexuality Sexual attraction and behavior directed toward the other sex

heuristic A cognitive (thought process) shortcut that may lead to a solution

homeostasis The body's tendency to maintain a steady internal state

homosexuals Persons who are sexually attracted to members of their own sex

hormones Chemicals that circulate through the blood and regulate the functioning (performance) or growth of the body

humanistic approaches to personality Theories that emphasize people's innate (inborn) goodness and desire to achieve higher levels of functioning (performance)

humanistic perspective on psychological disorders This perspective (view) suggests that all individuals naturally strive to grow, develop, and be in control of their lives; and emphasizes the responsibility people have for their own behavior, even when such behavior is abnormal (unusual)

humanistic therapy Therapy in which the underlying rationale (foundation) is that people have control of their behavior, can make choices about their lives, and are essentially (basically) responsible for solving their own problems

hypnosis A trancelike state of heightened susceptibility (openness) to the suggestions of others

hypochondriasis A disorder (illness) in which people have a constant fear of illness and a preoccupation (concern) with their health

hypothalamus A tiny part of the brain, located below the thalamus (see glossary definition), that maintains homeostasis (balance) and produces and regulates vital (essential) behavior, such as eating, drinking and sexual behavior

hypothesis A prediction (guess), stemming from a theory (supposition), stated in way that allows it to be tested

I

id The raw, unorganized, inborn part of personality (see glossary definition) whose sole purpose is to reduce tension created by primitive (ancient) drives related to hunger, sex, aggression, and irrational (unreasonable) impulses

identical twins Twins who are genetically identical

identification The process of wanting to be like another person as much as possible, imitating that person's behavior and adopting (taking on) similar beliefs and values

identity The distinguishing (unique) character of the individual: who each of us is, what our roles are, and what we are capable of

identity-versus-role-confusion stage According to Erik Erikson, a time in adolescence of major testing to determine one's unique qualities

implicit memory Memories of which people are not consciously aware, but which can affect subsequent (following) performance and behavior

incentive approaches to motivation Theories suggesting that motivation (see glossary definition) stems (comes) from the desire to obtain valued external goals, or incentives

independent variable The variable that is manipulated (controlled) by an experimenter

industrial-organizational (I/O) psychology The branch of psychology focusing on work- and job-related issues, including worker motivation, satisfaction, safety, and productivity

industry-versus-inferiority stage According to Erik Erikson, the last stage of childhood, during which children age 6 to 12 years may develop positive social interactions (exchanges) with others or may feel inadequate (not good enough, lacking) and become less sociable (friendly)

inferiority complex According to Alfred Adler, a problem affecting (influencing) adults who have not been able to overcome the feelings of inferiority (not being good enough) that they developed as children, when they were small and limited in their knowledge about the world

information processing The way in which people take in, use, and store information

informed consent A document signed by participants affirming (confirming) that they have been told the basic outlines of the study and are aware of what their participation (involvement) will involve

inhibitory message A chemical message that prevents or decreases the likelihood that a receiving neuron (see glossary definition) will fire

initiative-versus-guilt stage According to Erik Erikson, the period during which children ages 3 to 6 years experience conflict between independence (self-rule) of action and the sometimes negative results of that action

insight A sudden awareness of the relationships among various elements that had previously (before) appeared to be independent of one another

instincts Inborn patterns of behavior that are biologically (naturally) determined (fixed) rather than learned

intellectually gifted The 2 to 4 percent of the population who have IQ scores greater than 130

intelligence The capacity (ability) to understand the world, think rationally (logically), and use resources effectively when faced with challenges

intelligence quotient (IQ) A score that takes into account an individual's mental and chronological (physical) ages

intelligence tests Tests devised to quantify (measure) a person's level of intelligence (see glossary definition)

interference The phenomenon (event) by which information in memory disrupts the recall of other information

interneurons Neurons (see glossary definition) that connect sensory (sensation) and motor neurons, carrying messages between the two

interpersonal attraction (or close relationship) Positive feelings for others; liking and loving

interpersonal therapy (IPT) Short-term therapy that focuses on the context (situation) of current social relationships

intimacy-versus-isolation stage According to Erik Erikson, a period during early adulthood that focuses on developing close relationships

introspection A procedure used to study the structure of the mind in which subjects are asked to describe in detail what they are experiencing when they are exposed to a stimulus (see glossary definition)

J

James-Lange theory of emotion The belief that emotional experience is a reaction to bodily events occurring as a result of an external situation ("I feel sad because I am crying")

just noticeable difference *See* difference threshold

K

Korsakoff's syndrome A disease that afflicts long-term alcoholics, leaving some abilities intact, but including hallucinations (false, imagined sense perceptions) and a tendency (trend) to repeat the same story

L

language The communication of information through symbols arranged according to systematic (orderly) rules

language-acquisition device A neural (nerve) system of the brain hypothesized by Noam Chomsky to permit understanding of language

latency period According to Sigmund Freud, the period between the phallic stage and puberty during which children's sexual concerns are temporarily put aside

latent content of dreams According to Sigmund Freud, the "disguised" meaning of dreams, hidden by more obvious subjects

latent learning Learning in which a new behavior is acquired (obtained) but is not demonstrated until some incentive (motivation) is provided for displaying it

lateralization The dominance (control) of one hemisphere (see glossary definition) (side) of the brain in specific functions, such as language

learned helplessness A state in which people conclude that unpleasant or aversive stimuli (see glossary definition) cannot be controlled, a view of the world that becomes so ingrained (fixed) that they cease trying to remedy the aversive circumstances, even if they actually can exert some influence

learning A relatively permanent change in behavior brought about by experience

learning-theory approach to language development The theory suggesting that language acquisition (gaining of language) follows the principles of reinforcement (see glossary definition) and conditioning

levels-of-processing theory The theory of memory that emphasizes (stresses) the degree to which new material is mentally analyzed

life review The process by which people examine and evaluate their lives

limbic system The part of the brain that controls eating, aggression (hostility), and reproduction

linguistic-relativity hypothesis The notion that language shapes and may determine the way people in a particular culture perceive (see) and understand the world

lithium A drug made up of mineral salts that is used to treat and prevent manic (overexcited) episodes (incidents) of bipolar disorder (see glossary definition)

lobes The four major sections of the cerebral cortex (see glossary definition): frontal, parietal, temporal, and occipital

longitudinal research A research method that investigates behavior as participants age

long-term memory Memory that stores information on a relatively permanent basis, although it may be difficult to retrieve

M

major depression A severe form of depression that interferes with concentration (focus), decision making, and sociability (interaction with others)

mania An extended state of intense (strong), wild elation

manifest content of dreams According to Sigmund Freud, the apparent story line of dreams

masturbation Sexual self-stimulation

means-ends analysis Repeated testing for differences between the desired outcome and what currently exists

medical perspective on psychological disorders The perspective (view) that suggests that when an individual displays symptoms of abnormal (unusual) behavior, the root cause will be found in a physical examination of the individual, which may reveal a hormonal imbalance, a chemical deficiency (lacking), or a brain injury

meditation A learned technique for refocusing attention that brings about an altered (changed) state of consciousness

memory The process by which we encode (program), store, and retrieve (call back) information

memory trace A physical change in the brain that occurs when new material is learned

menopause The period during which women stop menstruating and are no longer fertile

mental age The average age of individuals who achieve a particular level of performance on a test

mental images Representations (visual pictures) in the mind that resemble the object or event being represented

mental retardation A condition characterized by significant limitations both in intellectual functioning and in conceptual *(see* concept), social, and practical adaptive (adjustable) skills

mental set The tendency for old patterns of problem solving to persist (keep on)

metabolism The rate at which food is converted (changed) to energy and expended (used) by the body

metacognition An awareness and understanding of one's own cognitive (thinking) processes

Minnesota Multiphasic Personality Inventory-2 (MMPI-2) A widely used self-report test that identifies people with psychological difficulties and is employed to predict some everyday behaviors

mood disorder An emotional disturbance (illness) that is strong enough to intrude on (interrupt) everyday living

motivation The factors that direct and energize the behavior of humans and voluntary movement

motor neurons Neurons (see glossary definition) that communicate information from the nervous system to muscles and glands

multiple personality disorder *See* dissociative identity disorder

myelin sheath A protective coat of fat and protein that wraps around the neuron (see glossary definition)

N

narcissistic personality disorder A personality (see glossary definition) disturbance characterized by an exaggerated (inflated) sense of self-importance

narcotics Drugs that increase relaxation and relieve pain and anxiety (unease, nervousness)

naturalistic observation Research in which an investigator simply observes some naturally occurring (happening) behavior and does not make a change in the situation

nature-nurture issue The issue of the degree to which environment (surroundings) and heredity (inherited) influence behavior

need for achievement A stable, learned characteristic in which a person obtains satisfaction by striving for and attaining (reaching) a level of excellence

need for affiliation An interest in establishing and maintaining relationships with other people

need for power A tendency to seek impact, control, or influence over others, and to be seen as a powerful individual

negative reinforcer An unpleasant stimulus (see glossary definition) whose *removal* leads to an increase in the probability that a preceding response will be repeated in the future

neo-Freudian psychoanalysts Psychoanalysts who were trained in traditional Freudian theory but later rejected some of its major points

neonate A newborn child

neurons Nerve cells, the basic elements of the nervous system

neuroplasticity Changes in the brain that occur throughout the lifespan, relating to the addition of new neurons (see glossary definition), new interconnections (relationships) between neurons, and the reorganization of information-processing areas

neuroscience perspective The approach that views behavior from the perspective (view) of the brain, the nervous system, and other biological functions

neurotransmitters Chemicals that carry messages across the synapse (see glossary definition) to the dendrite (and sometimes the cell body) of a receiver neuron (see glossary definition)

neutral stimulus A stimulus (see glossary definition) that, before conditioning, does not naturally bring about the response of interest

norms Standards of test performance that permit the comparison of one person's score on a test with the scores of other individuals who have taken the same test

O

obedience A change in behavior in response to the commands of others

obesity Body weight that is more than 20 percent above the average weight for a person of a particular height

object permanence The awareness that objects—and people—continue to exist even if they are out of sight

observational learning Learning by observing the behavior of another person, or model

obsession A persistent (constant) unwanted thought or idea that keeps recurring (returning)

obsessive-compulsive disorder A disorder (illness) characterized by obsessions (fascination) or compulsions (compelled behavior)

Oedipal conflict A child's sexual interest in his or her opposite-sex parent, typically resolved through identification with the same-sex parent

operant conditioning Learning in which a voluntary response is strengthened or weakened, depending on its favorable or unfavorable consequences (results)

operational definition The translation of a hypothesis (see glossary definition) into specific, testable procedures that can be measured and observed

opponent-process theory of color vision The theory that receptor (receiving) cells for color are linked in pairs, working in opposition to (opposite of) each other

optic nerve A bundle of ganglion axons (see glossary definition) that carry visual information to the brain

oral stage According to Sigmund Freud, a stage from birth to age 12–18 months, in which an infant's center of pleasure is the mouth

otoliths Tiny, motion-sensitive crystals within the semicircular canals (see glossary definition) that sense body acceleration (speeding up of the body)

overgeneralization The phenomenon (event, process) by which children apply language rules even when the application results in an error

ovulation The point at which an egg is released from the ovaries

P

panic disorder Anxiety (unease, nervousness) disorder (illness) that takes the form of panic attacks lasting from a few seconds to as long as several hours

parasympathetic division The part of the autonomic (automatic) division of the nervous system that acts to calm the body after an emergency or a stressful situation has ended

partial (or intermittent) reinforcement schedule Reinforcing of a behavior some but not all of the time

passionate (or romantic) love A state of intense absorption (interest) in someone that includes intense physiological (bodily) arousal, psychological interest, and caring for the needs of another

perception The sorting out, interpretation, analysis, and integration (combining) of stimuli by the sense organs and brain

peripheral nervous system The part of the nervous system that includes the autonomic (automatic) and somatic (bodily) subdivisions; made up of neurons (see glossary definition) with long axons (see glossary definition) and dendrites (see glossary definition), it branches out from the spinal cord and brain and reaches the extremities (outer parts) of the body

peripheral route processing Message interpretation characterized by consideration of the source and related general information rather than of the message itself

permissive parents Parents who give their children relaxed or inconsistent direction and, although warm, require little of them

personal stressors Major life events, such as the death of a family member, that have immediate consequences (results) that generally fade with time

personality The pattern of enduring (lasting) characteristics (traits, distinctive qualities) that produce consistency and individuality in a given person

personality disorder A disorder (illness) characterized by a set of inflexible, maladaptive (non-adapting) behavior patterns that keep a person from functioning appropriately (properly) in society

person-centered therapy Therapy in which the goal is to reach one's potential for self-actualization (see glossary definition)

phallic stage According to Sigmund Freud, a period beginning around age 3 during which a child's pleasure focuses on the genitals

phobias Intense, irrational (unfounded) fears of specific objects or situations

phonemes The smallest units of speech that affect meaning

phonology The study of the smallest units of speech, called phonemes

pituitary gland The major component of the endocrine system (see glossary definition), or "master gland," which secretes hormones that control growth and other parts of the endocrine system

place theory of hearing The theory that different areas of the basilar membrane (part of the inner ear) respond to different frequencies

placebo A false treatment, such as a pill, "drug," or other substance, without any significant (major) chemical properties or active ingredient

positive reinforcer A stimulus (see glossary definition) added to the environment (surroundings) that brings about an increase in a preceding response

posttraumatic stress disorder (PTSD) A phenomenon (event) in which victims of major catastrophes (disaster) or strong personal stressors feel long-lasting effects that may include re-experiencing the event in vivid flashbacks or dreams

practical intelligence According to Robert Sternberg, intelligence related to overall success in living

prejudice A negative (or positive) evaluation of a particular group and its members

preoperational stage According to Jean Piaget, the period from 2 to 7 years of age that is characterized by language development

priming A phenomenon (event) in which exposure to a word or concept (called a *prime*) later makes it easier to recall related information, even when there is no conscious memory of the word or concept

principle of conservation The knowledge that quantity is unrelated to the arrangement and physical appearance of objects

proactive interference Interference (intrusion) in which information learned earlier disrupts the recall of newer information

procedural memory Memory for skills and habits, such as riding a bike or hitting a baseball, sometimes referred to as *nondeclarative memory*

progesterone A female sex hormone secreted by the ovaries

projective personality tests A test in which a person is shown an ambiguous (unclear) stimulus (see glossary definition) and asked to describe it or tell a story about it

prosocial behavior Helping behavior

prototypes Typical, highly representative samples of a concept (see glossary definition)

psychoactive drugs Drugs that influence a person's emotions, perceptions (see glossary definition), and behavior

psychoanalysis Freudian psychotherapy in which the goal is to release hidden unconscious (see glossary definition) thoughts and feelings in order to reduce their power in controlling behavior

psychoanalytic perspective on psychological disorders The perspective (view) that suggests that abnormal (unusual) behavior stems from childhood conflicts over opposing wishes regarding sex and aggression

psychoanalytic theory Sigmund Freud's theory that unconscious (see glossary definition) forces act as determinants (causes, sources) of personality (see glossary definition)

psychodynamic approaches to personality Approaches that assume that personality (see glossary definition) is motivated by inner forces and conflicts about which people have little awareness and over which they have no control

psychodynamic perspective The approach based on the view that behavior is motivated by unconscious (see glossary definition) inner forces over which the individual has little control

psychodynamic therapy Therapy that seeks to bring unresolved past conflicts and unacceptable impulses from the unconscious (see glossary definition) into the conscious, where patients may deal with the problems more effectively

psychological tests Standard measures devised to assess (evaluate) behavior objectively; used by psychologists to help people make decisions about their lives and understand more about themselves

psychology The scientific study of behavior and mental processes

psychoneuroimmunology (PNI) The study of the relationship among psychological factors, the immune system, and the brain

psychophysics The study of the relationship between the physical aspects of stimuli (see glossary definition) and our psychological experience of them

psychophysiological disorders Medical problems influenced by an interaction of psychological, emotional, and physical difficulties

psychosexual stages Developmental (growth) periods that children pass through during which they encounter conflicts between the demands of society and their own sexual urges

psychosocial development Development of individuals' interactions and understanding of each other and of their knowledge and understanding of themselves as members of society

psychosurgery Brain surgery once used to reduce the symptoms of mental disorder but rarely used today

psychotherapy Treatment in which a trained professional—a therapist—uses psychological techniques to help a person overcome psychological difficulties and disorders (illnesses), resolve problems in living, or bring about personal growth

puberty The period at which maturation (maturity) of the sexual organs occurs, beginning at about age 11 or 12 for girls and 13 or 14 for boys

punishment A stimulus (see glossary definition) that decreases the probability that a previous behavior will occur again

R

random assignment to condition A procedure in which participants are assigned to different experimental groups or "conditions" on the basis of chance and chance alone

rapid eye movement (REM) sleep Sleep occupying 20 percent of an adult's sleeping time, characterized by increased heart rate, blood pressure, and breathing rate; erections (in males); eye movements; and the experience of dreaming

rational-emotive behavior therapy A form of therapy that attempts to restructure (reorganize) a person's belief system into a more realistic, rational (balanced), and logical set of views by challenging dysfunctional (not functioning) beliefs that maintain irrational behavior

reactance A disagreeable emotional and cognitive reaction that results from the restriction of one's freedom and that can be associated with medical regimens (programs)

recall A memory task in which specific information must be retrieved

reciprocity-of-liking effect A tendency (leaning) to like those who like us

recognition A memory task in which individuals are presented with a stimulus (see glossary definition) and asked whether they have been exposed to it in the past or to identify it from a list of alternatives

reflexes Unlearned, involuntary responses that occur (happen) automatically in the presence of certain stimuli (see glossary definition)

rehearsal The repetition of information that has entered short-term memory

reinforcement The process by which a stimulus (see glossary definition) increases the probability (chance) that a preceding behavior will be repeated

reinforcer Any stimulus (see glossary definition) that increases the probability (chance) that a preceding behavior will occur again

reliability The degree to which tests measure consistently what they are trying to measure

replication The repetition of research, sometimes using other procedures, settings, and groups of participants, to increase confidence in prior (earlier) findings

repression The primary (main) defense mechanism (device, tool) in which unacceptable or unpleasant id (see glossary definition) impulses are pushed back into the unconscious (see glossary definition)

resting state The state in which there is a negative electrical charge of about 270 millivolts within a neuron (see glossary definition)

reticular formation The part of the brain extending from the medulla through the pons and made up of groups of nerve cells that can immediately activate other parts of the brain to produce general bodily arousal (stimulation)

retina The part of the eye that converts the electromagnetic energy of light to electrical impulses for transmission to the brain

retroactive interference Interference (hinderance) in which there is difficulty in the recall of information learned earlier because of later exposure to different material

retrograde amnesia Amnesia in which memory is lost for occurrences (events) prior to a certain event

reuptake The reabsorption of neurotransmitters (see glossary definition) by a terminal button (see glossary definition)

rods Thin, cylindrical receptor (receiving) cells in the retina that are highly sensitive to light

Rorschach test A test that involves showing a series of symmetrical (balanced, proportional) visual stimuli (see glossary definition) to people who then are asked what the figures represent to them

S

Schachter-Singer theory of emotion The belief that emotions are determined jointly by a nonspecific kind of physiological (bodily) arousal and its interpretation, based on environmental (natural surrounding) cues

schedules of reinforcement Different patterns of frequency (occurrences) and timing of reinforcement (see glossary definition) following desired behavior

schemas Organized bodies of information stored in memory that bias (prejudice) the way new information is interpreted, stored, and recalled; sets of cognitions (thoughts) about people and social experiences

schizophrenia A class of disorders (illnesses) in which severe distortion (twisting) of reality occurs

scientific method The approach (view) through which psychologists systematically (scientifically) acquire knowledge and understanding about behavior and other phenomena (happenings) of interest

self-actualization A state of self-fulfillment in which people realize their highest potential, each in his or her own unique way

self-efficacy Belief in one's personal capabilities (abilities); underlies people's faith in their ability to carry out a particular behavior or produce a desired outcome

self-esteem The component of personality (see glossary definition) that encompasses (includes, surrounds) our positive and negative self-evaluations

self-report measures A method of gathering data about people by asking them questions about a sample of their behavior

self-serving bias The tendency (leaning) to attribute (attach) personal success to personal factors (skills, abilities, or efforts) and to attribute failure to factors outside oneself

semantic memory Memory for general knowledge and facts about the world, as well as memory for the rules of logic that are used to deduce (figure out) other facts

semantic networks Mental representations (visual depictions) of clusters of interconnected information

semantics The rules governing the meaning of words and sentences

semicircular canals Three tubelike structures of the inner ear containing fluid that sloshes through them when the head moves, signaling rotational (turning) or angular movement to the brain

sensation The activation of the sense organs by a source of physical energy

sensorimotor stage According to Jean Piaget, the stage from birth to 2 years, during which a child has little competence in representing the environment by using images, language, or other symbols

sensory (afferent) neurons Neurons (see glossary definition) that transmit information from the perimeter (outer part) of the body to the central nervous system (see glossary definition)

sensory area The site in the brain of the tissue that corresponds to each of the senses, with the degree of sensitivity related to the amount of the tissue allocated (set aside) to that sense

sensory memory The initial (primary) momentary storage of information, lasting only an instant

sequential research A research method that combines cross-sectional (representative sample) and longitudinal (long-term) research by considering a number of different age groups and examining them at several points in time

shaping The process of teaching a complex behavior by rewarding closer and closer approximations (similarities) of the desired behavior

short-term memory Memory that holds information for 15 to 25 seconds

significant outcome Meaningful results that make it possible for researchers to feel confident that they have confirmed their hypotheses (see glossary definition)

situational causes (of behavior) Perceived (apparent) causes of behavior that are based on environmental (surrounding world) factors

skin senses The senses of touch, pressure, temperature, and pain

social cognition The cognitive (thinking) processes by which people understand and make sense of others and themselves

social cognitive approaches to personality Theories that emphasize the influence of a person's cognitions—thoughts, feelings, expectations, and values—as well as observation of others' behavior, in determining personality (see glossary definition)

social influence The process by which the actions of an individual or group affect (influence) the behavior of others

social psychology The scientific study of how people's thoughts, feelings, and actions are affected (influenced) by others

social support A mutual network of caring, interested others

social supporter A group member whose dissenting (differing) views make nonconformity to (differing from) the group easier

sociocultural perspective on psychological disorders The perspective (view) that assumes that people's behavior—both normal and abnormal—is shaped by the kind of family group, society, and culture in which they live

somatic division The part of the peripheral nervous system (see glossary definition) that specializes in the control of voluntary (controlled) movements and the communication of information to and from the sense organs

somatoform disorders Psychological difficulties that take on a physical (somatic) form, but for which there is no medical cause

sound The movement of air molecules brought about by a source of vibration

spinal cord The neuron (see glossary definition) bundle that leaves the brain and runs down the length of the back and is the main means for transmitting messages between the brain and the body

spontaneous recovery The reemergence (reoccurrence) of an extinguished conditioned response (see glossary definition) after a period of rest and with no further conditioning

spontaneous remission Recovery without treatment

stage 1 sleep The state of transition between wakefulness and sleep, characterized by relatively rapid, low-amplitude (low-volume, low-size) brain waves

stage 2 sleep A sleep deeper than that of stage 1, characterized by a slower, more regular wave pattern, along with momentary interruptions of sleep spindles

stage 3 sleep A sleep characterized by slow brain waves, with greater peaks and valleys in the wave pattern than in stage 2 sleep

stage 4 sleep The deepest stage of sleep, during which we are least responsive to outside stimulation

status The social rank held within a group

stereotype A set of generalized (general) beliefs and expectations about a particular group and its members

stimulants Drugs that have an arousal (stimulating) effect on the central nervous system (see glossary definition), causing a rise in heart rate, blood pressure, and muscular tension

stimulus Energy that produces a response in a sense organ

stimulus discrimination The process that occurs if two stimuli (see glossary definition) are sufficiently distinct (different) from one another that one evokes (brings up) a conditioned response (see glossary definition) but the other does not; the ability to differentiate (tell the difference) between stimuli

stimulus generalization Occurs when a conditioned response (see glossary definition) follows a stimulus (see glossary definition) that is similar to the original conditioned stimulus (see glossary definition) ; the more similar the two stimuli are, the more likely generalization is to occur

stress A person's response to events that are threatening or challenging

structuralism Wilhelm Wundt's approach, which focuses on uncovering the fundamental mental components (parts) of consciousness, thinking, and other kinds of mental states and activities

subjective well-being People's own evaluation of their lives in terms of both their thoughts and their emotions

superego According to Sigmund Freud, the final personality (see glossary definition) structure to develop; it represents the rights and wrongs of society as handed down by a person's parents, teachers, and other important figures

survey research Research in which people chosen to represent a larger population are asked a series of questions about their behavior, thoughts, or attitudes

sympathetic division The part of the autonomic division (see glossary definition) of the nervous system that acts to prepare the body for action in stressful situations, engaging all the organism's (living thing's) resources to respond to a threat

synapse The space between two neurons (see glossary definition) where the axon (see glossary definition) of a sending neuron communicates with the dendrites (see glossary definition) of a receiving neuron by using chemical messages

syntax Ways in which words and phrases can be combined to form sentences

systematic desensitization A behavioral technique in which gradual exposure to an anxiety-producing stimulus (see glossary definition) is paired with relaxation to extinguish the response of anxiety (unease, nervousness)

T

telegraphic speech Sentences in which words not critical to the message are left out

temperament The basic, innate (inborn) disposition (tendency) that emerges early in life

teratogens Environmental agents such as a drug, chemical, virus, or other factors that produce a birth defect

terminal buttons Small bulges at the end of axons (see glossary definition) that send messages to other neurons (see glossary definition)

test standardization A technique used to validate (confirm) questions in personality (see glossary definition) tests by studying the responses of people with known diagnoses (an identified illness)

thalamus The part of the brain located in the middle of the central core that acts primarily to relay information about the senses

Thematic Apperception Test (TAT) A test consisting of a series of pictures about which a person is asked to write a story

theories Broad explanations and predictions concerning phenomena (happenings) of interest

theory of multiple intelligences Howard Gardner's theory that proposes that there are eight distinct spheres (areas) of intelligence

thinking The manipulation (handling, control) of mental representations of information

tip-of-the-tongue phenomenon The inability to recall information that one realizes one knows—a result of the difficulty of retrieving information from long-term memory

top-down processing Perception (see glossary definition) that is guided by higher-level knowledge, experience, expectations, and motivations

trait theory A model of personality (see glossary definition) that seeks to identify the basic traits necessary to describe personality

traits Consistent personality (see glossary definition) characteristics and behaviors displayed in different situations

transcranial magnetic stimulation (TMS) A depression treatment in which a precise magnetic pulse is directed to a specific area of the brain

transference The transfer of feelings to a psychoanalyst of love or anger that had been originally directed to a patient's parents or other authority figures

treatment The manipulation (handling, control) implemented (carried out) by the experimenter

trichromatic theory of color vision The theory that there are three kinds of cones in the retina, each of which responds primarily to a specific range of wavelengths

trust-versus-mistrust stage According to Erik Erikson, the first stage of psychosocial development, occurring from birth to age 1½ years, during which time infants develop feelings of trust or lack of trust

Type A behavior pattern A cluster of behaviors involving hostility, competitiveness, time urgency, and drive

Type B behavior pattern A cluster of behaviors characterized by a patient, cooperative, noncompetitive, and nonaggressive manner

U

unconditional positive regard An attitude of acceptance and respect on the part of an observer, no matter what a person says or does

unconditioned response (UCR) A response that is natural and needs no training (e.g., salivation at the smell of food)

unconditioned stimulus (UCS) A stimulus (see glossary definition) that naturally brings about a particular response without having been learned

unconscious A part of the personality (see glossary definition) that contains the memories, knowledge, beliefs, feelings, urges, drives, and instincts of which the individual is not aware

unconscious wish fulfillment theory Sigmund Freud's theory that dreams represent unconscious (see glossary definition) wishes that dreamers desire to see fulfilled

uninvolved parents Parents who show little interest in their children and are emotionally detached

universal grammar Noam Chomsky's theory that all the world's languages share a common underlying structure

V

validity The degree to which tests actually measure what they are supposed to measure

variable-interval schedule A schedule by which the time between reinforcements (see glossary definition) varies around some average rather than being fixed

variable-ratio schedule A schedule by which reinforcement (see glossary definition) occurs after a varying number of responses rather than a fixed number

variables Behaviors, events, or other characteristics that can change, or vary, in some way

visual illusions Physical stimuli (see glossary definition) that consistently produce errors in perception (see glossary definition)

W

wear-and-tear theories of aging Theories that suggest that the mechanical functions of the body simply stop working efficiently

Weber's law A basic law of psychophysics (see glossary definition) stating that a just noticeable difference is in constant proportion to the intensity of an initial stimulus (see glossary definition)

weight set point The particular level of weight that the body strives to maintain

working memory A set of active, temporary memory stores that actively manipulate (direct) and rehearse information

Z

zone of proximal development (ZPD) According to Lev Vygotsky, the level at which a child can almost, but not fully, comprehend (understand) or perform a task on his or her own

zygote The new cell formed by the union of an egg and sperm

PHOTO CREDITS

Page 1: © Royalty-Free/Corbis; 2: © Bettmann/Corbis; 3: © Paul Thompson/Getty Images; 4: Library of Congress; 14: © ImageDJ/Alamy; 23: © Digital Vision/Getty Images; 36: © PhotoAlto/JupiterImages; 40: © Kate Mitchell/Corbis; 43: © Creatas/PunchStock; 48: Brand X/Getty Images; 61: © Mike Kemp/Getty Images; 62: © Bettmann/Corbis; 73: © Royalty-Free/Corbis; 75: © Jules Frazier/Getty Images; 77: © BananaStock/PunchStock; 83: © PunchStock/Corbis; 86: © PhotoAlto/JupiterImages; 91: © Bill Anderson/Photo Researchers; 93: © PhotoDisc/Getty Images; 101: © Brand X Pictures/PunchStock; 105: © Bettmann/Corbis; 116: © The McGraw-Hill Companies, Inc./Gary He, photographer; 117: © Bettmann/Corbis; 121: © PhotoDisc/Getty Images; 126: © Andrea Morini/Getty Images; 132: © Laurent Hamels/PhotoAlto/JupiterImages; 143: © PhotoAlto/Getty Images; 146: Leigh Schindler/Getty Images; 148: Getty Images.

NAME INDEX

A

Adler, A., 149
Aiken, L. R., 152, 165
Allport, G., 149
Anderson, J. R., 86, 101

B

Balter, M. B., 64
Bandura, A., 72–73, 82, 151, 165
Bard, P., 108
Barston, S., 64
Benjamin L. T., Jr., 87, 101
Binet, A., 153
Bleuler, E., 189
Blumenthal, A. L., 3, 17
Boeree, C. G., 3, 4, 17, 72, 82
Bogen, J., 23
Bolger, N., 169, 180
Bowlby, J., 126, 143
Braid, J., 53
Breuer, J., 5
Broca, P., 21
Brooker, R. J., 47
Brown, P. K., 34, 47
Burton, L., 72, 82

C

Calkins, M. W., 7
Cannon, W. B., 19, 30, 108
Cartwright, R. D., 53, 64
Cattell, R. B., 149–150, 165
Chess, S., 123–124, 143
Clay, R. A., 6, 17
Crain, W. C., 128, 143

D

Darley, J. M., 210, 223
Darnton, R., 53, 64
Darwin, C., 153
Davis, S. F., 5, 7, 17, 21, 23, 30
Davis, S. M., 22, 30
de Benedictis, T., 64
Donnan, G. A., 22, 30

E

Ebbinghaus, H., 84–85, 101
Eber, H. W., 150, 165
Eckenrole, J., 169, 180
Ekman, P., 108
Engel, G. L., 6, 17
Erikson, E. H., 124–125, 143
Everitt, B., 180
Eysenck, H. J., 150, 165, 169, 180
Eysenck, M. W., 150, 165

F

Fancher, R., 165
Feldman, R., 32, 33, 47
Festinger, L., 105, 118
Fettiplace, R., 34, 47
Fisher, M., 22, 30
Freud, S., 4–5, 7, 53, 64, 104, 124, 147–148, 165, 187, 211

G

Gall, F. J., 147
Galton, F., 153, 165
Gardner, H., 154, 165
Gazzaniga, M., 23
Gelbart, W., 121, 143
Gibbons, A., 4
Goldstein, B., 38, 47
Graham, L. E., 47
Griffiths, A. J. F., 121, 143
Grossarth-Maticek, R., 180

H

Harlow, H. F., 126, 143
Heider, F., 208, 223
Helmholtz, H. v., 34
Hering, E., 34
Hippocrates, 147
Hobson, J. A., 53, 64
Holliday, R., 121, 143
Hopkins, J. R., 87, 101
Horney, K. D., 148–149
Hothersall. D., 5, 17
Hubel, D. H., 38, 47

J

James, W., 2, 3–4, 37, 47, 104, 107, 108, 118
Jones, E. E., 209, 223
Jung, C., 148

K

Kalat, J. W., 6, 17
Katz, J. Z., 37, 47
Kelley, H. H., 209, 223
Kemp, G., 64
Kleinginna, A., 104, 118
Kleinginna, P., Jr., 104, 118
Kobasa, S., 169, 180
Koffka, K., 38
Kohlberg, L., 128–129, 143
Kohler, W., 38
Kowalski, R., 72, 82

L

LaBerge, S., 64
Lahey, B., 2, 17
Lamberg, L., 53, 64
Lange, C., 107
Larson, H., 64
Latané, B., 210, 223
Lazarus, R. S., 108
Lewontin, R., 121, 143
Lindsay, P., 38, 47
Loftus, E. F., 87, 101
Lowenstein, J. H., 32, 47

M

Macleod, M., 22, 30
Madigan, S., 7, 17
Maslow, A., 6, 105–106, 118, 151–152
Matlin, M. W., 209, 223
May, R., 6
McCarley, R., 53, 64
Mellinger, G. D., 64
Melzack, R., 37, 47
Mendel, G., 121
Mesmer, F., 53

Milgram, S., 212
Miller, G. A., 86, 101
Miller, J., 121, 143
Moore, K. L., 120, 143
Münsterberg, H., 4

N

Nation, J. R., 87, 101
Nisbett, R. E., 209, 223
Nittrouer, S., 32, 47
Norman, D. A., 38, 47
Novelline, R., 22, 30

O

O'Hara, R., 7, 17

P

Palladino, J. J., 5, 7, 17, 21, 23, 30
Pavlov, I., 5, 67–68, 69
Piaget, J., 7, 126–127, 143
Prosser, I. B., 7

R

Rayner, R., 69–70, 82
Rescorla, R., 69, 82
Rogers, C., 6, 151
Roseman, R. H., 169, 180
Ross, D., 82
Ross, S. A., 82
Rossor, M. N., 122, 143
Rotter, J. B., 150–151, 165

S

Santrock, J. W., 210, 223
Schachter, S., 108
Schott, J. M., 122, 143
Segal, R., 64
Selye, H., 167–168, 169, 180
Shakow, D., 101
Sherrington, C. S., 23
Simon, T., 153
Singer, J. E., 108
Skinner, B. F., 5–6, 70–72, 82, 150
Spearman, C., 154, 165
Sperry, R., 23
Stang, D. J., 209, 223
Stern, W., 153
Sternberg, R. J., 154, 165, 210, 223
Stiling, P. D., 47
Strube, M. J., 208, 223
Sumner, F. C., 7
Suzuki, D., 121, 143

T

Tatsuoka, M. M., 150, 165
Terman, L., 153
Thomas, A., 123–124, 143
Thorndike, E. L., 73, 82, 208, 223
Triplett, N., 208, 223

U

Uhlenhurth, E. H., 64

V

Vogel, P., 23
Vygotsky, L., 127

W

Wald, G., 34, 47
Warren, W., 7, 17
Watson, J. B., 5, 69–70, 71, 82, 150
Weitzen, W., 2, 17
Wernicke, C., 21
Wertheimer, M., 38
Westen, D., 72, 82
Whyte, G., 223
Whyte, W. H ., 212
Widmaier, E. P., 47
Wiesel, T. N., 38, 47
Wolpe, J., 72
Wundt, W., 2–3

Y

Young, T., 34

Z

Zimbardo, P., 212

SUBJECT INDEX

A

Abdominal breathing, 170
Abnormal psychology, 183
  classification of mental disorders, 184–191
  defining abnormal behavior, 183
  medical model and, 183
  psychological model, 183–184
  therapies, 191
Absolute threshold, 32
Accommodation, in vision, 32–33
Acquisition, 69
Activation-synthesis theory, 53
Actor-observer bias, 209
Adaptation, 32
Adolescence, 129
Adulthood, 129–130
African Americans, in psychology, 7
Aggression
  defined, 211
  observational learning and, 73
  social psychology and, 212
Altruism, 210
Alzheimer's disease, 88, 130
Amnesia, 87–88
Amphetamines, 54
Amygdala, 21
Anal stage, 124
Animal magnetism, 53
Anosmia, 36
Anvil, 34, 35
Anxiety
  Freudian theory and, 148
  posttraumatic stress disorder (PTSD), 168
Anxiety disorders, 185–186
Appraisal theory, 108
Approach-approach conflict, 107
Approach-avoidance conflict, 107
Arousal theory, 105
Asperger's disorder, 190–191
Attachment, 126
Attention, perception and, 37
Attention deficit disorder (ADD), 190
Attention-deficit hyperactivity disorder (ADHD), 190
Attraction, 209–210
Attribution effect, 209
Attributions, 208
Attribution theory, 208–209
Auditory processes, 34–35
Autistic disorder, 190–191
Autonomic nervous system, 19
  fight-or-flight response, 19–20
  parasympathetic division, 19
  sympathetic division, 19–20
Avoidance-avoidance conflict, 107

B

Babinski reflex, 122
Barbiturates, 55
Behaviorism/behavioral perspective
  on abnormal behavior, 184
  history of, 5–6
  on personality, 150–151
  sleep restriction, 52
Behavior modification, 73
Binocular disparity, 38
Biofeedback, 171
Biological basis of psychology, 19–21
Biological theories, of motivation, 104–105
Biopsychosocial model, 167
  history of, 6
Bipolar disorder, 189
Bobo doll experiment, 73
Body dysmorphic disorder, 187
Brain
  Broca's area, 21
  functions of, 21–23
  hemispheres of, 23
  as part of central nervous system, 20–21
  parts of, 20–21
  during sleep, 49
  Wernicke's area, 21
Brain stem, 20
Brainstorming, 212
Broca's area, 21
Bystander effect, 210

C

Cannon-Bard theory, 108
Case studies, advantages/disadvantages of, 7
Central nervous system, components of, 20–21
Cerebellum, 20
Cerebral cortex, 21
Cerebrovascular accident, 22
Cerebrum, 20, 21
Childhood disorders, 190–191
Children
  cognitive development, 126–128
  infant development, 122–123
  language development, 128
  psychosocial stages of development, 124–125
  social bonds and attachment, 126
  temperament, 123–124
Chunking, 86
Cilia, 36
Classical conditioning, 67–70
  acquisition, 69
  defined, 67
  extinction, 69
  generalization, 69–70
  process of, 67–69
  stimulus discrimination, 70
Closure, as gestalt concept, 38
Cocaine, 54
Cochlea, 34, 35
Cognitive arousal theory, 108
Cognitive dissonance, 105
Cognitive perspective
  on abnormal behavior, 184
  history of, 6
  of motivation, 105
Collective unconscious, 148
Compliance, 212
Concrete operational stage, 127
Conditioned response, 67, 68
Conditioned stimulus, 67, 68
Cones, 33, 34
Conflict, 106–107

Conformity, 212
Conscious mind, 147
Consciousness, 49–55
  defined, 49
  dreams, 53
  drugs and altered states of, 54–55
  hypnosis, 53–54
  sleep issues, 51–53
  stages of sleep, 49–51
Conscious recall, 86
Conversion disorder, 187
Corpus callosum, 20, 23
Correlational research, advantages/disadvantages of, 8
Correspondence bias, 209
Crack, 54
CT scan, 22

D

Date rape drug, 55
Declarative memory, 86
Defense mechanisms, 148
Dementia, 88, 130
Demyelination, 22
Dendrites, 22, 23
Depersonalization disorder, 187
Depolarization, 34
Depressants, 55
Depression, 188–189
Depth perception, 38
Development, 120–130
  adolescence to adulthood, 129–130
  cognitive, 126–128
  conception to birth, 120
  dementia and Alzheimer's disease, 130
  genetics and, 121–122
  during infancy, 122–123
  of language, 128
  maturation, 123
  moral, 128–129
  nature via nurture, 120
  psychosocial, 123–126
  psychosocial stages of, 124–125
  social bonds and attachment, 126
Developmental disorders, 190
Dexedrine, 54
Diagnostic and Statistical Manual of Mental Disorders (DSM-IV-TR), 184–185
Diaphragmatic breathing, 170
Dichromate, 34
Difference threshold, 32
Discrimination, 208
Dissociative amnesia, 187
Dissociative disorders, 187–188
Dissociative drugs, 55
Dissociative fugue, 88, 188
Dissociative identity disorder, 188
Downers, 55
Dreams
  activation-synthesis theory, 53
  Freud and, 53
  latent content of, 53
  manifest content of, 53
  stages of sleep and, 53
  theories of, 53
Drive-reduction theory, 104–105

E

Ears, in hearing process, 34–35
Effectors, 19
Ego, 147–148
Electroencephalograph (EEG), 22
  REM sleep and, 50
Embryo, 120
Emotional state, 107
Emotions
  defined, 107
  nonverbal expression of, 108
  theories of, 107–108
Encoding, memory, 85
Episodic memory, 86
Eros, 104, 211
Experiments, advantages/disadvantages of, 8
Extinction, 69
Extraversion, 150
Eyes
  depth perception and, 38
  vision and, 32–33

F

Fears
  classical conditioning and, 69
  systematic desensitization, 72
Feature-analysis theory, 38
Feature detectors, 38
Fetus, 121–122
Fight-or-flight reaction, 168
Flashbulb memory, 86
Forebrain, 20–21
Forgetting, 88
Forgetting curve, 84
Formal operational stage, 127
Frontal lobe, 21
Frustration-aggression theory, 211
Fugue state, 87–88
Functionalism, 2
Fundamental attribution error, 209

G

Gate control theory, 37
General adaptation syndrome, 168
Generalization, 69–70
Generalized anxiety disorder (GAD), 186
Genetics
  basic concepts of, 121–122
  defined, 121
Genital stage, 124
Gestalt psychology, 38
  principles of perception, 38
GHB, 55
Group processing, 212
Groupthink, 212
Guided imagery, 171

H

Hallucinogens, 55
Halo effect, 208
Hammer, 34, 35
Hardiness, 169
Health psychology, 167–171
  biopsychosocial model, 167
  effects of stress, 167–168
  sources of stress, 168
  stress and coping skills, 169
  stress and illness, 169
  stress reduction and relaxation, 170–171
Hearing, 34–35
Hierarchy of needs, 105–106, 151–152
Hindbrain, 20
Hippocampus, 21
Homeostasis, 106–107
Hues, 32
Humanistic perspective
  on abnormal behavior, 184
  history of, 6
  of motivation, 105–106
  on personality, 151–152
Hypersomnia, 52
Hypnosis, 53–54
  procedure of, 54
Hypochondriasis, 186
Hysteria, 187

I

Id, 147–148
Immune system, stress and, 168
Impression formation, 208

Incentive theory, 105
Infants, development, 122–123
Insomnia, 51–52
Instinct theory, 104
Instrumental conditioning, 70
Intelligence, 153–154
Intelligence tests, 153
Interpersonal attraction, 209–210

J

James-Lange theory, 107–108

K

Ketamine, 55

L

Language, development of, 128
Latency stage, 124
Learning, 67–73
  behavior modification, 73
  classical conditioning, 67–70
  memorization vs., 88
  observational learning, 72–73
  operant conditioning, 70–72
Learning curve, 84
Librium, 55
Light waves, 32–33
Limbic system, 21
Little Albert experiment, 5, 69–70
Locus of control, 151
Long-term memory, 85–86
LSD, 55

M

Marijuana, 55
Maturation, 123
Mechanoreceptors, 37
Medical model of abnormal behavior, 183
Meditation, 171
Medulla oblongata, 20
Meiosis, 121
Meissmer corpuscles, 37
Memory, 84–88
  chunking, 86
  declarative, 86
  disorders of, 87–88
  encoding, 85
  episodic, 86
  flashbulb, 86
  forgetting, 88
  forgetting curve, 84
  learning curve, 84
  long-term, 85–86
  memorization vs. learning, 88
  overlearning effect, 85
  physiology of, 87
  procedural, 86
  rehearsal, 85
  retrieval, 85, 86–87
  semantic, 86
  sensory, 85–86
  short-term, 85–86
  stages of formation, 85
  working, 85, 86
Mental disorders
  anxiety disorders, 185–186
  childhood disorders, 190–191
  defining abnormal behavior, 183
  dissociative disorders, 187–188
  medical model of, 183
  mood disorders, 188–189
  overview of *DSM-IV-TR,* 184–185
  personality disorders, 189–190
  psychological model of, 183–184
  schizophrenia, 189
  somatoform disorders, 186–187
  therapies for, 191
Meridia, 54
Merkel receptors, 37
Mescaline, 55
Mesmerism, 53
Methamphetamine, 54
Midbrain, 20
Middle ear, 34, 35
Mitosis, 120
Monochromat, 34
Mood disorders, 188–189
Moral anxiety, 148
Moral development, 128–129
Moro reflex, 122
Morpheme, 128
Motivation, 104–106
  arousal theory, 105
  biological theories of, 104–105
  cognitive dissonance, 105
  cognitive theories of, 105
  defined, 104
  drive-reduction theory, 104–105
  hierarchy of needs, 105–106
  humanistic theory of, 105–106
  incentive theory, 105
  instinct theory, 104
Motor nerves, 20
MRI scan, 22
Multiple sclerosis, 22
Myelin sheath, 22

N

Narcolepsy, 52
Naturalistic observation, 7–8
Nature via nurture, 120
Needs, hierarchy of, 105–106, 151–152
Negative reinforcement, 71
Nerves
  motor, 20
  sensory, 20
Nervous system
  autonomic, 19
  central, 21–22
  drugs that alter, 54–55
  fight-or-flight response, 19–20
  neurons, 22
  neurotransmitters, 23
  peripheral, 19–20
  somatic, 19
Neurons, 22
  transmitting information, 23
Neuroscience
  defined, 32
  history of, 6
Neurotic anxiety, 148
Neuroticism, 150
Neurotransmitters, 23
Neutral stimulus, 67
Nightmares, 49, 50
Night terrors, 49–50
Nodes of Ranvier, 22
Non-REM (NREM) sleep, 49
Nonverbal cues, 108

O

Obedience, 212
Observational learning, 72–73, 151
Obsessive-compulsive disorder, 186
Occipital lobe, 21
Olfaction, 36
Olfactory epithelium, 36
Oligodendrocytes, 22
Operant conditioning, 70–72
  positive and negative reinforcement, 71
  punishment, 71
  schedules of reinforcement, 72
  shaping, 72
  Skinner box, 71
  systematic desensitization, 72

Opioids, 55
Opponent process theory, 34
Optic nerve, 33
Oral stage, 124
Ossicles, 34, 35
Oval window, 34, 35
Overlearning effect, 85
OxyContin, 55

P

Pacinian corpuscles, 37
Pain, sensation of, 37
Pain disorder, 187
Palmar (grasping) reflex, 122
Panic disorder, 186
Parasomnia, 52–53
Parasympathetic division of autonomic nervous system, 19
Parietal lobe, 21
Parkinson's disease, 23
Pattern perception, 37–38
PCP, 55
Penis envy, 148–149
Perception
  attention and, 37
  defined, 32
  depth, 38
  gestalt principles of, 38
  pattern, 37–38
  perceptual constancy, 38
  phi phenomenon, 38
  process of, 37–38
Perceptual constancy, 38
Percocet, 55
Peripheral nervous system
  autonomic nervous system, 19
  components of, 19
  fight-or-flight response, 19–20
  somatic nervous system, 19
Personality, 146–153
  assessing, 152–153
  behaviorist perspective of, 150–151
  biological/evolutionary approaches to, 146–147
  defined, 146
  humanistic approach to, 151–152
  psychodynamic approaches to, 147–149
  social learning theory, 150–151
  stress and coping skills, 169
  trait approach to, 149–150
Personality disorders, 189–190
Personality inventories, 152
Personality trait, 149–150
Persuasion, 211
PET scan, 22
Phallic stage, 124
Phi phenomenon, 38
Phobias
  classical conditioning and, 69
  overview of, 185
  systematic desensitization, 72
Phonemes, 128
Phrenology, 147
Physiological perspective, 6
Pinna, 34, 35
Pleasure principle, 148
Pollyanna principle, 209
Pons, 20
Positive reinforcement, 71
Positivity bias, 209
Posttraumatic stress disorder (PTSD), 168
Prejudice, 208
Preoperational stage, 127
Primacy effect, 85
Primary reinforcer, 70
Principles of Psychology (James), 4, 37
Procedural memory, 86
Progressive muscle relaxation, 170
Projective tests, 152–153
Prosocial behavior, 210
Proximity, as gestalt concept, 38
Psilocybin, 55
Psilocyn, 55
Psychedelic drugs, 55
Psychoanalytic perspective
  on abnormal behavior, 184
  history of, 4–5
  instincts and, 104
  personality and, 147–149
  psychosocial stages of development, 124–125
Psychological disorders. *See* Mental disorders
Psychological model of abnormal behavior, 183–184
Psychology
  biological basis of, 19–21
  branches of, 4–6
  defined, 2
  diversity in, 6–7
  history of, 2–4
  research methods in, 7–8
Psychophysiological, 169
Psychosocial analysis, 148
Psychosocial stages of development, 124–125
Psychosomatic, 169
Psychoticism, 150
Puberty, 129–130
Punishment, 71

R

Rapid eye movement (REM) sleep, 49–50
Reality anxiety, 148
Recall, 87
Recency effect, 85
Receptors, 19
Recognition, 87
Recollection, 87
Reflexes, 20
Reflexive behavior, 67, 69
Rehearsal, memory, 85
Reinforcement
  defined, 70
  positive and negative, 71
  schedules of, 72
Reinforcer, 70
Relaxation, 170–171
Relearning, 87
REM sleep, 49–50
Research methods, overview of, 7–8
Response
  defined, 19
  fight-or-flight, 19–20
Retina, 33
Retrieval, memory, 85
Ritalin, 54
Rods, 33
Rohypnol, 55
Rooting reflex, 122
Rorschach test, 152–153
Ruffini endings, 37

S

Schachter-Singer theory, 108
Schema, 86
Schizophrenia, 189
Schwann cells, 22
Secondary reinforcer, 70
Self-actualization, 106, 151–152
Semantic memory, 86
Sensation
  adaptation, 32
  defined, 32
  hearing, 34–35
  skin senses, 37
  smell, 36

Sensation—*Cont.*
- taste, 35–36
- thresholds, 32
- vision, 32–34

Sensorimotor stage, 127
Sensory memory, 85–86
Sensory nerves, 20
Septum, 21
Serial position curve, 85
Shaping, 72
Short-term memory, 85–86
Simplicity, as gestalt concept, 38
Skinner box, 71
Skin senses, 37
Sleep
- bed-wetting, 53
- deep sleep stage, 49
- dreams, 53
- drowsiness stage of, 49
- hypersomnia, 52
- insomnia, 51–52
- light stage, 49
- making up for lost, 51
- muscle twitching, 52–53
- narcolepsy, 52
- need for, 50
- nightmares, 49, 50
- night terrors, 49–50
- non-REM, 49
- parasomnia, 52–53
- percentages of, in different stages, 50
- problems with, 51–53
- REM sleep, 49–50
- sleep apnea, 52
- sleep deprivation, 51
- sleep restriction, 52
- sleep talking, 53
- sleep walking, 52
- stages of, 49–50

Smell, sense of, 36
Social bonds, 126
Social facilitation effect, 208
Social learning theory, 72–73
- on personality, 150–151

Social psychology, 208–212
- aggression, 211
- attribution theory, 208–209
- group processing, 212
- obedience, conformity, and compliance, 212
- overview of, 208
- persuasion, 211
- prosocial behavior, 210
- social relationships, 209–210

Somatic nervous system, 19
Somatization disorder, 187
Somatoform disorders, 186–187
Somatosensory processing, 37
Sound wave, 34
Spinal cord, 20
Spontaneous recovery, 69
Startle reflex, 122
Stereotypes, 208
Stimulants, 54
Stirrup, 34, 35
Stress
- coping skills, 169
- effects of, 167–168
- illness and, 169
- immune system and, 168
- posttraumatic stress disorder (PTSD), 168
- sources of, 168
- stress reduction and relaxation, 170–171

Structuralism, 2
Subcortical structures, 20–21
Superego, 147
Survey research, 8
Sympathetic division of autonomic nervous system, 19–20
Synapse, 23
Synaptic button, 22, 23
Synaptic cleft, 23
Syntax, 128
Systematic desensitization, 72

T

Target response, 70
Tastants, 35
Taste, 35–36
Taste buds, 35–36
Taste receptor cells, 35
Tectum, 20
Temperament, 123–124, 147
Temporal lobe, 21
Thalamus, 21
Thanatos, 104, 211
Thematic Apperception Test (TAT), 152–153
Therapies, 191
Thermoreceptors, 37
Thresholds
- absolute, 32
- difference, 32

Tongue, in taste sensation, 35–36
Top-down processing, 86
Tract, 20
Trait, personality, 149–150
Transduction, 32
Trichromatic theory of color vision, 34
Trichromats, 34
Type A personality, 169
Type B personality, 169

U

Umami, 35
Unconditioned response, 68, 69
Unconditioned stimulus, 67, 68
Unconscious mind, 147
Uppers, 54

V

Valium, 55
Vertebrae, 20
Vertical column, 20
Vicodin, 55
Vision, 32–34
- color, 34
- process of, 32–33

Vitreous humor, 33

W

Wernicke's area, 21
Womb envy, 149
Women, in psychology, 7
Working memory, 85, 86

X

Xanax, 55

Y

Yoga, 171

Z

Zygote, 120